Improving Your Memory For Dummies®

P9-CQY-579

Cheat Sheet

Keeping a Vintage Memory Well Pruned

You don't know less as you grow older. You probably know much more, and you certainly are a lot wiser than when you were young. But your information processing speed slows down as you age — that's just a fact of life. To retain your power to learn and recall, remember to

- **Reduce your stress level.** See Chapter 7.
- **Improve your blood circulation — exercise!**
- **Correct any reduction in your hearing or eyesight.**
- **Push your temporal lobes into more activity.** For example, listen to lectures and discuss them afterwards. (I talk about lobes in Chapter 3.)
- **Keep your occipital lobes humming.** Attending photo and art shows is one way. Going on sightseeing trips is another.
- **Share jokes with friends.** Join in the kinds of activities that your friends say are fun.
- **Change your routines.** Try new routes that cause you to think.
- **Turn off the TV.** Use the time to start a new hobby.
- **Go back to school.** Attend adult-education classes.
- **Spend time with young people.** They can inspire you and keep you quick on your feet.

See Chapter 10 for more details.

How to Remember a Name

Most people forget names because they stumble at the first step — getting the name right upon hearing it the first time. So follow these steps closely:

- **Pay attention.** Make sure that you hear the name clearly. If you don't, ask him to repeat it.
- **Give the name special meaning.** Connect the name with some aspect of his physical appearance or personality by:
  - **Exaggerating:** Imagining an artist drawing a caricature of the person and highlighting that one physical feature
  - **Associating:** Linking that one physical feature with some aspect of his personality, such as the way he moves or expresses himself or wears his clothes.
- **Repeat the name.** Use it in conversation with him — but don't overdo it. Repeat the name silently to yourself.
- **Review afterwards.** Think again about the clever association you've made between his name and some aspect of his appearance or personality.

See Chapter 14 for more details on remembering names and faces.

How to Remember a Birthday

One way to remember an important date like a birthday is to use the Loci technique. *Loci* means location. For example, suppose the birthday you want to remember is November 4. Using familiar locations, here are the steps:

1. **November:** In most temperate regions of the Northern Hemisphere, deciduous trees lose their leaves by November. Your first loci clue is bare trees on the way to work.
2. **Four:** You pass four barns during a stretch of your daily commute. So after you notice the leafless trees, the four barns cue you to remember that the birthday is on November 4.
3. **Birthday present:** The crass commercial billboards along your route remind you to buy a gift.

Of course, you may have to change your location cues if you move to the treeless desert or if the four barns are torn down to accommodate 600 new houses. But you can invent a new loci story with help from Chapter 9.

For Dummies: Bestselling Book Series for Beginners

Improving Your Memory For Dummies®

Cheat Sheet

Feeding Your Brain for Maximum Memory

What you eat and drink directly affects the chemistry of your brain and thus the keenness of your memory. For best results, adopt these habits (and check out Chapters 4 and 5):

- Eat three balanced meals per day, each meal consisting of three parts:
  - Fruit or vegetable
  - Complex carbohydrate, like whole-wheat bread
  - Protein
- Stay hydrated:
  - Drink water and juices
  - Moderate your caffeine intake
  - Minimize sodas and sugar drinks
- Take the following supplements:
  - Vitamins, such as C, E, and the Bs
  - Minerals, such as calcium, magnesium, and zinc
  - Herbs, such as Gingko (unless you're taking blood-thinning medications)

Protecting Your Memory from Overload in a High-Speed World

Chapter 16 goes into details, but because you're in a hurry:

- **Avoid multitasking, like talking on the phone while e-mailing, or watching TV while reading.** Divided attention dampens memory. Be selective. Be exclusive.
- **Finish each project before moving on to the next.** If that's impossible, make a clean break as you move back and forth. For example, stand up and stretch.
- **Keep your cellphone and pager turned off when you don't absolutely need to be in touch.**
- **Check e-mail and phone-mail messages a few times a day, not continuously.**
- **Watch TV selectively.** Don't watch just to see "what's on."

Improving Your Memory

FOR

DUMMIES®

Improving Your Memory FOR DUMMIES®

by John B. Arden, Ph.D.

Wiley Publishing, Inc.

Best-Selling Books • Digital Downloads • e-Books • Answer Networks • e-Newsletters • Branded Web Sites • e-Learning

Improving Your Memory For Dummies®

Published by
Wiley Publishing, Inc.
111 River Street
Hoboken, NJ 07030
www.wiley.com

Copyright © 2002 by Wiley Publishing, Inc., Indianapolis, Indiana

Published simultaneously in Canada

For general information on our other products and services or to obtain technical support, please contact our Customer Care Department within the U.S. at 800-762-2974, outside the U.S. at 317-572-3993, or fax 317-572-4002.

Wiley also publishes its books in a variety of electronic formats. Some content that appears in print may not be available in electronic books.

Library of Congress Cataloging-in-Publication Data:

Library of Congress Control Number: 2002106046

ISBN: 0-7645-5435-2

Manufactured in the United States of America

10 9 8 7 6 5 4

1B/TQ/RS/QT/IN

About the Author

John Boghosian Arden, Ph.D., is the Director of Training for Psychology in the Kaiser Permanente Medical Centers in Northern California. In this capacity, he oversees 20 training programs in as many medical centers. He is also the local Director of Training at Kaiser Permanente in Vallejo, California, where he served in the past as Chief Psychologist.

Dr. Arden is the author of four other books: *Consciousness, Dreams, and Self* (winner of the 1997 Outstanding Academic Book of the Year Award by *Choice* — a publication of the American Library Association); *Science, Theology, and Consciousness* (nominated by an international panel of jurists for the Templeton Prize); *Surviving Job Stress;* and *Creating the Lowest Common Denominator Society*.

Dedication

This book is dedicated to my wife, Vicki, and our two sons, Paul and Gabe, who were more than patient and supportive of me during the long hours and months I spent writing this book. Vicki also read every page of this book before I sent it on to my editor, always forcing me to be clear and straightening out my grammatical stumbling.

Author's Acknowledgments

No book is written in a vacuum or is the product of just one person's effort. Many people deserve my hearty thanks and acknowledgment. To begin with, many thanks go to my always pleasant and hardworking agent, Elizabeth Frost-Knappman, for asking me to put together a proposal to write this book and for working out the contractual details that are well beyond me. I am very fortunate to be represented by Elizabeth and her husband, Ed.

To Greg Tubach, Acquisitions Editor, for working with both Elizabeth and me to help me get into the ballpark and learn to write a book of this style. He was more than gracious.

To my Project Editor, Norm Crampton, who was my partner. Norm worked with me for all the months that it took for this book to develop, and it was his job to make sure that it took the proper form and became the best that it could be. He was always there, not only to provide helpful suggestions and forcing me to be practical and down to earth, but also to be a friend. Our many pleasurable conversations touched on everything from politics to family and were always enlivened by his warmth and humor.

Finally, to Norm's associate, Senior Copy Editor, Patricia Yuu Pan, who, with her colleagues Chrissy Guthrie and Mary Fales went over every page and word to make sure that what you read is clear and complete. Her running dialog with Norm, which I was privy to, was not only helpful, but quite fascinating, because it all took place in the amazing high-tech environment of e-mail.

Publisher's Acknowledgments

We're proud of this book; please send us your comments through our Dummies online registration form located at www.dummies.com/register/.

Some of the people who helped bring this book to market include the following:

Acquisitions, Editorial, and Media Development

Project Editor: Norm Crampton

Acquisitions Editor: Greg Tubach

Copy Editors: Patricia Yuu Pan, Christina Guthrie, Mary Fales

Technical Editor: Michael Shore, Ph.D.

Editorial Manager: Christine Beck

Editorial Assistant: Melissa Bennett

Cover photo: © Royalty-Free/Corbis

Composition

Project Coordinator: Dale White

Layout and Graphics: Scott Bristol, Brian Drumm, Jackie Nicholas, Barry Offringa, Betty Schulte, Mary J. Virgin

Proofreaders: Dave Faust, TECHBOOKS, Inc.

Indexer: TECHBOOKS, Inc.

Publishing and Editorial for Consumer Dummies

Diane Graves Steele, Vice President and Publisher, Consumer Dummies
Joyce Pepple, Acquisitions Director, Consumer Dummies
Kristin A. Cocks, Product Development Director, Consumer Dummies
Michael Spring, Vice President and Publisher, Travel
Brice Gosnell, Associate Publisher, Travel
Suzanne Jannetta, Editorial Director, Travel

Publishing for Technology Dummies

Richard Swadley, Vice President and Executive Group Publisher
Andy Cummings, Vice President and Publisher

Composition Services

Gerry Fahey, Vice President of Production Services
Debbie Stailey, Director of Composition Services

Contents at a Glance

Table of Contents

Introduction

So you want to improve your memory. Good! You've come to the right place. Your memory can be the key to success and enjoyment on the one hand or the key to mistakes and concern on the other hand. Practically all of us have first-hand experience on *both* hands.

Improving your memory is a worthwhile activity no matter how old you are, from high school student studying for exams to carefree retiree making new acquaintances.

Wherever you are, whatever you're doing, you can improve your memory, and I can show you how.

About This Book

This book is about your memory — what it is, what it isn't, and how to improve it. This book is a resource that you can count on not only to explain how your memory works, but also to provide you with ways to improve it.

Because there's no single, all-purpose way to improve your memory (and no magic memory pill), this book addresses the wide variety of ways that you can boost your memory skills. You can discover how to enhance your brain's ability to remember and how to avoid those things that drag it down. I also show you how to use a number of tricks to remember what you want to remember.

Whether you want to remember facts and ideas for an upcoming exam, improve your memory of work processes on the job, or just remember the people you meet, you can discover ways to do all that and much more in this book.

Who Needs This Book

I don't know what your age is, but I do know that you have memory skills. You simply can't live without them. How good those memory skills are is another question. However, the opportunity is the same for you, me, and everyone else: There's always room to improve memory skills.

So the answer to "Who Needs This Book" is simple: We all do. Everyone can benefit from using *Improving Your Memory For Dummies* as a reference and guide.

How to Use This Book

Because you can improve your memory in a wide variety of ways, you can think of this book as a general resource and reference. I suggest that you use each chapter as a self-contained mini-book on a special aspect of improving your memory.

For example, in the chapter on nutrition, you find tips on improving your memory by what you eat. In the chapter on mnemonics (nee-MON-iks), you can discover useful little tricks for remembering things — for example, associating something you know well with something else that you want to remember.

Each chapter in this book is an independent unit, but each is also one part of the bigger picture concerning ways you can improve your memory. I hope that you dip into every chapter and consider all the advice I provide in this book — but you don't have to. Browse, if you want to. Take what you need at the moment and save the rest for later. It's okay to skip around and read the chapters out of order. If a topic, such as improving your memory at work, is important to you right now, you can start with Chapter 12, and then you can jump to, say, Chapter 5, which covers food supplements that have a good effect on memory. Your route and pace through this book are strictly up to you.

I do recommend, however, that you read the entire book, over time, because there's no *one* way to improve your memory. The more ways you discover and learn to use memory skills, the better those skills become.

How This Book Is Organized

This book is organized in parts. Each of the five parts covers a broad area associated with your memory.

Part 1: Understanding Memory

Use this part to discover what your memory is and what it isn't. Find out how your memory works and what kinds of things affect it, from body chemistry to outside environment. Basically, Chapter 1 gives you the big picture.

Chapter 2 sorts fact from fiction concerning memory, so that you can cast away the myths and concentrate on strategies that actually do have an effect on memory.

Chapter 3 tells you all about how your brain remembers. Your brain works as a system of systems to form your memories. Various parts of the brain are specialized to perform specific roles in your memory. Chapter 3 explains how short-term memories move into long-term memory, how attention and association are important parts of your memory, and more.

Part II: Establishing Memory Power

You can improve your memory in many ways. You can also diminish your memory in many ways. Part II covers this territory in detail.

Chapter 4 explains how important a balanced diet is to your memory. What you eat has a major effect on your brain chemistry, which, in turn, has a major effect on how well you remember.

Chapter 5 takes you on a tour of dietary supplements — vitamins, minerals, and herbs — that help support your brain's ability to remember. I explain which ones are helpful.

Chapter 6 identifies illnesses and warns you away from lifestyle habits (smoking, poor diet, and so on) that suppress your memory.

In Chapter 7, you discover why relaxing is so important to remembering, and I suggest relaxation techniques. You also discover how to pull yourself out of a depression, so that you're not distracted and can remember better. The chapter also covers sleep and exercise — two vital parts of a strong memory.

Part III: Preserving Your Memory

Chapters 8, 9, and 10 serve as your memory "maintenance manual" where I show you a number of all-purpose strategies and tricks for remembering the things you *want* to remember (the central topic of Chapter 8). I cover a variety of mnemonic techniques, such as loci, peg, and story links.

Chapter 9, "Troubleshooting Your Forgetfulness," shows you how to "over-learn," so that you can tell yourself with pride, "I've got that down cold!" (Don't you love the sound of those words?) The chapter also explains how to apply other useful remedies called tagging, chunking, rhyming, and serializing.

Chapter 10 is your "sooner or later" chapter. Sooner or later, as people grow older, they worry that their memory is withering away. Chapter 10 explains what's what about aging and memory, and shows you how to maximize your memory skills as you age.

Part IV: Exercising Your Memory Every Day

You test your memory skills in a variety of arenas every day of your life. In this part, you find out how to enhance your memory as you meet challenges at work, school, and in social situations.

In Chapter 11, you can discover how to maximize your memory skills while you try to learn as much as you can at school.

When you're at work, your memory is working every minute. In Chapter 12, you find out ways that you can stretch your memory skills while on the job.

Whether at school or at work, your memory is put to the test regularly. Chapter 13 shows you how to ace those exams.

Human beings are social creatures. You've probably met hundreds, if not thousands, of people in your lifetime. You may not remember them all, but, in Chapter 14, you find out how to remember the ones you *want* to remember.

If remembering dates, appointments, and anniversaries is important to you, Chapter 15 is your key reference to practical ways that you can make sure you don't forget.

The last chapter of Part IV contains my best advice on preserving a strong memory in a Post-Modern world that's saturated with cell phones, e-mails, pagers, instant messaging, and so on. Remembering who just called, e-mailed, or paged you can be hard if you're off to something else before you can digest the conversation. Chapter 16 shows you how to avoid the memory perils of multitasking or jumping from one engagement to another with barely a break in between.

Part V: The Part of Tens

The three chapters in Part V provide information about memory in a top-ten format. Chapter 17, "Ten Best Ways to Improve Your Memory," is a quick list of reminders. Chapter 18 covers ten frequently asked questions about memory and provides the answers. Finally, Chapter 19 is your reference to ten sites on the World Wide Web where you can find many more fascinating facts and helpful hints about improving your memory.

Icons Used in This Book

The margins of this book contain little pictographs called icons. Here's what they mean:

Targets information that you can apply at once to improve your memory.

Cautions you away from certain kinds of behavior that can derail your memory improvement effort.

Presents information about memory gathered from my practice as a psychologist.

You could tag the whole book with this icon, but I reserve it for big ideas about memory.

Gives you the deep background on a few selected topics.

Part I

Understanding Memory

The 5th Wave   By Rich Tennant

"Nothing shows up on the tests. I think your memory loss is probably just stress-related."

In this part . . .

Human beings have wonderful imaginations. You and I can imagine all sorts of things about our memories — some of it true, some of it not. This part sorts fact from fiction and shows you around the brain's anatomy so that you're familiar with memory land. I explain how the brain works and how it performs amazing gymnastics for you, 24-7.

Chapter 1

Cultivating Your Memory Skills

. . . .

. . . .

*N*ine out of ten people say that they want to improve their memory. Are you one of them? Are you also one of the six out of ten people who tell pollsters that they've had the awkward experience of walking into a room — and forgetting why?

These numbers seem to suggest that planet Earth is experiencing an epidemic of declining memories, but that's not the case. Nearly everyone wonders from time to time whether he or she is losing memory power.

By reading this book, you're demonstrating that you want to have the best memory possible. Therefore, my job is to show you how to improve your memory and how to avoid losing it.

In this chapter, I cover the main points of the book and address the initial concerns you may have about your memory. I also recommend tactics you can employ to improve your memory. What's more, you find out how your brain works, how to feed it, and how to minimize exposing it to harmful parts of the world that we all live in. You also discover the variety of memory systems that you possess, along with techniques for expanding your memory abilities.

Your journey to a better memory begins now!

Wondering about Skips in Your Memory

Nobody's memory is perfect all the time. You've probably noticed some forgetfulness and absentmindedness on occasion. Some types of memory loss — like forgetting your keys and forgetting names — are quite common. But when memory glitches occur more often and more severely, that's another thing entirely.

The types of memory loss that are reasonable cause for alarm include repeatedly getting lost on a familiar route home; having difficulty finding words to express yourself; having difficulty identifying common objects; not knowing where you are; not knowing the time of the day; and asking the same question over and over again when you aren't hoping to get a different answer than you got previously.

If you've noticed an abrupt and severe loss of memory, you should consult your doctor right away. This sudden and severe loss could be a symptom of a major health problem that needs immediate attention. You could be suffering from a wide variety of major medical problems, or you could be taking medications that have side effects, such as those that affect your memory.

Although I address some of these issues in Chapter 6, don't wait to read that chapter before consulting with your doctor. This book isn't meant to be an alternative to first-line medical help.

Being present rather than absentminded

No doubt, you're like most people who've locked themselves out of the house or who've forgotten what they were going to buy after they arrived at the store. I'll never forget the time that I locked my keys in the trunk of my car. This experience wouldn't have been so bad had I done it in my driveway; I easily could have gone back into the house for my wife's keys or called AAA and sat waiting in the comfort of home, reading, and sipping an espresso. No, the location I picked for this misadventure was the North Rim of the Grand Canyon at the trailhead parking lot. I was 2 miles from the lodge, which wouldn't have been a problem had I not just hiked rim to rim, 24 miles down to the bottom and back up to the top — a change in elevation of about 5,280 feet, twice!

My absentmindedness occurred just after I arrived on top and was changing from shorts to long pants. I put the shorts in the trunk of the rental vehicle, and an elderly man walked up asking where I had been. I politely satisfied his curiosity by proudly telling him that I had just made my 17th hike to the bottom, and then I slammed the trunk closed. Oops!

If you lose your keys somewhere other than on the North Rim of the Grand Canyon, you may want to imagine walking around your house. Try to go from room to room in your imagination, remembering what you did in each room (see Chapter 8).

If you can't locate your keys in your mind, retrace your steps and try to make associations when you enter each room. You may remember opening the refrigerator door to pull out a container of orange juice and putting the keys down on the counter so you could open the cabinet door to grab a glass.

Absentmindedness means what it says: Your mind is absent from where you are in the present. Don't expect to remember what you were doing if your mind was elsewhere.

Most people in their 40s and 50s experience absentmindedness and other minor memory problems. Usually, these instances are normal and are no cause for concern.

People 60 and up commonly experience some loss in short-term memory. Unless these problems are progressive and severe, there is also no cause for concern.

Before going to bed each night, I find myself checking to see that the doors are locked — sometimes twice! I waste this time not because I have obsessive-compulsive disorder (OCD), but because I'm thinking about something else or talking. My mind is absent from what I am doing.

If you don't need the exercise of checking the doors two times every night, make the check only one time with your mind in gear. Make it part of a routine, like brushing your teeth. Find yourself noticing the differences in the locks, like their firmness or loose hardware. Be mindful of the process of checking (see Chapter 16).

On the tip of your tongue

You're probably familiar with this experience: You're in the middle of a conversation, and even though you know the word you want to utter, you can get out only a few syllables, or maybe just the first letter.

Perhaps you know that the word starts with two letters, T and I, and you begin to start your search. Tianna? No, Timumu? You know that you're looking for a northern city in the country of Mali, and you remember how far away the city is and how the name is often used as the epitome of remoteness, "Oh yeah, Timbuktu."

In fact, you can go to Timbuktu or any other place in the world and find people who've had this problem. In Korean, the tip-of-the-tongue (TOT) phenomenon is referred to as *hyeu kkedu-te-man-dol-da.* In Afrikaans, it's *op die punt van tong;* in Italian, *sulla punta della lingua;* and in Estonian, *kee le otsa peal.* (See if you can remember those expressions!)

The TOT phenomenon provides clues about the complexity of memory. When you feel that you know a word but can't seem to recall what it is, you're still recalling something. You know that a word applies succinctly to what you're trying to say.

As you get older, you'll find that the number of times you want to utter a word that you can't remember increases. These TOT experiences are quite common and have been described as being on the verge of a sneeze.

Memory is not an all-or-nothing skill. It's a skill that can be improved upon (see Chapter 2). There's a difference between whether you remember something in detail and whether you remember it at all. Like the TOT problem, you remember that you have memory somewhere in your mind, but now you need to recover it.

If you want to recall a word that's eluding you, think around it. Look for associations — connections between that word and other ideas and concepts. (See Chapter 8 for more on association.) In the Timbuktu example, instead of focusing on the sound of the word (Tim . . . Tutt . . . Tot), think of the meaning of the word. With Timbuktu, you may want to focus on the metaphoric meaning of the word. Next, think about how the name has a unique sound that in many ways reflects its remoteness. By thinking around the actual word, the association brings you sooner or later to the word itself.

Unblocking the block

Chances are, you've forgotten your PIN or password when using one of the multitude of automated so-called conveniences. If you are caught in the maze of a phone-tree system that won't let you out without your password, you may think that you're losing your mind — not because of the password, but because of the happy, recorded voices repeatedly telling you how important your business is. If you could only talk to a real person!

Most people have had the experience of feeling as if they know something but something else is "blocking" their memory. Some people even say, "I'm blocking on that." This blockage is similar to the tip-of-the tongue problem, but it doesn't involve trying to remember a name or something else discrete; it involves a more complex memory, such as what Carol said yesterday at work.

The more you "try" to remember, the more you feel "all bottled up." Forcing out a memory compounds the problem, as if you have your foot on the gas pedal and the brake at the same time.

A good way to allow the block to ease up is to take your foot off the gas for a moment. In other words, stop trying. Take a brief break and a few deep breaths. Go do something else for a moment. If you're with other people, say, "It'll come to me in a minute." Talk about something else for a while. Allow your mind to wander. In a matter of moments, you'll likely pick up an association that will trigger the full spectrum of memories you were trying so hard to dig up.

The ancient memory tradition

Well before Gutenberg developed his printing press and the written word was widely available, many of the great thinkers in history praised memory as a window to the divine and a means of absorbing wisdom.

Pre-Socratic poet Simonides regarded memory as the means through which the arts and wisdom interact. He was the originator of mnemonic techniques to aid memory. Roughly a century later, Plato believed that knowledge is latent in our memories. (We already know, so all we have to do is remember.) His student, Aristotle, is said to have written a book on mnemonics, which, if ever written, is lost. Nevertheless, he proposed that memory is what makes higher processes of thought possible.

The Romans, so dependent on Greek thought, cultivated memory techniques as part of their rhetoric (the art of using words). Cicero and Quintilian wrote books focusing on the techniques of memory that were used through the Middle Ages. The Roman philosopher and a teacher of rhetoric, Seneca, was said to be able to repeat 2,000 names in the order given to him. Several centuries later, St. Augustine boasted that his friend could recite Virgil backwards. And at the end of the Middle Ages, St. Thomas Aquinas was famed for having a phenomenal memory.

Memory skills were indeed highly useful until the advent of the printing press. With the proliferation of books, "external memory" could give a handicap to those needing a little support.

Clearing the Air of Random Noise and Ridiculous Ideas

We're a society inundated with stimuli that demand our attention. E-mail, faxes, cell phones, and the constant bombardment of commercials litter our minds and clutter our memories. Life was simpler in years past. Today's world puts more demands on our memory skills.

How many things can you pay attention to at the same time? Some people keep the television on all the time, thinking it's "only in the background." They mistakenly think that the distraction is "no bother unless I look at it." Some teenagers do their homework with loud rock-and-roll music blasting their ears. If you have a teenager at home, you've probably asked him to turn down the music, thinking it's interfering with his ability to remember what he's studying — and you're right.

Although he may think that he's taking in what he needs to be remembering, he is limited in how much he can actually absorb. Think of your brain as capable of multitasking, but at a cost. When you multitask, you spread yourself out, diluting your attention. If your attention is compromised, so is your ability to remember.

How do you know what to pay attention to and what to remember? If you say, "I need to pay attention to everything," you're being terribly unrealistic. You need a way to sift the wheat from the chaff. That is, you need to develop the ability to pay attention to what's important and allow yourself to forget what's not.

Before you can improve your memory, you need to be realistic about your potential memory capabilities. You can probably do a lot to improve it, but you don't want to set impossible goals, such as:

- Being able to pay attention to several things at once and remember them with great accuracy
- Expecting to improve your memory without effort
- Assuming that you'll remember everything you've ever experienced

Sorting fact from fiction

You've probably read sensational claims that you can "boost your brain power." Some hucksters claim that you're using only 10 percent of your brain. Some even claim that you're using only 1 percent of your brain. The fact is, the percentage of your brain that you're using isn't what's important. You're using all of it now. The more precise way to address this issue is not how much (quantity) but how well (quality) you're using it. If you improve the way you use your brain's thinking ability, your memory can improve tenfold.

Some so-called experts offer a single method to improve memory; with this single tool, you can supposedly master any memory task, impress your friends, and thrill yourself. Of course, the idea that a single tool can improve your memory is ridiculous because your mind is far too complex. In this book, you discover numerous ways that can improve your memory skills.

Some books offer "the secret" to a good memory. But just as there's no single tool to improve your memory, there's no one secret about memory. In fact, what psychologists know about memory isn't a secret at all. It's a secret only because you haven't discovered it. Psychologists have been amassing information about memory for more than 100 years, and they haven't been storing it away in a secret chamber.

Some books even claim that your mind can become a gigantic sponge that won't forget anything. This notion is not only impossible, but also absurdly impractical. Do you really want to remember everything? Imagine the debris of memories you'd have to wade through when trying to retrieve an important memory. This would be like not being able to distinguish a crusty rock from a diamond. You must forget so you can remember. Putting it another way, being able to forget unimportant experiences allows you to remember the ones that are important.

The shortness of your working memory is necessary for you to maintain an ongoing presence in the world. The rapid cleaning of the slate of working memory allows your mind to clear for the next series of moments. By remembering what just happened, you can move on to the next moment with crucial information. You're able to make decisions based on what you just did and what you just thought about.

Imagine how cluttered your mind would be if you remembered each and every useless detail. Your mind transfers into long-term memory information that will be important to you later and readies itself to collect new impressions of the world around you.

Some books claim that by reading them, you can develop a "super mind" with memory powers beyond that of normal humans. These books imply that your memory can be psychic, remembering beyond your own experience. What's more, some books claim that your memory can leap beyond your computer in a single bound.

My point? Yes, you can improve your memory, but not by psychic ability or by becoming like a computer. Your memory is a psychological skill, and by reading this book, you find out how to improve that skill.

The good-news/bad-news reality

I have good news and bad news about your memory. The bad news is that there isn't a single trick, pill, or secret that can magically move your memory into high gear. The good news is that a wide variety of techniques can improve your memory skills.

The bad news is that laziness makes your memory skills dull. The good news is that, with effort, you have tremendous opportunity to improve your memory. But this effort doesn't mean torture. It can be fun, stimulating, and invigorating.

The old adage "Use it or lose it" applies to your memory. Using it can be so rewarding that you wonder why you ever chose to sit back and watch your memory skills drift away.

You may worry that people with a higher IQ have better memories than you do. It's true that psychological memory tests are highly correlated with scores on IQ tests. But stop to think about it for a minute. How did the people with high IQ scores do so well on the tests? Their memory skills help bolster their IQs. If you improve your memory skills, you can help support your IQ.

Your memory skills support the foundation for just about all your thinking abilities. Improve these skills, and you find yourself better able to reach your potential in numerous areas of your life.

Improving Your Memory

You can employ a number of techniques to improve your memory. But because you're a complex human being, no one method alone can do the job. You need to do a number of things all at once to improve your memory.

Never fear! Improving your memory isn't difficult if you do the following:

- Understand the facts and myths of how your memory works (see Chapters 2 and 3).
- Make sure that your brain is capable of remembering (see Chapter 4).
- Avoid memory depressors (see Chapter 6).
- Keep your mind sharp by challenging yourself intellectually.
- Learn memory techniques, such as mnemonics (see Chapter 8).
- Apply your memory skills on the spot, such as at school, at work, or in social situations (see Chapters 12–14 and 16).

I address all these aspects of your memory in the coming chapters. By using this comprehensive approach, you not only enjoy improved memory skills but also enhance the quality of your life.

Discovering what your memory skills are

To improve your memory, you need to know what memory is and isn't. You need to understand the facts about your memory and discard the myths.

Some of the following facts may surprise you:

- **Your memories are constantly reshaping throughout your life.** They aren't snapshots of information, frozen in time. Throughout your life, you go through all sorts of changes: You mature, learn from previous mistakes, and even get tainted by unfortunate experiences. Your perspective changes over time, and the lens that you use to look back at your memories colors those memories. Your brain is far too complex and is always changing, which affects the way you look at your memories. They're subject to modification by everything you experience.

- **Your memory is a skill that you can cultivate and improve upon, no matter what your age, intelligence level, or socioeconomic class.** Your memory isn't something that you have or don't have. It can't be lost or found like a memory chip. However, if you do incur damage to your brain, the amount and type of damage can limit your memory skills (see Chapters 3 and 6).

✔ **Your entire brain works together as one system.** Each memory has input from a wide variety of different parts of your brain. Memories aren't stored in one place in your brain. Your brain codes memories like a system of different units. Some areas of your brain have unique talents in coding memories that correspond to shapes. A few other areas have unique talents in coding words. Your entire brain works together, so when you're trying to remember a 1969 Volkswagen Beetle, you remember the shape with one part of your brain (the right hemisphere) and the words Volkswagen Beetle with another part of your brain (the left hemisphere — see Chapter 3).

The more dimensions and parts of your brain you can involve in a memory, the more easily you can remember it later. Remembering a 1969 Volkswagen Beetle is easier than remembering a 1969 Plymouth Valiant because of the shape of the Beetle and the word Beetle (see Chapters 3, 8, and 9).

✔ **Your brain possesses several key parts that play a major role in forming the foundation of your memory.** One the key parts of your brain is called the *hippocampus,* which moves short-term memories into long-term storage. (You can find more details about the parts of a brain in Chapter 3.)

The short-term memories that you move into long-term memory depend largely on three factors:

- **Your attention:** Generally, a measure of short-term memory.

- **The meaningfulness of the information:** The more meaningful or relevant the information, the greater your chances of remembering it.

- **How well the memory fits into what you already know:** A foundation of memory helps with new learning.

✔ **Your memory depends on your attention.** Your memory simply doesn't work unless you're paying attention. But when you're paying attention, your brain is capable of extraordinary mental gymnastics. If you protect and care for it, you can possess keen memory skills.

Your phenomenological loop

At the interface between short-term memory and long-term memory, a *phenomenological loop* acts as a gateway for new words. You use this when building your vocabulary, by learning specific words, or when learning a new language. The phenomenological loop is centered in the left hemisphere of your brain. If your left pre-frontal cortex is damaged, you have trouble expressing words. If the back part of your left temporal lobe is damaged, you have trouble understanding what's being said to you.

Feeding your brain properly

Your ability to remember depends on a number of factors, first of which is maintaining a healthy brain through adequate nourishment. To ensure that your brain works at an optimum level, follow these guidelines:

- **Maintain a balanced diet.** What you eat affects your brain's chemistry. Eating the right foods at the right time gives your body the building blocks to manufacture brain chemicals called *neurotransmitters*. Neurotransmitters not only affect your mood and ability to think clearly, but also your ability to remember.

  A simple, balanced meal consists of a carbohydrate, a protein, and a fruit or vegetable. Eating a balanced meal three times a day can provide you with a sound foundation for your brain and its memory. (See Chapter 4 for more details on brain chemistry and nutrition.)

- **Take the right supplements.** Vitamins and herbs can support your brain's ability to produce good memory skills. Specific vitamins, such as some of the B vitamins, help form the building blocks for healthy brain chemistry. Other vitamins, such as vitamin E, help your brain cleanse itself of bad chemicals. It helps combat the destructive but subtle brain-wasting changes, such as free-radical damage, glycation, and homocystine. Herbs, such as gingko, have been used to enhance the circulation of blood in the brain. Gingko dilates the *capillaries* (small blood vessels), which can help your brain cells get the vital nourishment they need. (For more information on vitamins and herbs, see Chapter 5.)

- **Get regular exercise.** Exercise enhances your memory because it helps your brain receive the nutrients that it needs. Every time you exercise, you increase your respiratory rate, your metabolism, and your energy level. (For more details on exercise and memory, see Chapter 7.)

Avoiding food, drink, and drugs that depress memory

Foods, drinks, and chemicals that your brain is exposed to have major effects on your memory. I explore this in detail in Chapter 6.

If you eat junk food loaded with sugar, you set yourself up to crash, finding yourself full of anxiety and short of short-term memory. Similarly, if you drink too much caffeine, the liquid anxiety scatters your thoughts and shatters your memory ability. If you consume caffeine and sugar on an empty stomach, your mood and memory skills will plummet quickly.

Keep these two guidelines in mind:

> ✔ Avoid heavy amounts of sugary foods (like candy, cookies, and so on).

> ✔ Minimize caffeine (and never drink coffee on an empty stomach).

If you treat your brain badly, your long-term memory can erode, and your brain will reward you with few memory skills. You can avoid devastating your brain and memory by staying away from the following substances:

> ✔ **Alcohol:** It kills not only your brain cells but also what they produce — a good memory. Alcohol causes your thinking skills, which are so critical to a good memory, to erode away.

> ✔ **Drugs:** Marijuana and other drugs can cloud your memory so badly that you lose the ability to focus. The chemical found in marijuana, called *tetrahydrocannabinol* (THC), can really put a damper on your short-term memory as well as your motivation.

> ✔ **Neurotoxins:** These poisons include petrochemicals, solvents, and herbicides. They kill brain cells when you're exposed to them.

> ✔ **Food "enhancers":** *Monosodium glutamate* (MSG) and artificial sweeteners are damaging to brain cell operations.

Growing older and wiser

You may be like most people who worry that aging will make their memory wither away in time. Aging can affect your brain and its ability to remember.

It's true that your brain shrinks and loses mass as you age. You can slow down this deterioration by:

> ✔ Maintaining a balanced diet that is low in saturated fats.

> ✔ Eating foods high in vitamin, mineral, and antioxidant content.

> ✔ Taking vitamin supplements, including a broad-based multivitamin.

> ✔ Exercising on a regular basis.

> ✔ Pushing yourself to be mentally active, taking classes, going to lectures, reading, and maintaining stimulating conversation.

One of the factors that comes into play as you age is that you're compared to younger adults in thinking ability. Younger adults may have more practice in particular types of intellectual tasks and, as a result, be more skilled at these tasks.

But if you're elderly and have practiced a particular mental task, your skill level will not only rise but also rival your younger counterparts.

Working your memory systems

Whatever your age or background, you can improve your memory skills using numerous memory techniques, such as *mnemonics* (*nee-MON-iks:* cues that you can use to remind yourself of information). Some mnemonic techniques include Peg, Loci, and Story Link. I define all these terms and provide other details in Chapter 8.

Mnemonics can remind you by associating a letter or number to information. For example, if you're trying to remember the names of the Great Lakes, use the first letter as a cue. For example, by using the word HOMES you can remember each of the lakes: **H**uron, **O**ntario, **M**ichigan, **E**rie, and **S**uperior. Or use the phrase **H**ealthy **O**ld **M**en **E**xercise **S**ome.

Priming: To retrieve "lost" information

A process known as *priming* can also help you remember. When you're priming memories, you remember some related things in hopes of remembering the "lost" information. For example, if you forget where you've put your keys, you retrace your steps. You try to remember where you were and what you were doing, priming out the memory of where you left your keys.

You can structure information all sorts of ways to help you remember it. You can overlearn the material you want and get feedback while you're learning it. If you organize the information by serializing, chunking, or even rhyming it, you can remember it.

When you chunk information, you break it up into bite-size segments that are easier to remember. For example, when you learned to remember your social security number, you didn't memorize it as one long chain of 9 numbers, such as 235482971. You broke it up in three chunks, such as 235-48-2971.

Associating: When you can't remember the person's name

If you're like most people, you've felt embarrassed because you've blocked on a person's name. You've probably seen a few people at the supermarket and found that, though they look familiar, you can't remember their names.

You can remember a person's name by associating it with:

- ✔ Her occupation
- ✔ A physical characteristic, such as height
- ✔ A unique facial feature, such as a sharp chin
- ✔ The way she moves

Driving in the fast lane

Because stress can be a drain on your memory skills, job stress can bog down your memory while you're at work.

Have you ever felt like you're juggling several tasks at once while trying to do your job? It's one thing to be under pressure because of the workload, but quite another thing if the pressure you feel is self-imposed.

In our fast-paced society, where we talk on cell phones while we drive through fast-food restaurants before going home to check our e-mail while we simultaneously check our voice mail, we are at risk of feeling stressed and scattered. Our memory skills also will be stressed and scattered. If we import this scattered lifestyle into work and constantly try to juggle four or five tasks at once, we needlessly deplete our short-term memory.

You may say, "Yeah, but it's hard to maintain a slower pace than everyone else. The go-go mentality is contagious!" Yes, it's hard to resist what we can call the ADD society (where everyone seems to have Attention Deficit Disorder), even when you're at work. But if you don't resist, your memory at work can't reach its potential.

The bottom line is that each of the tasks that you juggle gets only a portion of your attention. None of the tasks can be completed in a thorough and comprehensive way. You find yourself forgetting what you were doing on each task. They begin to blur together.

Take a few steps back from the frenzied social climate and resist the temptation to juggle. Follow each task through to its completion before going on to the next task.

Putting your memory skills to the test

You can use memory techniques at school, at work, in social situations, and during exams. There are good ways and bad ways to prepare for exams, and all the details are in Chapter 13. Waiting for the last minute to study and trying to "cram" the information into your memory is one of the worst ways. On the other hand, if you organize your studying time, spreading out the time well before the exam, you'll do much better on the exam.

Cramming information before taking an exam is a good way to forget it.

Here are some of the main ways you can bolster your effort to remember information for an exam:

- ✔ Stretch out your learning instead of waiting until the last minute to cram.
- ✔ Organize your studying by starting with the outline and main subject areas and then homing in to the specific.
- ✔ Cover the main points and the "main main" points by using underlining and highlighting.

Sleeping well to remember well

Losing sleep can also mean losing some of your memory ability. Short-term insomnia is far less problematic than long-term insomnia. Short-term insomnia is usually the result of a poor diet, alcohol, caffeine, and/or stress, and it's easier to resolve quickly.

Long-term insomnia, however, fouls up your circadian rhythm. You may want to try the Sleep Scheduling Technique (described in Chapter 7) if you're experiencing long-term insomnia.

Overall, you can minimize insomnia by trying the following:

✔ Cut down on sugar and caffeine.

✔ Avoid alcohol.

✔ Minimize bright light late in the evening (including light from your computer monitor).

✔ Maximize bright light in the daytime.

✔ Do some exercise 3 to 6 hours before you go to sleep.

As you improve the quality of your sleep, you find that the quality of your memory skills also improves. So, get some good sleep.

✔ Get feedback early and adjust accordingly.

✔ Use mnemonics, symbols, and visual images.

Keeping your mind sharp

By maintaining a mind free of distractions, you increase your readiness to remember. Anxiety, depression, and sleep deprivation can put a damper on your memory skills (see Chapter 7 for details).

Learn to relax and stay alert enough to form memories. You can practice several relaxation techniques, such as progressive relaxation, meditation and/or prayer, self-hypnosis, imagery, and exercise.

Depression not only depresses your mood but also your memory. Pulling out of the dumps can help your memory skills bounce back from the pit of gloom. By learning how to correct your faulty thinking, you can pull out of the pit and enjoy the memory skills you once had.

Much of your memory skills depend on your ability to pay attention. If you're not mentally present because you're distracted, you wish you were somewhere else, or you're anxious, you won't code into memory or retrieve memories to your fullest ability.

You can try *mindfulness* to be fully present (see Chapter 16). This approach not only improves your memory because of your attentiveness and clarity of mind, but it also improves the quality of your life. Mindfulness involves being fully attentive to the moment, feeling and savoring every sensation, and slowing down to live in the present or the "now."

So get going. Cultivate your presence in the now. Clear your mind and improve your memory skills.

Chapter 2

Tossing Out Those Memory Myths

• •

• •

*Y*ou were born with a bad memory. Your memory is like a light switch —
sometimes on, sometimes off. You have a memory problem beyond repair.

If you agree with any of the above statements, here's some good news: You've
been held captive by the memory myths. You can break out of those memory
myths that hold you captive and improve the way you remember.

To get on the road to memory improvement, you need to throw away the
myths you've heard about memory. Some of these myths are so wrong that
simply believing in them adds to your stress level.

These myths include the following:

✔ Believing that you *will* lose your memory no matter what

✔ Believing that your memories are little files of information found in
specific parts of your brain

✔ Believing that your memories are true snapshots in time, uncontami-
nated by all the living you've done

✔ Believing that you don't have to pay attention to remember

✔ Believing that you're too old, too young, or too dumb to improve
your memory

In this chapter, you find out about the most common myths and replace them
with the facts about memory. These facts form the foundation for your effort
to improve your memory skills.

Myth: Thinking that You're Losing Your Memory

If you're like most people, you worry about losing your memory. You may forget someone's name in the middle of a conversation or misplace your keys and spend the next half-hour looking for them.

Never fear. You aren't losing your memory, because it's not a thing to be lost. Sweep away this and other myths and discover that your memory is a skill that can be sharpened.

Your memories aren't stored in specific corners in your brain. They're widely dispersed throughout your brain (see Chapter 3 for details about the brain). After more than 100 years of research, those experts who study the brain haven't found a specific place where memories are stored.

Many people are fond of using the image of a computer as a way to describe how their brain works. You may be one of these people who says, "My brain is like a computer that's obsolete. I can't access files because my brain's not quick enough, and I have no more room for new information."

Your brain and your memory skills are far more complex than any computer. Your memory skills can improve and aren't pre-programmed like a computer. Memory isn't a hard-wired part of your brain.

Your memory isn't a possession; it's an ability. It's not something you either have or don't have. Think of the word *memory* as a verb rather than a noun.

When I say that I enjoy hiking, I know that it's not a thing. It's an activity. Since childhood, I've become more skilled at hiking. When I use the word *memory* in this book, I mean your ability to remember, how you remember, and your style of remembering. Memory is what you do with greater or lesser skill.

You may think, "Well, that's all fine and good, but I was able to remember more in the past." This statement may be true. A person's memory ability can worsen over time in a variety of ways.

Here are some of the reasons why you may experience a decrease in your memory:

- A poor diet
- Alcohol or drug use
- Stress (including anxiety and depression)
- Medications with memory-depressing side effects
- Sleep deprivation

✔ Difficulty with paying attention

✔ Decreased mental activity

✔ Utilizing poor memory techniques

Many of these problems can be resolved. You can support your brain's ability to remember by doing the following:

✔ Maintaining a balanced diet (See Chapter 4 for details.)

✔ Taking vitamins and other supplements (I talk more about vitamins in Chapter 5.)

✔ Avoiding alcohol and drugs (I talk about these substances in Chapter 6.)

✔ Avoiding food supplements, such as MSG and aspartame (I also discuss these substances in Chapter 6.)

✔ Exercising on a regular basis, getting some sleep, and relaxing (I discuss the importance of these activities in Chapter 7.)

You can also figure out how to use memory techniques to enhance your memory skills, such as:

✔ Using mnemonic cues (see Chapter 8)

✔ Overlearning and stretching out your learning (see Chapter 9)

✔ Organizing the information you wish to remember into a pattern, such as serializing it or rhyming it (see Chapter 15)

✔ Developing a sense of meaning with the information

Myth: Memory Is Like a Filing Cabinet— F for Food, T for Travel

If your memory is an ability and not a thing, what kind of ability is it? Is it like riding a bicycle, driving a car, or cooking tonight's dinner? Sort of. However, memory is far more complex and underlies each one of these activities.

Memory is the basis for everything that you do and everything that you learn. You can't learn without it. Some people who have suffered severe brain injury have also lost the ability to remember in a variety of ways, depending on what area of the brain they injured. Memory skills work together as one memory system. If part of that system is damaged, they can still remember, but with specific limitations. For example, they may not be able to remember the shapes of objects as well as they did before the brain injury. Yet, they retain the ability to remember in ways the healthier parts of their brains allow.

Measuring memory

Psychologists don't use just one simple test to measure memory. We have several tests available to assess different types of memory. Some tests measure how well you remember what you hear. Others measure how well you remember shapes, touch, and so on. The mother of all memory tests is called the *Wechsler Memory Scale.* This battery of smaller subtests has gone through a few revisions over the years. Each time this test is revised, it gets more complicated, and more types of memory can be measured. Its many subtests measure different types of memory, such as the ability to remember words, lists of numbers, letter/number sequencing, and stories. Other subtests measure the ability to remember faces, family scenes, shapes, and the sequences of patterns. Scores are calculated to help a psychologist measure auditory and visual memory, both delayed and immediate. Overall, the index scores correspond to percentiles. Also, General Memory, Working Memory, and Immediate Memory scores can be compared to IQ scores.

When I told Dr. Ralph Reitan, the father of American neuropsychology (the study of how the brain affects behavior) that I was writing a book on memory, he said, "Make sure that you stress how memory is *systemic.*" What he meant was that memory involves systems of the brain that are associated with specific capabilities.

You have basic memory abilities, such as remembering what you hear, what you feel, and how you move. You also have complex types of memories. You remember shapes of various objects and faces, and you remember tunes, words, and numbers. Finally, you have even more complex types of memories, such as whole sentences, whole pieces of music, mathematical equations, the names of the capitals of the countries of South America, and so on.

Even the simplest of tasks involves multiple memory systems. When you drive your car, you're relying on a variety of different memory abilities. As you pull up to an intersection, you remember that it's a time for caution. You see a red, eight-sided sign and remember that it's a signal to stop (visual/spatial memory). You notice that the red sign has the word *Stop* painted on it, and you remember that the word means that you must make sure that your car comes to a complete stop (advanced verbal memory). You automatically remember that you need to remove your right foot from the gas pedal and place it on the brake pedal to bring the car to a halt without locking your tires (movement, touch, and spatial memory). Then, after you've come to a complete stop, you abide by the rules of traffic, remembering that the driver to the right has the right of way if you arrive at the same time (conceptual memory, involving many systems). You acknowledge that it's his turn to go ahead, so you look at him and wave (complex conceptual memory). He drives off. When it's safe, you take your foot off the brake and place it on the gas pedal, gradually applying pressure (movement and touch memory).

Even in this simple experience of coming to a stop at an intersection, you're accessing multiple systems of memory. Almost everything you do involves *systems* of memory rather than one discrete memory.

 Because so many systems in your brain all work together to form even the most simple memories (such as driving), the more ways you code a memory, the easier it'll be for you to remember it.

If I use the driving example again, even the stop sign itself has at least three different ways to be coded. You can remember the distinctive shape of the sign. Or you can remember the distinctive red color of the sign. Or you can read it and remember what the word *stop* means.

So if you're illiterate, in which case you can't read the sign, you can still remember the shape and the color. But if you're color blind, you can remember it by shape and the word *stop*. If you're completely blind, you'd better not be driving.

Myth: Memories Are Snapshots, and Cameras Don't Lie

Who you are in the present determines what you remember about your past. Think about that, and you can see why you're sometimes surprised by your memories.

Have you ever gone to visit the elementary school that you attended as a child and found yourself shocked that it's a lot smaller than you remember? Have you ever reflected on an early romance gone awry and found yourself remembering many of the idealized high points and few of the low points?

Just as memories aren't things, they also aren't etched in stone. Your memories aren't snapshots in time, to be remembered with complete accuracy later in life. Your memories are reworked, or re-remembered, from your perspective in the present. You look back at your life through the filter of all the experiences you've had since the events that you're trying to remember.

When you think about your return to the elementary school, your memory is affected by who you were then and who you are now. When you were a child, your school was "big" to you. In this sense, your memory that your school was big represented who you were at the time. You were smaller then, so everything looked larger to you. But you've probably even exaggerated the memory by making the school larger than it actually was because you experienced so much at that school. It was one of the primary centers of your childhood experiences.

Remembering becomes even more complicated when you try to remember events surrounding a romantic relationship. You look back at the love affair, remembering all those passionate moments. Somehow, you overlook the events that led to your breakup. You don't remember the whole picture because your memory of those passionate moments is so vivid.

Not only were those romantic experiences very important to you, but you remember them from the vantage point of the present. You probably exaggerate those memories of the high points if you're between relationships or in a bad one now. On the other hand, if you're in a good relationship, your memories of a past romance may not be as exaggerated.

This tendency has been shown to be the case with couples. If the relationship has soured, their memories of past times together may be tainted. For instance, a wife who's feeling that her husband is now cold and aloof may say, "He's always been that way."

When you try to remember events from your past, think about how you've changed since. By taking this moment to review your memories, you have the opportunity to see how you've grown and matured over time.

Brainwashing memories

Cults "brainwash" their members. They accomplish this feat partly by reworking the memories of their new members. To make sure that the new members are true believers in their new "family," cults convince them that their real families and old friends were mean or evil. They covertly, often through smothering kindness, pressure the new members to distort their memories of their past. The job of a re-programmer is to reconnect former cult members with the reality of their past and re-cultivate positive memories of their families and old friends.

Sometimes, it's too late for reprogramming. The cult takes them into the "new world" or to some illusive deliverance, as was the case with the Jonestown massacre in 1978 or the Heaven's Gate mass suicide, which occurred as cult members waited for the spaceship (hidden in the tail of the comet Hale-Bopp) to take them back to their "home planet." This phenomenon led many in popular culture to sport bumper stickers saying, "So many idiots, so few comets."

But the people who fall prey to the cults suffer from far more problems than the simplistic term "idiot" could possibly describe. They experience a loss of self, and that loss involves tremendous distortions of their personal memories.

Now that you understand that memories aren't simple snapshots of information, consider the highly controversial subject of *repressed memories.* Repressed memories are traumatic memories that have been pushed back into a person's unconscious. Over the past 20 years, some mental health professionals have tried to help their clients discover memories that may have been repressed. A therapist may try to help the person fill in the "gaps" in their memory of childhood.

You may wonder why you can't remember much about your life between birth and age 5. This memory gap is quite common and is no cause for alarm.

When you try to "dig up" early memories, don't forget that they're reworked and colored by your life in the present. Whatever you remember has been tainted and contaminated by what has happened in your life since the events that you're trying to remember originally took place.

Sometimes, these "discovered" memories involve the highly charged issue of childhood molestation. Although our society has done right by beginning to come to terms with this tragic issue, too many well-meaning mental health professionals have conjured up memories of events that didn't even happen.

Creating false memories

The contamination of memories even takes place when children are asked to "remember" events in the not-so-distant past. An unfortunate example occurred some years ago in California when the operators of a daycare center were wrongly accused of child molestation based on what the children "remembered." The children who attended this preschool were interviewed countless times by "trained professionals." These professionals "discovered" evidence that scores of children were abused in the school. Later, it was found that the "trained professionals" had led the children toward remembering events that solid evidence indicated never happened. For example, the interviewer used an anatomically correct doll and asked the child if he or she could "remember where you were touched." After several leading interviews, the children began to help the interviewers "discover" what they expected.

When children are asked repeatedly about a particular event, they eventually begin to feel that it must have happened. Because their abilities to remember objectively are limited, they patch together pieces of what the interviewer asks with what they may be familiar with — adult workers at the school, for instance. Some children were asked, "Did he touch you there, in your private spots?" If children are asked that several times, eventually it becomes familiar. Then, when the interviewer encourages, praises, or even rewards the children in any way by smiling and acting pleased, the children cooperate and confirm the so-called repressed memory. This technique hurt the adults, who were falsely accused, and the children, who became confused and overwhelmed.

I'm certainly not saying that memories of real childhood abuse aren't buried and distorted over time. However, a therapist must look for a number of other symptoms of abuse first, before trying to bring forth memories. (See the related sidebar titled, "Creating false memories," earlier in this chapter.)

People are more likely to push away a memory of childhood sexual abuse if the perpetrator is a family member rather than a neighbor or unfamiliar person. Accepting the fact that a family member could abuse you is simply much harder than accepting that a stranger could. This acceptance is especially difficult for children who are dependent on the adult family member.

Another way that many people believe they can recover lost memories is by the use of *hypnosis*. Some people still believe that, under hypnosis, you can capture memories untainted by the filter of your present life. This belief is based on the idea that, when in a hypnotic trance, you're in a separate reality, cut off from the nuisances of your conscious daily life.

After being trained in hypnosis, I came to appreciate how it can promote focus, relaxation, and suggestion. But I've also grown to appreciate how you can't tear a person away from his or her current beliefs or perspective when making post-hypnotic suggestions.

Neither can you use age regression to recover memories that are independent of who you are now. You simply can't go back in time to capture memories that haven't been influenced by your present life.

The bottom line is that memories aren't set in stone. They're reworked by all the experiences that you've had in your life since that time. You're not a computer. You're a highly complex human being who is growing and changing all the time — even now, as you learn about memory.

Because you aren't a computer with static memories, but are a complex human being, you can view your memories as reference points for the journey ahead. Whatever your age and educational background, think of yourself as being fully capable of making many more changes in your life.

To take a very basic example, you pick up tennis as a hobby and a way of getting exercise. But now, you're worried that you've hit a plateau in your playing ability. Though your learning curve may not be as steep as it was when you were first learning, think about how far you've come and how frustrated you were at different points along the way. From this perspective, you can keep going and continue learning.

As you review your memories of the past ten years in a particular area in your life, you not only have an opportunity to see how far you've come, but also how much farther you can go. This principal applies no matter what your age may be. Even if you're 80 years old, you can challenge yourself to develop a broad-based wisdom and reverence for life.

Myth: You Can Learn in Your Sleep and Other Nonsense

Ever since the 1950s, when advertisers were reported to have manipulated television and theater audiences with ads, accusations of "mind control" have popped up now and then. Large corporations, in fact, do a lot more than just convince people to buy their products. They have had a tremendous power over what we're served on television and even what we see on the news. But they exercise this power only when you're paying attention.

Think about the highly publicized series of incidents called *subliminal learning*. (Subliminal means "below your attention.") Theater audiences were subjected to split second, below-consciousness, flashes of the word *popcorn* on the screen. Popcorn sales reportedly shot through the roof because of this subliminal learning.

Well, popcorn sales did shoot up, and here's the rest of the story: When researchers asked the people buying popcorn why they were buying it, they said they had seen a quick picture of popcorn and had been reminded that they wanted some. The "subliminal" message wasn't hidden at all!

The truth is, for you to remember anything that you will later act on, you have to be alert to remember it. Advertisers have figured out that you'll remember their product only after they get your attention and teach you to associate their product with something important to you. For example, think of how an ad tries to convince you to buy a certain brand of automobile. This ad may fill your ears with a catchy tune that you'll have a hard time forgetting. It may also teach you that driving that brand of car can help you attract the opposite sex or be regarded as a person with class.

The take-home point here is that, to remember, you need to be attentive. Also, what you're trying to remember must be relevant to your life. A split-second flash of the word *popcorn* doesn't do the job.

This point leads to another myth about memory — sleep-learning. For many years, the United States and the former Soviet Union funded numerous studies that explored the use of sleep-learning. However, the results showed that sleep-learning wasn't a good way to learn. Some people did learn what they were hearing on tape — but because it woke them up! If we did this all the time we'd never sleep, and exhaustion is fatal to memory.

Some companies sell audiotapes that purport to "teach" you while you sleep. You're asked to believe that, as the tape drones on beneath your pillow, you're learning and will remember what you've learned the next day or even weeks later. My advice: If you're learning Spanish in your sleep to prepare for a trip to Latin America, make sure that you pack a good Spanish dictionary. Better still, take a translator.

Viva Las Vegas

You may have learned about idiot savants by watching the film *Rain Man*. Dustin Hoffman played a middle-aged man who had limited mental skills barely beyond that of a child. But he did have the uncanny ability to remember long strings of numbers. His unscrupulous brother, played by Tom Cruise, put that skill to use in Las Vegas. The term "idiot savant" means "learned idiot." These exceedingly rare people have developed one skill to such a point that they far surpass most people who have greater intellectual abilities overall. Idiot savants may be masters at calculation or remembering a complete piece of music, but they're generally limited in most other areas.

Sleep-learning isn't an effective way to learn. You're far better off trying to remember material when you're awake by reading, studying, or listening to lectures.

You've probably heard about people who can see something one time, even for a brief moment, and then remember it forever. Such a person is said to have a "photographic memory." You may have also heard of people who can hear a string of numbers once and repeat them with acute accuracy, even though they have few other skills. Such a person is referred to as an "idiot savant." (See the related sidebar titled "Viva Las Vegas.")

The truth is that very few people have such limited skills as to remember just one dimension with acute accuracy. Even those people who do possess these skills go over the material repeatedly in their minds.

To remember anything for any length of time, you have to go over the material. If, for example, you're trying to remember a picture or string of numbers, you'll need to reflect on specific details of that picture or repeat the numbers to yourself over and over again.

Also, you can benefit from using *associations, mnemonic devices, chunking,* and *peg systems* with the material that you're trying to remember. (I talk about all these things in Part III.)

The point is that a brief, snapshot exposure to something you're trying to remember isn't enough. What's the point of even trying? You're not a camera; you're a human being. Absorb the information. Don't wink at it.

You need to review the material repeatedly, *overlearning* it. If you're trying to learn material for a class you're taking, make sure that you overlearn the material. Overlearning involves studying the material thoroughly over an extended period. You want to study it from as many angles and perspectives as possible. Learn as much as you can about the subject matter, the history, the context, and the main issues. If you do, you'll remember more — simple as that.

For example, if you're trying to put to memory the political structure of Nigeria for an international relations class, you'll undoubtedly remember more if you read about the history, economics, and ethnic breakdown of the country. By reading about the three main ethnic groups (the Ibo, Hausa, and the Yoruba), you shade in one layer, one dimension. Then, you learn that the Hausa has been the dominant political group for some years. You learn that the Hausa occupy the center of the country as well as the northern part and have been largely Muslim. Then, you come across the history of the struggle between these groups and how, during the Biafran War, the Ibo were beaten back. You then turn to economics and learn that for the past 30 years, oil has dominated not only the economy but also foreign relations.

With all these dimensions committed to memory, you have a greater chance of remembering any one of these aspects of Nigeria. If you're tested on one aspect, thinking about another will allow you to link back. Say that you were asked about the Biafran War. Knowing about the three main ethnic groups can help you remember information about the war.

When you stretch out your learning or studying for an exam over a few weeks, you allow yourself the ability to remember the complexity of the material. In contrast, "cramming" the information the night before an exam is a very inefficient way to learn (see Chapter 13 for more on why cramming isn't a good idea). You don't retain the information you cram, possibly not even long enough to pass the exam.

The difference between cramming and stretched-out learning is similar to the difference between hastily sketching and producing an oil painting. With the sketch, you'll reveal the scene you're drawing in a one-dimensional way. With an oil painting, you're representing the scene with many different layers of complexity, including line, color, dimension, and texture. You want your memories to be more like the oil painting than a rough sketch.

Myth: You're Too Old, Too Young, or Too Dumb to Improve Your Memory

You likely have heard someone excuse himself or herself for a memory lapse by saying, "Sorry, I guess I'm having a senior moment." However, being a senior doesn't mean that you're doomed to lose your memory.

Yes, psychologists have shown that people do experience some decline in memory as they age. But this decline isn't as great as is popularly believed (see Chapter 10). Neither do all seniors experience memory decline at the same rate. Though some evidence suggests that visual and spatial memory erodes faster than verbal memory, everyone doesn't lose this memory at the same pace.

The fact is that those seniors who maintain a rich and active life experience fewer declines in memory and thinking ability. This trend supports the adage, "Use it, or you lose it." Actually, *how* you use your brain is important, just using it isn't enough. But, with practice, seniors can outperform their younger counterparts.

Speaking of the younger set, whether you have a teenager at home or are a teenager yourself, you may have heard people say, "He just doesn't seem to have his head screwed on tight." Being a teenager, or being a child for that matter, doesn't mean that you have to expect memory lapses.

Children and teenagers can improve their memory skills not only through maturation, but also through application of memory techniques. Why not get a head start and do better in school?

Henry Ford said, "Whether you think you *can* or whether you think you *can't*, you're right!" Why not be right about improving your memory?

Chapter 3

Discovering How Your Brain Remembers

*Y*ou possess the most complex organ on the planet. Your brain is more powerful than any computer — it can leap beyond any PC in one single memory. Your brain remembers with feeling, with the rich context of experience. No computer can do that.

In this chapter, you discover how your brain forms memories. I explain how your brain remembers, the stages that each memory goes through, and how the pathways through which your memories are coded illustrate the dynamic and ever-evolving nature of your memory skills.

Navigating Through Your Hemispheres and Lobes

Your brain has two large hemispheres: the left cerebral hemisphere and the right cerebral hemisphere. Each hemisphere consists of four lobes: the frontal, temporal, parietal, and occipital. (See Figure 3-1.) These lobes provide a great deal of area to store memories. Each of the four lobes offers a unique talent and way of coding memories, as I explain in this chapter.

The right hemisphere controls the left side of your body, and the left hemisphere controls your right side. The crossover of nerve fibers from the right side of your brain to the left side, and vice versa, takes place deep within your brainstem in a structure called the *medulla oblongata*.

The right hemisphere is adept at storing visual and spatial memories. Spatial memory involves anything that occupies physical space — remembering the shape of this book, for example. The left hemisphere is more adept at storing verbal memories. The two hemispheres work together in everything you do.

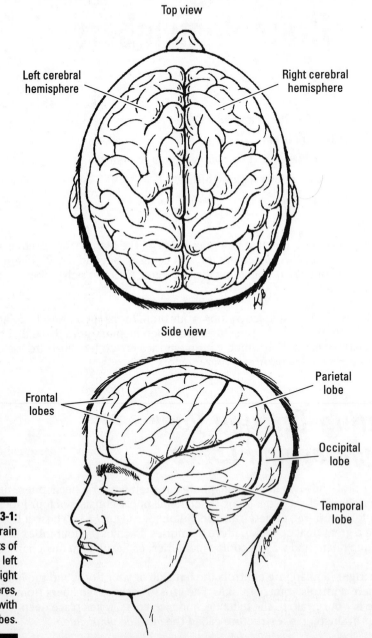

Top view

Left cerebral hemisphere

Right cerebral hemisphere

Side view

Parietal lobe

Frontal lobes

Occipital lobe

Temporal lobe

Figure 3-1: The brain consists of the left and right hemispheres, each with four lobes.

Introducing your right hemisphere, the emotional side

Your right hemisphere has more extensive connections than does your left hemisphere with certain other parts of your brain, especially the limbic system. In other words, the right hemisphere can pick up the emotional climate of conversations better than the left hemisphere. (For more detail about the limbic system, see the section titled, "T is for temporal: Remembering what you hear," later in this chapter.)

The band of fibers that bind your two hemispheres together is called the *corpus callosum.* This band serves to connect distant neurons in each hemisphere enabling them to fire together, adding dimension and depth to everything you do and think.

If you're a woman, you'll be interested to know that your corpus callosum is denser than that of men, which means your two hemispheres work more evenly together. Perhaps the denser corpus callosum is one reason that women seem to be more intuitive — by accurately sensing the emotional climate of a conversation or situation.

In spite of some hard-wired gender differences, people can become more balanced in the way they lead their lives. You may be familiar with the caricature of a "typical" man — someone who isn't in touch with his feelings, not wanting to be bothered by the nuisance of emotions. Yet, twenty-first-century men are becoming more sensitive and women more assertive. The sexes are beginning to achieve more balance @ md whether through changes in culture or in the way people think.

Meeting your left hemisphere, the orderly side

The left hemisphere tries to bring order to the world and has been called the interpreter. It is particularly talented at picking up the details in whatever you learn.

The right hemisphere tries to take in the "whole" picture and takes information literally. When both halves of the brain work together, you get a system of checks and balances that enables you to be flexible and adaptive. You need to be open, yet capable of interpreting the world around you.

Your memories don't lie stored away in compartments in your brain, lost and decaying in time. Rather, memories are dispersed throughout your brain and colored by the unique talents of these lobes. In fact, as people age, it isn't their long-term memories that wither away, it's their ability to store new memories that may become more difficult. (See Chapter 10 for more on how older people can sharpen their memory skills.)

Because each of the two hemispheres adds a different emphasis, the four lobes carry the overall character of each hemisphere. Further, each lobe also has primary areas specific to the skills of hearing, sensing, seeing, and moving.

T is for temporal: Remembering what you hear

Your *temporal lobes* contain your primary area for hearing. These lobes also help you remember the gist of an experience. All right-handers and 80 percent of left-handers use their left temporal lobes for language.

The top part of your left temporal lobe is called *Wernicke's area,* which involves making sense of words. This part of your brain helps you comprehend what's being said.

Deep within your brain and bordering your temporal lobes is an area called the *limbic system.* This system, which is very involved in recalling your emotions, contains two key structures involving memory:

- ✔ The amygdala
- ✔ The hippocampus

The almond-shaped *amygdala* plays a big role in recording the emotional context of your memories. When you experience an event, your amygdala records your emotional reaction to it.

Right-brain and left-brain people

Plenty of hype centers on the character of the two halves of the brain. So-called right-brain people are said to be more creative and even more spiritual than so-called left-brain people. Left-brain people are viewed as more rigid and meticulous. That hype, born in the 1970s, still wears on. Many people who were instrumental in stirring up this fad, however, have long since abandoned it — your brain is far more complex than that simplistic idea suggested. The premise isn't entirely faulty, though, because each hemisphere does specialize in creating and storing specific types of memory.

Carl Wernicke's discovery

In 1881, physician Carl Wernicke found a man who suffered from damage to the upper-left temporal lobe with what later became known as *Wernicke's aphasia.* The term *aphasia* means difficulty with language. The type of aphasia that this patient had is called "associative apha-sia." The patient couldn't understand what he was being told, but he could speak fluently. The only problem was that his words made no sense because he didn't understand the meaning of words.

A person with a damaged amygdala has trouble remembering the emotional context of an event, perhaps by underreacting or overreacting to it. For example, if she again meets a person who in the past was emotionally abusive, then she may react to him with indifference — as if she has totally forgotten about the incident.

The amygdala evaluates the personal significance of new experiences. If fear is appropriate, then the amygdala kicks into gear hormones that get you activated.

If you've been traumatized by a particular event, your amygdala helped record the emotional reaction to that trauma. People with post-traumatic stress disorder have persistent memories of their traumatic event.

Another part of your limbic system that's centrally involved in your memories is your *hippocampus,* shown in Figure 3-2. The hippocampus is the key structure that moves short-term memory into long-term memory. If an experience is important enough, your hippocampus codes the memory of it away so that you can recall it later.

If your hippocampus receives personally significant information, it moves that information along for long-term memory. If you experience something over and over again, even if it annoys, your hippocampus transfers it to long-term memory.

Take a look at this principle at work: The folks who produce television commercials may not know specifically about brain anatomy and your hippocampus, but they do know that repetition equals retention. When you repeatedly see or hear a particular commercial — especially when laced with a catchy tune or silly joke — you have trouble forgetting it. As you walk down the aisle at the supermarket, you may find yourself humming the tune for bath soap and end up with six bars of it in your grocery basket!

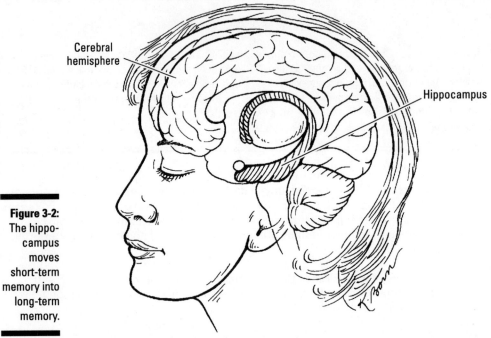

Cerebral hemisphere

Hippocampus

Figure 3-2:
The hippo-
campus
moves
short-term
memory into
long-term
memory.

Your hippocampus is tucked away deep within your temporal lobes. If it's damaged in any way, you have trouble moving short-term memories into long-term memories. (See the related sidebar titled, "H.M.'s new day.")

F is for frontal, as in "frontal assault"

Your *frontal lobes* contain your primary area for initiating movement. These lobes are more complex than that of any other species on the planet and involve far more than movement. The frontal lobes represent what's most human about you: This part of your brain helps you form a sense of identity. Although all mammals have frontal lobes, your far frontal area represents the biggest evolutionary leap. This area is your executive control center and the last to mature as you grow up.

Teenagers often struggle with questions such as "Who am I? How do I find my place in the world?" Teenaged boys and girls work hard to find identity. A friend of mine once said, "The only thing an adolescent knows is that they aren't you." Moreover, it's this part of their brain that they're using to remember that they aren't.

H.M.'s new day

One of the most famous neurosurgery patients of the twentieth century was someone referred to by his initials, H.M. This patient suffered from severe epilepsy until a neurosurgeon removed most of his temporal lobes and all of his hippocampus and amygdala.

The surgery was a success with respect to curing H.M.'s epilepsy; he no longer experienced seizures. Unfortunately, a severe side effect occurred: H.M. lost his ability to set down new memories. While his long-term memory was intact for events that took place in his life before the surgery, H.M. was put into a perpetual state of "now." The patient couldn't transfer new information from his short-term memory to his long-term memory. H.M. couldn't form new memories from his life following the surgery. When distracted, H.M. would lose all of his short-term memory.

If you were to meet H.M., you'd probably enjoy a good conversation with him. However, if you walked out of the room for a few minutes, he would forget who you were upon your return. H. M. would greet you as if you were someone completely new to him. He was in a state of perpetual novelty — everything was new to him. H.M. could watch the same movie repeatedly, as if he had never seen it each time.

Despite having both his right and left hippocampus removed, along with the inner parts of both temporal lobes, H.M. was able to deal well with his immediate world. The patient was intellectually capable; he scored as well on intelligence tests after the surgery as he had done before.

For the remainder of his life, H.M. was incapable of forming new memories. He was in the position of always being lost in the moment.

Although H.M. lost the ability to code memories into long-term storage and then recall them later, he could savor each fresh new experience as if it were the first time. For him, repeated experiences were first-time experiences.

Savor not just new experiences but repeated experiences, too — just as if you were having them for the first time. You don't need to have your hippocampus removed to be able to enjoy your life with freshness.

The back parts of your frontal lobes direct your movements and mature before other parts do. Your first movements came from major muscle groups, such as your limbs, and then came fine motor control in your fingers. You could grab toys before you could put toys together.

The lower parts of your left frontal lobes help you elaborate memories before they are encoded in your long-term memory. This area doesn't work well when you get distracted. Absentmindedness occurs when this area is not working to its fullest potential, such as when you're paying attention to too many things at once.

Going up on the left side of your left frontal lobe, you come to an area that helps you find the words you need when you're speaking. The name for this area is *Broca's area*. People with damage to Broca's area have "expressive aphasia." With this condition, people have trouble expressing themselves but have no problem with comprehension. No, just because you periodically get stuck recalling a name doesn't mean you have *expressive aphasia*.

Conversation stopper

In 1861, Emil Broca performed an autopsy on a man who had a great deal of difficulty finding words to express himself. All he could say was "Tan, Tan." Broca found a lesion the size of a silver dollar in the man's left frontal lobe. Broca correctly surmised that this area was responsible for finding the correct words during a conversation.

Your left frontal lobe is quite involved in reflecting on your memories and trying to make sense of them. In depressed patients, the left frontal lobe is underactive and stumbles at this task.

Depressed people experience persistent negative memories and overgeneralize future events based on these negative memories.

In general, every effort you make to initiate or inhibit a behavior involves your frontal lobes. Damage to this area can make you listless or terribly impulsive.

It's hard to believe, but back in the 1930s, one of the treatments for severe mental illness was a *frontal lobotomy*. In this procedure, doctors would sever the frontal lobes from the other parts of the cerebrum. Patients who had this procedure became listless and unmotivated.

P is for parietal — sensory stuff

The primary area of the *parietal lobe* deals with sensory feelings. Your parietal lobes help you know where on your body you've been touched; where you are in space; and with spatial sensation, in general. The sensory area lies at the very forward part of your parietal lobes, bordering your *motor strip* — the area of your far back frontal lobes that controls your movements; together, they're called the *sensory motor strip*.

The back parts of your parietal lobes help you sense yourself in space. Your right parietal lobe is especially adept at remembering shapes and forms. When I tested a person with right parietal lobe damage, he had a great deal of difficulty remembering spatial forms. When I asked this person to draw a form that I showed him ten minutes before, his right parietal lobe seemed to falter while his left parietal lobe didn't. His drawing showed many of the details of the drawing (left parietal lobe) but none of its form (right).

O is for occipital — visual stuff

Your *occipital lobes* involve themselves in your visual capabilities. If your occipital lobes are damaged, you can become blind. The occipital lobes in some animal species are much larger than that in humans. For example, gorillas have much larger occipital lobes so that they can visually detect what would seem to us as subtle changes in the dense forest.

The occipital lobes don't have a monopoly on your visual memories, however. Even your memory of a specific object, for example the chair you sat in at your friend's house, is dispersed throughout your brain. You remember the elegant shape of the chair (right parietal lobe). You remember how firm it felt as you squirmed in it during your friend's long-winded monologue (the sensory motor strip). You remember looking back at the chair as you were leaving the room and noticing its deep cinnamon color (further back toward the occipital lobe).

Brain Cells: Zooming in for a Closer Look

Your brain is an electrochemical organ that functions partly on chemistry and partly on its electrical firing. The word *electrical* doesn't mean your brain has electricity running through it. Rather, the word highlights the fact that your neurons fire impulses in an on and off way like an electrical current. Between neurons, however, your brain relies on chemistry. Your neurons communicate with one another by chemical messengers called *neurotransmitters.*

Understanding your chemical messengers

You have more than 50 types of neurotransmitters operating in your brain enabling you to think, feel, and remember. Your neurons specialize in particular neurotransmitters.

Some neurotransmitters, such as *dopamine,* activate you, keeping you alert; others, such as the one called *GABA,* mellow you out and calm you down. Still others, such as *serotonin,* help keep you from becoming depressed. The activating neurotransmitter *norepinephrine* keeps your mood up and helps you code memories.

The neurotransmitter *acetylcholine* plays a critical role in learning and memory. When acetylcholine becomes blocked in some way, your memories suffer. On the other hand, when acetylcholine is present and accounted for, your ability to remember improves. (For more on acetylcholine and nutrition, see Chapters 5 and 6.)

Synapses help form memories

Your neurotransmitters operate in your synapses to form memories. Here's how the process works: Neurons release neurotransmitters, which other neurons pick up by finding binding sites that are receptive to the neurotransmitters. The neurotransmitter has to have the right chemical structure (like a key) to get into the receptor (the lock) of the post-synaptic membrane. If the chemical structure is correct, the neurotransmitter unlocks and opens a channel in the new neuron, making that neuron fire. The firing neuron sends its own neurotransmitter out into another synapse, and the entire process goes on and on.

Another way to look at the way neurotransmitters work is to visualize differently shaped pegs all trying to get through a Pegboard with assorted shapes cut out. Only the round peg can get through the round hole on the board, the square peg through the square hole, and so on. When the right peg gets through the right hole, it sets off a reaction. (In the case of a neurotransmitter that enters a neuron, the reaction is that the neuron fires.)

All of these neurotransmitters work by jumping across a gap between your neurons called a *synapse*. On one side of the synapse, the presynaptic membrane of one neuron contains little sacs of specific neurotransmitters that release if the neuron fires. When the neurotransmitter is released, it floats around in the synapse until another neuron picks it up or until the one that released it reabsorbs it.

Every time you remember a new piece of information or learn a new fact, changes occur at the synaptic level. Those connections between neurons adjust to accommodate the new memories. The more times the memory is remembered or repeated, the stronger those connections become.

Sometimes, these repetitive connections serve memories you'd probably rather forget. The neurotransmitter norepinephrine helps record into memory particularly emotionally laced events. If you suffer from post-traumatic stress syndrome and get a big boost of norepinephrine each time the memory occurs, chances are you'll experience intense and intrusive replays of the memories of that traumatic event.

Your brain is a charged, constantly evolving electrochemical soup; it modifies itself as you live your life. Two other ways your brain changes over time as you experience and remember are through the processes of myelination and dendritic branching.

Coating your axons

Myelination and dendritic branching involve parts of the neuron, shown in Figure 3-3. At the heart of your neuron lies its nucleus. Other parts of a neuron consist of the axon, which sends out information, and dendrites, which pick up information. (For details on dendrites, see the section titled, "Branching out for new thoughts and memories," later in this chapter.)

As you grow and mature, your axons become *myelinated*. In this process, axons develop a coat of a fatty substance produced by oligodendroglia. These coats, or myelin sheaths, help your axons have better conduction to send information more efficiently and quickly.

Think of ripping off the wall paneling in an old house to reveal the electrical wiring. You can see that many of the wires are frayed and exposed. The wires probably short out constantly, and chances are good that a fire can develop.

In another wall, you find newly installed wiring that has plastic sheaths as insulation. No shorting or fire to worry about here. You then realize that this wall feeds the plug that services the TV, which never seems to fail.

The bad wall wiring services the plug in the kitchen that you have your toaster plugged into. You realize that the bad wiring is the reason your toaster seems to always go on the blink. Once, you even brought the toaster in for repair but even that didn't fix it. Now you know why.

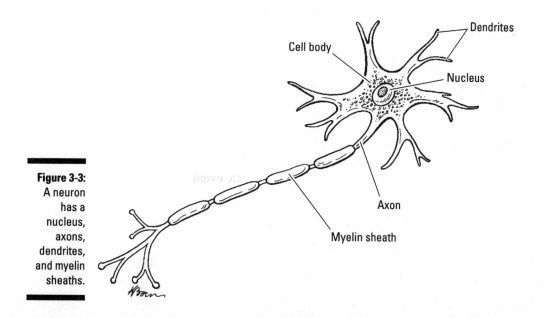

Figure 3-3:
A neuron has a nucleus, axons, dendrites, and myelin sheaths.

Dendrites

Cell body

Nucleus

Axon

Myelin sheath

Consequently, just like poor wiring in the house, your axon can have poor conduction. The signals that those axons send will falter.

Under healthy conditions, the myelination of your brain, the maturation of your brain, and the increase in your basic skills, all go together. In other words, as you mature and gain specific skills, myelination supports the neurons supporting those skills.

When you were an infant, those neurons in your brain that aided your primary senses of hearing, seeing, and feeling and your ability to move had their axons myelinated in the primary areas of your temporal, occipital, parietal, and frontal lobes. As you expanded your capabilities beyond those rudimentary abilities, those areas of your brain that supported more-complex skills became myelinated.

Branching out for new thoughts and memories

The more you think in novel ways, such as learning new skills or curiously exploring new information, the more your brain adjusts to make that happen. Specifically, your dendrites branch out to make new connections with other neurons. This process is called *dendritic branching* or *dendric arborization*. Picture a tomato plant that is growing three long stalks. To make your plant branch out, you pinch off the ends of the stalks, and out of each stalk grow three more. Keep arborizing your plant, and you'll have much more opportunity for tomatoes to grow.

When you face having to relearn a skill, do just as you did with your plant. Pinch off or resist doing the task the same old way, and your dendrites will branch out in search of other neurons for input for new solutions. The more you think in novel ways, the more your brain will dendritically branch out.

Einstein didn't have more neurons than you or I do. Einstein had more connections between his neurons because he was always branching out in novel thoughts. Although the chances of either of us coming up with a major modification of the Theory of Relativity are pretty slim, we can branch out in new thought and, in doing so, make our dendrites branch out.

Keeping your mind active and curious develops a brain that can support that curiosity. Your memory ability could expand because you'll be able to code and remember with the richness that your brain provides.

Staging Your Memories: Long Term, Short Term

More than 125 years ago, German philosopher Herman Ebbinghaus performed a series of memory experiments on himself. Ebbinghaus tested his own ability to remember thousands of strings of letters. He found that after a short period, he forgot much of what he tried to remember.

These days, psychologists refer to two different memory processes: short-term and long-term memory. Each type corresponds to a length of time:

- **A short-term memory** (or *working memory*) generally lasts for no more than 30 seconds.
- **A long-term memory** can last a lifetime.

Short-term memory is one gateway to long-term memory — it's the gateway to acquiring a memory. Recently, psychologists have begun to use the term *working memory* to refer to short-term memory. The phrase derives from the fact that you're always working with your memory.

Working memory has a lot to do with your attention span. One of the numerous ways that other psychologists and I measure working memory is to ask you to repeat a string of numbers, draw a design, or identify an image that you saw just seconds before. The longer the string of numbers that you remember, the better your attention and working memory is.

Never fear — you can't clutter your mind with too many memories. Your brain has an extraordinary ability to remember vast quantities of information in long-term memory. As for your working memory, you shed almost all of them seconds after you pick them up. When I give you another string of numbers, you'll most likely forget the set I gave you before. Only the important stuff goes into long-term memory. So, how do you decide what's important?

Imagine that you're talking to someone and you overhear two other people talking about an amusing person you'd like to get to know better. Who do you listen to? Who you pay *attention* to is the key.

Attention is the gateway into short-term memory. You may forget the other conversation. You purge it out of your working memory. The importance you place on the conversation that you *do* listen to dictates what you store in your long-term memory. Because you paid attention to the two people talking about an amusing person you'd like to get to know better, you'll probably remember that story.

Riding your bike down Memory Lane

You may have noticed you can do many things over and over and that you don't even have to try to remember how to do them. Riding a bicycle is a great example. When you first learned to ride, you had to try to remember each step. You probably said to yourself at one point, "Okay, I need to stop this thing! Where's the brake? Oh yeah — I remember — there it is!" Later, these steps became so ingrained that you didn't have to try to remember. You were on automatic pilot.

Psychologists differentiate between these two types of memory. *Explicit memory* requires that you consciously search memories. This type of memory operates when you're trying to remember where the brake is on that bike you're just learning to ride. However, if you have ridden all your life, as you hop on the bike you're relying on *implicit memory*.

While implicit memory is well ingrained in your long-term memory, explicit memory goes through three steps before getting there:

1. **Acquiring a memory.** Sometimes, this phase is called recording or coding a memory. This process occurs as you learn the basics of riding a bike.

2. **Storing or recording a memory.** At this stage, you file the memory for later use as you work at learning to ride.

3. **Retrieval of a memory.** At this point, you recall the memory back into consciousness. In short, you remember it the next time you hop on the bike.

One of the interesting facets to long-term memory is that memories trigger each other. For example, if you begin to describe an event earlier in your life, you may be surprised by how much you remember. As you begin to describe the event, you're reminded of other circumstances surrounding the event. You unleash a whole chain of associations and rekindle a much wider spectrum of memories.

Try this: Think back to an event in your childhood. Reflect on where that event took place and who was there at the time. Chances are good that a wider picture of what occurred on that day will open up.

Working and long-term memory differ in many ways. Not only is time a main distinguishing factor, but so is storage capacity. While a limit exists on how much you can store in working memory, your long-term memory has no such constraints.

Disruptions to your working memory can occur in a number of ways. Because attention and concentration have such close ties to short-term memory, any distraction can hamper your memory. If you're distracted, you may forget what you were holding in working memory. This principal doesn't apply to long-term memory, because it's relatively permanent. Damage to your brain, as well as using drugs and alcohol, can wreak havoc on your short-term memory. (See Chapter 6 for more detail on the various things that damage your brain and its capacity to remember.) Long-term memory remains generally intact, but your ability to retrieve those memories may erode.

Assuming the ideal circumstances, you can count on the following as being the key demands of a good memory:

- ✔ **Attention:** This is the key to your short-term memory.
- ✔ **The degree of importance that information holds for you:** This drives the strength of the memory into long-term storage.

Sorting and Recovering Your Memories Down Pathways

You retrieve your long-term memories by going down many pathways. Each pathway has a lot to do with how you learned the information and how you recall it. You may be a visual learner. You may be a verbal learner. If you're a visual learner, you learn better if you try to remember by visualizing the information. If you're a verbal learner, you learn better by coding the information in sentences or separate words. On the other hand, you may learn better by hearing information or by movement.

You can label the more common pathways with simple terms like these:

- ✔ Emotions
- ✔ Smells
- ✔ Sounds
- ✔ Sights
- ✔ Movement
- ✔ Tactile sensation (touch)

Feeling memories

One of the ways that your brain codes memories relates to your emotions. How you felt emotionally at the time of the event is bound up with your memory of the event. This combination of memory and emotion is often called *state-based*. The emotional state that you were in at the time of the event carries your memory.

Perhaps, out of the blue, the thought of a particular person, place, or event pops up. The emotional state you're in at the time of the recollection triggers the parts of your brain associated with that memory.

For example, have you ever gotten a whiff of a particular aroma and found yourself overwhelmed by a memory of an event long since past? For example, sometimes, when I walk past a honeysuckle bush, I find myself with vivid memories of early childhood, where I was catching bees in jars along a fence covered with honeysuckle. I hadn't tried to recall that memory; it just occurred without my conscious attention.

Why does this sudden memory happen? Is it some kind of magic? In a way, it is — it's the magic of evolution. You and I are mammals, the product of millions of years of evolution. Your olfactory bulbs, which record the sense of smell, are some of the most primitive parts of your brain. The olfactory bulbs lie almost on top of your hippocampus.

I'll never forget the time I held a human brain in my hands. My neuropsychology professor said, "Look at these little fingerlike structures here. They have a direct route to your hippocampus. Smells are remembered without being bothered by the rest of your brain thinking about it!" The olfactory bulbs are like two elongated petals that act like sensory shortcuts for memory.

The sense of smell is a powerful memory trigger, but it's not the only trigger. Consider this example: You're driving down the highway and there's a road crew working. You see that up ahead, one lane is closed off. Immediately, you worry that you're not going to get to work on time. Just as you pull up in front of the person holding the Stop sign, you feel that your fears have been realized.

You resent the worker as if he has chosen just you to torment. Then he turns to you with a smile and rotates his sign to read Slow. Your feelings about him transform into gratitude, as if he is paternally taking care of you. As you drive away, you find that out of the blue, memories of your father pop into your head. Those memories are state-based memories! (See the related sidebar titled, "Your emotional ancestry.)

Because you and I are mammals, we have emotionally based experiences. Yet, we also have a large cerebral cortex sitting right on top of this limbic system complex that tempers those emotions.

Your mammalian heritage enables you to use emotions adaptively. This means that emotional memories are psychological tools. Keeping your emotions and thoughts in sync with your goals enables you to achieve those goals.

You'll remember an event far more easily if it has emotional meaning for you. The more important the information is to you, the more prominent it will be in your memory.

Similarly, the more motivated you are to remember an event or information, the better chance you'll have remembering it.

Types of memory

Psychologists identify a number of types of memory. For example, as I type this sentence into my laptop, I'm using a type of memory called *procedural memory*. After more practice than most people need, I can finally look at the screen rather than the keyboard as I type, because I remember this procedure from years of practice.

The sentences that I'm using to describe the pathways of memory require that I tap into *semantic memory*. This type of memory involves using the most appropriate words to describe what I'm trying to explain to you. It deals with the recording of facts. When you use semantic memory, your left hemisphere is involved in expressing and understanding language.

Event-based prospective memory comes into play when you're trying to remember to do something later. When the outrageous electricity bill comes, you remember that you're supposed to pay the bill.

Time-based prospective memory is tied to a specific time, such as when you remember to go to one more meeting that you wish you had forgotten about.

If you begin to reflect on when you discovered how memory works, you're using what's referred to as *episodic memory*. This type of memory involves remembering the when of personal events. It's active when you remember how bored you were at the last meeting.

Hearing memories

If you have the sense of hearing, then your memories for what you hear are found largely in your temporal lobes. (See the section titled, "T is for temporal: Remembering what you hear," earlier in this chapter.) Sounds of all types carry with them memories colored by when and how you hear them. The sound of a purring cat can bring one person to feel warm and soothed, while another person finds that it reminds her of play and laughter.

I've seen people who have a wide variety of different memories associated with the sound of a firecracker. One person may remember Fourth of July fireworks, while another person, such as a war veteran with post-traumatic stress disorder, may feel a surge of fear.

You may have experienced driving down the road and hearing a piece of music on the radio that lifted you to memories that you hadn't tried to recall. You may remember the first time you heard it or a time you spent with someone you loved. Memories of that person pepper the highway in front of you.

Music therapists know that emotionally troubled people perk up when they hear upbeat music. The mood of the music can change your mood.

Your emotional ancestry

Humans are mammals, and all mammals are emotional creatures. If you own a dog or a cat, you know what I mean. These pets, like other mammals, react to everything around them emotionally. This response is an evolutionary advance over reptiles, which react only instinctively.

Think of the evolutionary advantage that humans gained from that development. Instead of reacting repeatedly in the same way to similar experiences, we developed emotional flexibility.

We remember the emotional experience, such as fear, when we encounter a similar experience. You probably have seen a dog shy away from a person who has been cruel to it in the past. The dog is responding to a state-based memory.

 Music can also create the reverse effect. For example, some people who suffer from depression play music that gets them more depressed by activating their sad memories. Don't be one of these people. Your memory for your immediate surroundings will suffer. (See details on how you can clear your mind of depressing memories in Chapter 7.) Pull yourself out of the negative spiral — be your own music therapist.

You have your own associations to different types and pieces of music, especially if you've heard the music in more than one setting and on many occasions. Exploit and cultivate these memories to edify your positive and aspiring goals.

I'm a big consumer of music with tastes that range from *avant-garde* jazz to classical. Before I learned to talk, I was accustomed to hearing Beethoven played at high decibels at my house. My father was obsessed with Beethoven.

At one point, my grandparents called me Little Ludwig because I would stand conducting as my father had taught me. Now, as I listen regularly to music by Beethoven, I seem to remember every note and know personally the intensity of his driving passionate nature. Listening to Beethoven motivates me to strive ahead toward my goals.

 You have similar associations to all types of sounds. Those associations carry with them a complex collage of memories. Whether you're hearing the sound of wind gusting through the pines or the surf at the beach tumbling and dragging out your worries, use your memories to savor the past and motivate you for your future.

Seeing memories

The phrase "A picture is worth a thousand words," may be trite, but the saying is true. You use visual imagery to code a vast number of your memories. Each visual image carries with it numerous words, and trying to remember all of those words is much more difficult than remembering the image itself.

Words that evoke visual images are far more potent as future memories than those that don't evoke visual imagery. This dual coding creates a stronger memory: You code not only the word, but also the visual image associated with it.

The power of visual images can resonate with you for years. Take a moment to prove this to yourself: Lift your eyes from the page and look at some object in the room, say a chair or table. Now close your eyes. For a few seconds, you'll notice an afterimage. However, that image fades away as you go on to note new sensations and thoughts. Now, go back to reading and don't look back at the chair. Notice that many of the details of the chair have faded. The image probably isn't as sharp as it was before.

That image is affected by your mood and what you've been thinking about since originally seeing it. Now, when you try to visualize that image, it's no longer an objective representation of the image but one colored by your mood and your most recent thoughts.

You don't need a "photographic" memory, however, to use visual images as memory enhancers. A simple visual image can carry with it an association to an abstract concept whereas a simple word may not.

Suppose you are trying to recall the abstract concept *religion.* You can use a simple image of a church, temple, or mosque. The image carries with it far more meaning and depth than if you simply use the word *church, temple,* or *mosque.*

Following are other examples of how using visual images can help you remember:

- You want to remember the abstract idea of *location.* The location includes a lake, and that's much easier to remember. With the word *lake,* you have an opportunity to visualize an image of a lake. You may even embellish that image with the sun gently reflecting on the still waters of the lake. The word lake can even carry a personal association. Perhaps you vacation each summer on a lake. Alternatively, maybe you're a hearty ice fisher who braves below-freezing temperatures as you sit above a hole cut into the ice. Now think of the word location. Which location? Perhaps a lake?

- Suppose you want to try to remember the *decadence* of the late Roman emperors such as Caligula and Nero. Try to imagine a banquet with toga-clad people gorging themselves with food and even tossing it at one another. I'd remember that scene more easily than I would if someone told me to remember the words Caligula, Nero, and decadence. Chances are you would too.

✔ You're trying to remember to *ship documents* to your sister across the country. You need to try to remember the words *ship* and *package*. Imagine a large package floating in the sea with two large masts with sails being blown across the water.

✔ You have a cat at home and you're going to try to remember to vacuum the cat hairs off the carpet. You may envision your cat vacuuming the carpet. In this way, you're tying in motion and substitution into the memory. You're bringing it alive. You may try to envision your cat's friends teaming up, each with a vacuum cleaner feverishly cleaning. The cats' vacuum cleaners bump together in their mad rush to make you happy. Finally, you may even substitute the vacuum cleaners for magnets, and the cats manage to pick up their hair as if magnetized.

The embellishments on the cat image pull the image into greater vividness. Maybe the image becomes so indelible that you may have trouble forgetting it later, especially if you lie on the carpet and envision the sharp metallic cat hair puncturing your sensitive skin!

✔ Imagine that you're an oceanographer and will be playing basketball after work with friends — if you can remember to show up. Try to imagine dolphins playing basketball. Each team tries to move the basketball down the court until they can bump it into the nets, which just happens to hang over the tank at both ends. By remembering this scene, you may show up at the court.

Choose images that represent the information you want to remember and put them into an exaggerated scene.

Verbal memories

Obviously, visual images aren't useful if you're blind. Other senses and memory triggers come into play, such as smell, touch, sound, and words.

The degree to which words are useful as memory cues depends on how adept you are at using words. If you're very highly talented in using words and have a high linguistic intelligence, the subtle nuances of words can carry complex memories. Poets are masters of this talent. Even if you're not a poet, I provide a number of tricks for remembering words in Chapter 9.

The combination of visual imagery and words as cues for memory is the most powerful of all. Any time you have an opportunity to try to remember something by using multiple channels, your memory will be stronger and your recall will be easier.

Compared with adolescents or adults, young children are more adept at visual imagery than at verbal memories. This conclusion comes as no surprise, because young children are just beginning to learn language. A child's vocabulary jumps astronomically between the ages of 1 and 5 and continues to expand into adulthood. Accumulated vocabulary then slows down as people age. You can learn new words constantly, however, by taking classes, reading, or doing crossword puzzles. Doing so increases your capacity to remember, based on verbal cues. My grandfather spoke five languages, and, until the last few weeks of his life, was diligently learning six new words each day.

Part II
Establishing Memory Power

The 5th Wave — By Rich Tennant

"I've been working over 80 hours a week for the past two years preparing for retirement, and it hasn't bothered me OR my wife, what's-her-name."

In this part . . .

You can improve your brain's readiness to remember in a number of ways, such as eating a balanced diet and taking supplements. You also change certain habits that prevent your brain from operating at peak memory power, such as eating too much sugar or consuming too much wine. This part gives you the low-down on brain food, covers relaxation techniques, and provides suggestions for improving your sleep. Yes, getting enough sleep is crucial to waking up with full memory power at your command.

Chapter 4

Eating To Remember

• •

• •

*T*he old adage "You are what you eat" is certainly true when it comes to brainpower. What you eat directly affects your body biochemistry, and that's the connection to how well your brain functions. Your brain consumes more energy than any other organ in your body, so any change in your food intake can have a major impact on your ability to remember.

What you eat is so important that national and international conferences have addressed diet as an important health concern. The following recommended dietary guidelines come from nutritionists and medical professionals:

✔ Eat more fruits and vegetables.

✔ Replace foods containing processed white flour with those consisting of complex grains, such as whole wheat.

✔ Eat less red meat.

✔ Avoid egg yolks, butter, and margarine.

✔ Minimize salt on foods.

✔ Use low-fat milk and cheeses instead of whole milk and cheeses.

✔ Try to have each meal include a protein, complex carbohydrate, and a fruit or vegetable.

✔ Drink lots of water.

✔ Eat a balanced breakfast.

Follow these guidelines and not only will your health improve, but so will your memory. You'll be eating to remember. In this chapter, you find out which foods are best for memory health and which ones to avoid.

Breaking a Fast — Breakfast

Breakfast is called breakfast because when you eat it, you're breaking a fast. The period between dinner and breakfast is the longest span of time between any of your meals. You need a balanced breakfast to fuel your memory.

Yes, most of us sleep during that span of time we are not eating, but your body isn't lying in stasis, where everything stops while you snooze. Your body is still using glucose and other nutrients — especially during dreaming sleep — from food you took in during the last few meals. (For details on how sleep affects memory, head over to Chapter 7.)

I've seen too many patients over the past 25 years who have failed to eat breakfast and then complain of low energy, depression, anxiety, and thinking and memory problems. They say, "I'm not a breakfast person." Too often, they can't see any importance in eating, complaining, "I just don't have the taste for it." I tell them, "Your brain is like your car." You don't expect your car to run on empty, do you? It's the same with your brain. When your brain runs on empty, you can't think and remember clearly."

Scores of studies prove that people who eat breakfast can think more clearly and remember more than people who skip breakfast. Many of the subjects of these studies were young, healthy college students. Those students who ate breakfast scored higher on tests than those who didn't.

The message here is simple: Eat a balanced breakfast that consists of a protein, a carbohydrate, and a fruit or vegetable. The following are examples of a balanced breakfast:

- Bowl of cereal (carbohydrate), milk in the cereal (protein), glass of orange juice (fruit)
- Bowl of oatmeal, glass of juice
- Eggs and whole-wheat toast, glass of juice
- Pancakes, yogurt, glass of juice
- French toast, glass of juice
- Whole wheat bagel, cream cheese, glass of juice

Some of my patients create attention problems and short-term memory problems for themselves by skipping breakfast and compounding that mistake by drinking coffee and eating donuts instead. Drinking coffee on an empty stomach makes you doubly anxious and unable to concentrate. (For more on how coffee affects memory, see the section titled, "Brewing a cup of anxiety," later in this chapter.) If you drink coffee at breakfast, always drink a moderate amount (no more than two cups of coffee) and only after you have eaten a balanced breakfast.

Avoid sugar at breakfast — donuts, for example — otherwise, you likely will become anxious and have trouble concentrating, and your short-term memory will plummet two hours later. (For more about the ill effects of sugar on memory, see the section titled, "Carbo Loading: Go Complex Instead of Simple," later in this chapter.)

Vegging Up

Thirty years ago, I was a strict vegetarian. When I left the United States (circling the globe for one year), I tempered the strict emphasis of that diet because I needed to be flexible in the countries I visited. Vegetarians have to pay very close attention to making sure that they get enough protein, and I couldn't be sure I could complement my diet with enough protein during my travels.

Since that time, I try not to eat red meat because of the high fat and cholesterol contained within. Instead, I emphasize fish, skinless poultry, tofu, and eggs (hopefully without the yolks). I have always been a salad fanatic, learning early from my Armenian mother that salads can be delicious. I'm lucky that now, after a half century of daily salads, I have a low cholesterol count. I can't imagine how bad my memory would be if I hadn't watched my diet.

Most people in the United States eat too much protein and not enough other nutrients. I hope you're not one of them. If you depend on animal products for your protein, all you need each day is a piece of meat or fish the size of a full deck of cards. If you have too much protein coming in, you'll overtax your kidneys and set yourself up to be vulnerable to osteoporosis in old age.

At the other extreme are those people who don't get enough protein. You can be a health-conscious vegetarian and still not be eating healthily. Although you don't eat animal products, you may not eat enough foods rich in protein. Protein is critical for your brain and its memory.

One of the easiest ways to take in protein is to eat moderate amounts of foods rich in protein, such as egg whites, fish, skinless chicken or turkey, tofu, legumes, rice, and beans.

A diet rich in plant foods lowers your risk of heart disease, cancer, stroke, and a vast list of other medical problems while making your brain more capable of better memory skills.

A diet rich in plant foods provides the highest source of antioxidant vitamins and minerals. Antioxidants help prevent the destructive effect of free radicals. For example:

- Green leafy vegetables contain minerals and vitamin A.
- Orange-colored vegetables, such as sweet potatoes, contain beta carotene.
- Whole grains, nonprocessed oils, and raw nuts contain vitamin E.
- Citrus fruits, green peppers, and berries contain vitamin C.

A diet rich in plant foods is a diet rich in nourishment. If you emphasize more plant foods, you benefit from many of the vitamins and minerals you need to operate a brain capable of vibrant memories.

Carbo Loading: Go Complex Instead of Simple

When you eat foods rich in carbohydrates, you provide your body with a rich source of energy. Enzymes in your gastrointestinal tract break down carbohydrates into sugars, specifically glucose. Your bloodstream absorbs that glucose, which in many ways can be thought of as fuel.

Your brain is a high glucose consumer, demanding 25 percent of the total glucose that your body uses. You need a good supply of glucose for your brain and carbohydrates are a source, but not all carbohydrates are the same. Improving your memory requires carbohydrates that can keep your energy high for a long time.

Carbohydrates come in two forms: simple and complex. Always try to steer toward complex carbohydrates. Here's why: Simple carbohydrates, such as sugar and processed white flour, convert into glucose much more quickly than do complex carbohydrates.

You may ask, "So what's so bad about that?" The short answer is that you lose your energy more quickly. This sudden crash in energy is what you try to avoid. You benefit by a slower and sustained rise in your blood glucose that will stay with you longer.

By providing yourself with a slow and sustained glucose conversion, your brain will operate at an optimal level, and you'll be able to pay attention to and remember what you want to remember.

Complex carbohydrates — including most vegetables, starches, and grains — break down more slowly than simple carbohydrates do and give you the slow rise of glucose that stays with you longer without the sharp decline. As a result of consuming complex instead of simple carbohydrates, your pancreas doesn't have to pump out insulin to try to balance out your body's sharp rise in glucose that comes with eating simple carbohydrates.

Many people wonder why white bread isn't as nutritious as whole grain breads. The white bread, and white-flour products in general, contains refined flour that has been stripped of many nutrients. As a result, these products convert to glucose, as other simple carbohydrates do. Similarly, you get a short burst of energy and then you crash.

Nutritionists sometimes note the difference between simple and complex carbohydrates by the *glycemic index,* which is a measure of basic structure (glyceraldehydes) in carbos. The lower the glycemic index value, the slower a carbohydrate gets converted to blood glucose — and slower is better. The lower the glycemic value of the foods you eat, the less chance you'll have of suffering from low blood sugar — and its extreme, hypoglycemia.

Low blood sugar means that you are less able to concentrate and, as a result, your short-term memory isn't what it could be. Low blood sugar is what you may experience as that 2 o'clock slump.

Low-glycemic foods	*High-glycemic foods*
Legumes, beans, peas	Sugar, honey, molasses
Whole-grain breads	Processed-flour breads
Whole grains, brown rice, bulgur	Corn
Soy products	Crackers, snack chips made from refined flour
Vegetables	Sweetened fruits
Fruits	Fruit cocktails, applesauce

Many lecturers don't like to make their presentations to people after lunch, because chances are high that their audience will be suffering from low-blood-sugar slump. Inattentive audiences like these remember less of the presentation than an audience that attends in the morning (assuming audience members had a breakfast with complex carbohydrates instead of simple carbohydrates).

Getting Your Fats Right

You're a fathead, and so am I. Sixty percent of our brains consist of fat. Fats serve many functions in the brain, including serving as energy reserves, as insulation, and as a coating for the axons to promote conduction. Eating foods that contain the right fat makes sense. (See the related sidebar titled, "Getting enough 'smart fat'.")

Good fats are called *unsaturated fats,* and the not so good ones are *saturated fats.* Most people in the United States eat too much saturated fat. You can identify saturated fats easily: When they sit at room temperature, they remain solid. Most meats and dairy products contain saturated fats. Tropical oils such as coconut and palm oil also contain saturated fats.

Getting enough "smart fat"

Polyunsaturated fats contain essential fatty acids (EFAs), which help your brain stay in tip-top shape. EFAs come in two types: omega-3 and omega-6 fatty acids. These two EFAs must be in balance with one another. If you get more of the omega-6 type, it acts as a precursor to the highly inflammatory prostaglandins that cause swelling and clotting of your blood. Unfortunately, most of us consume too much of the omega-6 type because it's found in vegetable oils (such as corn, safflower, and sunflower oils). The omega-3 fatty acids are in cold-water fish such as salmon, mackerel, and sardines. The two main fats in your brain are *docosahexaenoic acid,* usually referred to as just DHA, and *arachidonic acid,* also referred to as AA (not to be confused with Alcoholics Anonymous). While AA is an omega-6 fatty acid, DHA is an omega-3 fatty acid.

If you're like most people, abundant dairy and meat products supply plenty of omega-6 fatty acids; your AA intake is probably fine. Your DHA (omega-3) levels, however, may be deficient. Nutrition researcher Dr. Michael Schmidt has called DHA the "smart fat." Indeed, low levels of DHA have been associated with memory problems. On the other hand, DHA supplements have been shown to help memory.

One easy way to supply yourself with this essential fatty acid is to take supplements of omega-3, fish oil, or flaxseed oil; or use flaxseed on your cereal in the morning.

Pushing away those saturated fats

Saturated fats make your blood platelets stick together and consequently clog up your arteries. If you eat too much saturated fat, you run the risk of suffering from heart disease and or strokes, and your memory difficulties will be severe.

A diet rich in butter, dairy products (that aren't low-fat), red meat, poultry skin, and margarine is a diet rich in saturated fats. Soon, you'll have to call a plumber to clean out your arteries. Remember to take it easy on foods such as:

- Butter
- Coconut oil
- Egg yolks
- Lard
- Meats
- Palm oil
- Whole milk

If you eat eggs, separate the yolks from the whites. Whereas egg yolks are loaded with cholesterol, egg whites are rich with a wonderful protein source called albumin.

Eating saturated fats at dinner tonight won't make your memory ability plummet for the after-dinner conversation. The negative effect of saturated fats is cumulative and depresses memory indirectly.

Reaching for (certain) unsaturated fats

The unsaturated fats come in two varieties, *monounsaturated* and *polyunsaturated*. The monounsaturated fats include olive oil, canola oil, and peanut oil. Most people think these oils are good for one's health, and generally, that's right, but they have one problem. If you heat these vegetable oils to a very high temperature, a chemical alteration occurs that forms harmful substances called trans fatty acids. These trans fatty acids contribute to obesity and diabetes, so watch your fried food intake!

The most helpful type of fat is the polyunsaturated type, which occur in cold-water fish, some vegetable oils, seeds, and nuts. Polyunsaturated fats are involved in the membrane structure of your cells and in producing energy.

The following foods supply polyunsaturated fats:

- ✔ Albacore tuna
- ✔ Anchovies
- ✔ Broccoli
- ✔ Flaxseed
- ✔ Haddock
- ✔ Mackerel
- ✔ Salmon
- ✔ Scallops
- ✔ Spinach
- ✔ Walnut oil

Boosting Your Neurotransmitters

Many foods supply the raw ingredients to manufacture the brain chemicals called neurotransmitters. You need an adequate supply of neurotransmitters so that your brain can remember what you want it to. (For details about neurotransmitters, see Chapter 3.) These neurotransmitters play a major role in how your brain operates. The brain has at least 40 different types of neurotransmitters.

Your body synthesizes specific amino acids that are contained in the food you eat, thus forming neurotransmitters. Each neurotransmitter has a specific function. For example, when your body digests the amino acid L-Glutamine from foods such as peas, your body synthesizes it into the neurotransmitter called GABA. GABA is very involved in your ability to stay calm. When you're calm, you remember more.

You can find L-Glutamine in the following foods:

- ✔ Avocado
- ✔ Eggs
- ✔ Peaches
- ✔ Granola
- ✔ Grape juice

  ✔ Peas

  ✔ Sunflower seeds

The amino acid L-Tryptophan affects the neurotransmitter serotonin. Serotonin improves your mood; when levels are low, you can get depressed. When you're depressed, so is your ability to remember.

You can find L-Tryptophan in the following foods:

  ✔ Almonds

  ✔ Cottage cheese

  ✔ Milk

  ✔ Shredded wheat

  ✔ Soybeans

  ✔ Turkey

The amino acid L-Phenylalanine affects the neurotransmitter norepinephrine. Norepinephrine increases your energy, keeps you from getting depressed, and helps with memory.

You can find L-Phenylalanine in the following foods:

  ✔ Chicken

  ✔ Lima beans

  ✔ Milk

  ✔ Peanuts

  ✔ Soybeans

  ✔ Yogurt

Vitamins: Eating Foods that Put the Bs in Your Brain

Vitamins aren't only important as building blocks for the body, but a lack of vitamins affects your ability to think clearly and to use your memory skills effectively. Vitamins have a direct effect on brain chemistry.

The B-vitamins influence the manufacture of specific neurotransmitters. For example, if you're low in vitamin B_1 (thiamin) you may have the following problems:

- ✔ Decreased alertness
- ✔ Decreased reaction time
- ✔ Emotional instability
- ✔ Fatigue

You can find B_1 in the following foods:

- ✔ Bran
- ✔ Brewer's yeast
- ✔ Oatmeal
- ✔ Peanuts
- ✔ Vegetables
- ✔ Wheat

If you're low in vitamin B_2 (riboflavin), you may find yourself suffering from:

- ✔ Depression
- ✔ Eye problems
- ✔ Sluggishness
- ✔ Stress
- ✔ Tension
- ✔ Trembling

You can find B_2 in the following foods:

- ✔ Brewer's yeast
- ✔ Cheese
- ✔ Eggs
- ✔ Fish
- ✔ Liver
- ✔ Milk

If you're low in B_6, you could experience:

- ✔ Depression
- ✔ Headaches
- ✔ Irritability
- ✔ Muscle weakness
- ✔ Nervousness
- ✔ Tingling feet and hands

Replenish your vitamin B_6 levels by eating:

- ✔ Beef
- ✔ Cabbage
- ✔ Cantaloupe
- ✔ Liver
- ✔ Wheat germ
- ✔ Whole grains

If you're low in vitamin B_{12}, you may have the following problems:

- ✔ Confusion
- ✔ Limb weakness
- ✔ Mental slowness
- ✔ Psychosis
- ✔ Stammering

Replenish your vitamin B_{12} level with:

- ✔ Beef
- ✔ Cheese
- ✔ Eggs
- ✔ Kidneys
- ✔ Liver
- ✔ Milk

Avoid an AGE problem

Glycation can subtly damage your brain over time. The glycation process occurs when proteins in your body react to excess glucose or blood sugar and produce what's referred to as advanced glycation end products (AGEs). These AGEs build up in your tissues and damage your central nervous system, including your brain.

If you're diabetic, you're particularly vulnerable to glycation. You need to pay extremely close attention to your diet, making sure that your blood sugar is in balance. Follow the diabetic dietary guidelines religiously. (For all the specifics on this condition, get a copy of *Diabetes For Dummies,* by Alan L. Rubin, M.D., published by Wiley.)

Many pre-diabetics are also quite vulnerable to glycation. If you're pre-diabetic, manage your blood sugars as closely as if you're diabetic.

If you're not diabetic or pre-diabetic, you're not off the hook. Although the effects of glycation may not be as dramatic as for diabetics and pre-diabetics, it's still a risk of consuming too much sugar. Even before glycation gets you over the long term, a high sugar intake contributes to poor concentration at least over the short term.

Minimize your sugar intake. Not only will you avoid the sugar crash, which can cause your short-term memory to go on the blink, you'll also minimize the risk of glycation.

If you're low in folic acid (another B-type vitamin), expect the following:

- Irritability
- Memory problems
- Mental sluggishness

Replenish your levels of folic acid with:

- Cantaloupe
- Carrots
- Dark leafy vegetables
- Whole wheat

A poor diet has long been associated with contributing to health problems. If you suffer from health problems, then you're adding to your memory problems. The combination of poor diet and health problems further depletes your ability to absorb important vitamins and minerals that can help you remember. (I have much more to say about vitamins and minerals in Chapter 5.)

I hope you don't eat too many of the wrong foods that rob your brain of its potential for achieving maximum memory ability. If your diet is too high in fat, cholesterol, and empty calories, it's all going to catch up to you. The cumulative effect of all these excesses can contribute to major health problems. However, well before you get heart disease or have a stroke, you'll undoubtedly want to avoid the memory problems that result from a poor diet.

Avoiding Foods that Aren't

Many foods and condiments aren't foods at all because they lack any nutritional value. When you eat such foods, you're also taking away your brain's ability to remember.

These snacks aren't substitutes for food:

✔ Candy

✔ Cookies

✔ Potato chips

✔ Salted pork rinds

✔ Salt water taffy

Salting a slippery slope

If you overuse salt, you decrease your ability to pay attention enough to form memories. By consuming excessive amounts of salt, your body depletes itself of potassium. Low potassium can increase anxiety. Because anxiety lowers your ability to concentrate, it also causes your short-term memory to falter.

When you're under considerable stress or if you drive yourself too hard, you may develop hypertension. Salt can exacerbate hypertension. Salt raises blood pressure because it causes fluid retention, which adds stress on your heart and circulatory system. High blood pressure can make you feel like you're on edge.

These foods have an unnecessary amount of salt and it's best to avoid them:

✔ Corn chips

✔ Salted pretzels

✔ Salted white-flour crackers

Caffeinism

Insomnia, racing thoughts, and free-floating anxiety brought on by consuming too much caffeine form the guidelines in diagnosing *caffeinism,* according to the *Diagnostic and Statistical Manual of Mental Disorders, 4th Edition* *Revised,* published by The American Psychiatric Association. The bottom line is that mental health professionals refer to caffeinism as a mental disorder. The cure is to cut down your caffeine intake.

Hey, Sugah — you put me in a slump

When you feel worn down and need something to get through the day, you may think a sugar boost will help with your energy and memory. You'd be right — candy, cookies, or soda will give you a boost. The high price you pay for consuming processed sugar, however, outweighs the benefit. (See the related sidebar titled, "Avoid an AGE problem," earlier in this chapter.)

Your renewed energy will be short-lived — what goes up must come down. Here's how it works: Your pancreas releases insulin to counterbalance the overdose of sugar. After the momentary sugar high, you have an energy dip, or crash. Instead of going back to the level of energy you felt before the sugar high, you fall lower than you were before. To make matters worse, feelings of nervousness accompany that energy crash, creating a nervous depression.

Sugar is a pure but simple carbohydrate that has no minerals, vitamins, or enzymes to aid in its digestion. When you eat sugar, it takes nutrient supplies such as B-vitamins from parts of your body. When you're low in B vitamins, you have a variety of problems, including anxiety, depression, difficulty concentrating, and memory problems.

I have seen numerous patients who have binged on foods containing sugar, such as cookies or candy bars. Many of these patients come in complaining that they have attention deficit disorder (ADD). Not surprisingly, they also complain that they have had a difficult time sleeping and are plagued by anxiety, depression, and memory loss. When I tell them about the ill effects of sugar, they quit and feel immediate relief.

Consider the following:

- ✔ Use sugar minimally
- ✔ Never consume sugary foods in place of nutritious foods

Brewing a cup of anxiety

Drinking a cup of coffee can make you alert (and ahhh, that aroma!). However, consuming too much coffee — or, rather, caffeine — can make you unable to concentrate and use your memory skills.

Caffeine is a stimulant that increases the blood flow to your brain; it dilates your blood vessels and increases your heart rate. Caffeine also depletes B vitamins (especially thiamin) and raises stress hormones. If you eat or drink a large amount of caffeine, you put your body into a prolonged state of stress and hyper alertness. Consuming large amounts of caffeine is like drinking liquid anxiety.

Effects of caffeine

When you consume caffeine, the levels of your activating neurotransmitters, dopamine and norepinephrine, increase. Norepinephrine is the scientific name for adrenaline, which is why you may feel adrenaline-charged after you consume a great deal of caffeine. A high level of caffeine in your system throughout the day overcharges your adrenal glands, putting you in a chronic state of stress. (See the related sidebar titled, "Caffeinism," in this chapter.)

Caffeine in high amounts is notorious for contributing to tension headaches (not to be confused with migraines). To make matters worse, withdrawal from caffeine can cause headaches.

Coffee isn't the only caffeine culprit. The stimulant shows up in more edibles than you may have thought — for example, certain pain relievers, cold/flu remedies, diet aids, frozen desserts, and candy bars. Table 4-1 reveals the caffeine content in some common foods.

Table 4-1	Caffeine Content in Various Sources
Sources	*Amounts in Milligrams (mg)*
Coffee (8 ounces)	
Drip	88–280
Percolated	27–64
Decaffeinated	1.6–13
Tea	
Black	45–78

(continued)

Table 4-1 *(continued)*

Sources	Amounts in Milligrams (mg)
Green	24–56
Oolong	20–64
Darjeeling	45–56
Instant	40–58
Soft drinks (12 oz.)	
Jolt	70
Mountain Dew	55
Coca-Cola	30–45
Dr Pepper	30–45
Cocoa and chocolate	
Baking chocolate	18–118
Sweet chocolate	5–35
Milk chocolate	1–15
Chocolate car	4
Hot cocoa (8 oz.)	16–56
Over-the counter medications (per tablet or capsule)	
Dexatrim	200
No-Doz	100
Excedrin	65
Anacin	32
Dristan	16

If you consume more than 250 milligrams of caffeine (2–3 cups of brewed coffee), you may have some of the problems that appear in the list below. (If you have memory problems plus five or more of these symptoms, your memory problems may be caused by poor attention brought on by high caffeine consumption.)

✔ Diuresis (the feeling that you have to urinate often)

✔ Excitability

✔ Flushed face

✔ Gastrointestinal disturbance

✔ Insomnia

✔ Muscle twitching

✔ Nervousness

✔ Rambling flow of speech

✔ Rapid heart beat

✔ Restlessness

To make matters worse, after the caffeine wears off, you'll crash, which can result in headaches, fatigue, and still more difficulty concentrating and remembering.

Caffeine and sleep

Caffeine lowers your level of adenosine, a neurotransmitter that helps you calm down and become sleepy. If you consume high levels of caffeine, especially in the afternoon or evening, you likely will have insomnia or at least a poor quality of sleep.

Caffeine suppresses your Stage 4 sleep, which is the deepest, most restful stage of the sleep cycle. (For more information on sleep, see Chapter 7.) You don't want to lose Stage 4 sleep because it recharges your immune system; otherwise, you'll get more colds and wake up feeling less rested.

Caffeine also puts a damper on Stage 5, otherwise known as REM (rapid eye movement) sleep. You have your most intense dreams during this stage. If you suppress your REM sleep, you increase your irritability and have difficulty concentrating the next day. Less concentration means less short-term memory.

Caffeine and an empty stomach

If you drink coffee on an empty stomach in the morning, you create a variety of problems for yourself. Skipping breakfast compromises your thinking ability and destabilizes your emotions. Add caffeine to that equation, and your problems magnify. You end up so wired that you can't pay attention long enough to form memories.

The ill effects of drinking caffeine on an empty stomach are not immediately obvious. Just wait one to two hours after you consume caffeine, and you'll experience a bigger crash than had you eaten breakfast. You'll probably have more difficulty concentrating.

You expend energy from your fat cells when you fast, are starving, or when you consume caffeine on an empty stomach. However, after this compromised burst of energy that you borrowed, you'll feel more exhausted and depleted than before and probably feel free-floating anxiety.

Caffeine and sugar

Many caffeinated soft drinks have as many as four to five tablespoons of sugar in one can. Not only do you get the buzz and crash from the caffeine, but you also feel the ill effects of the sugar.

If your diet consists of a lot of caffeine and sugar and you don't eat three balanced meals, don't expect to be able to concentrate and remember what you want to remember. If you fall into this pattern, you may be addicted to these non-foods. When you don't consume your regular dose of sugar and caffeine, you may feel that you need more of it to keep yourself going.

Now with all this said about the evils of caffeine, I want to emphasize that I am not an anti-caffeine fanatic. (That must be hard to believe after reading this section!)

My confession is that I drink a double espresso each morning. I know, it's not good for me. However, I never drink it on an empty stomach and always eat a balanced breakfast. I never drink it after lunch and never use sugar or eat donuts or junk food. Does that make it right? No. It's just easier to drink it and be able to think clearly.

If you use caffeine, do follow these guidelines:

  ✔ Make sure you use caffeine in moderation and on top of a healthy diet.
  ✔ Always consume it after a healthy meal.

Making Sure You're Hydrated

Your body consists of roughly 60 percent water. Most people don't realize how much water they need to drink each day to prevent dehydration. You can go a few weeks without eating and not die, but you'll die going just a few days without drinking water.

If you get a headache and find yourself very thirsty, you're already dehydrated. Your brain, which consists of about 75 percent water, simply needs enough water to function. The subtle effects of dehydration include an unclear mind, difficulty paying attention, and, of course, short-term memory problems.

To keep your body and your brain functioning at optimum levels, drink about 1 ½ quarts (or 1 ½ liters) of water per day. Be sure to increase the amount during hot weather or if you're exercising. I keep a bottle or glass of water near me at all times.

Keep in mind that many beverages are diuretics, meaning they make you urinate, causing further dehydration. Coffees, teas, beer, wine, and spirits, actually do less to liquefy you than you may think. What you need is water, pure and simple.

A significant benefit of drinking an adequate amount of water is fewer illnesses. Whenever I feel a cold coming on, I drink more water than I usually do and sometimes that can put on the brakes before I plunge into a cold.

When drinking fluids, follow these guidelines:

- Drink at least four large glasses of water a day.
- Limit your consumption of diuretic beverages.
- If you're exercising or if the day is hot, drink more water than usual.

Chapter 5

Supplementing Your Memory

• •

• •

*Y*ou will always hear talk about magic memory pills. No one pill can magically make you possess a mega memory. However, many vitamins, hormones, and minerals form the foundation for a good memory.

Vitamins, minerals, and hormones provide you with the nourishment and chemistry necessary to support your memory. However, you must think of vitamins and other supplements as just that, supplements to a good diet, not a replacement for it.

In this chapter, you discover how vitamins, minerals, and hormones help form the building blocks to your brain's chemistry and your memory.

Vitalizing Your Memory with Vitamins

Vitamins are essential to your health. These organic compounds are available in many foods and help all parts of your body function. By using vitamins, you enable your brain to remember; without them, your brain will stumble, sputter, and forget.

Vitamins help your memory in two principal ways:

✔ Many vitamins can act as antioxidants, which stabilize free radicals from their destructive attack on your brain (see Chapter 6). Vitamins A, C, and E are all highly touted antioxidants.

✔ Some vitamins, such as those in the B family, are critical for many of your neurotransmitters.

Vitamins are either water-soluble or fat-soluble. Water-soluble vitamins operate in the watery areas of your brain. Fat-soluble vitamins operate in the fatty areas of your brain.

Powering up the watery areas of your brain with vitamins

The water-soluble vitamins include the B vitamins and vitamin C. They operate in the watery areas of your brain.

The brainy Bs

The B vitamins are crucial for your brain. If you have a balanced supply of them, your brain appreciates it and rewards you with memory. If you don't get enough vitamins, you won't remember that you have a brain.

The B vitamins support your body's ability to perform methylation, which is the process of removing the toxic by-products of cellular metabolism (see Chapter 6). If methylation doesn't happen properly, you run the risk of building up the toxic substance called homocystine, which increases your risk of atherosclerosis, heart disease, and stroke. Excessive homocystine has been linked to poor memory. Don't let that happen to you. Make sure you have the Bs.

Vitamin B_1

Each of the B vitamins has a chemical name. Vitamin B_1, for example, is thiamine. It was the first found of the B vitamins, which is why it's called number 1. Thiamine is heavily involved with converting glucose to energy in your brain by helping to produce three important enzymes that do the job.

Vitamin B_1 is also closely tied to the acetylcholine-like activities (see Chapter 3). If you don't get enough of this vitamin, you'll suffer from problems with attention; probably become confused; and, in extreme B_1 deprivation, develop beriberi, which is marked by severe mental confusion and depression.

Plenty of foods contain B_1. Here are some good sources:

✔ Beans

✔ Lean pork

✔ Many grains

✔ Oatmeal

- ✔ Peanuts
- ✔ Unrefined cereals

Vitamin B₂

Vitamin B₂ (also called riboflavin) helps your body digest and use carbohy-drates and protein, which are so critical to a healthy brain. This vitamin also helps support your mucous membrane.

Good sources of B₂ include:

- ✔ Brewer's yeast
- ✔ Broccoli
- ✔ Cheese
- ✔ Dark leafy vegetables
- ✔ Eggs
- ✔ Liver
- ✔ Whole grains

Vitamin B₃

Vitamin B₃, also called niacin, is another important vitamin you need to supply to your brain. Niacin is very much involved in lowering cholesterol, facilitating nerve impulses, and metabolizing your oxygen supply. If you're low in B₃, you'll probably have problems with short-term memory and confusion.

A word of caution if taking a B₃ supplement: Don't take the time-released vari-ety. It has been known to cause liver damage.

Good sources of B₃:

- ✔ Lime-treated corn meal
- ✔ Liver
- ✔ Milk
- ✔ Yogurt

Vitamin B₅

Vitamin B₅, also called pantothenic acid, is involved in the synthesis of red blood cells — which carry oxygen through your body including your brain — and adrenal hormones. Vitamin B₅ converts choline into acetylcholine, which is very much involved in supporting your memory (see Chapter 3).

Good sources of B_5 include:

- ✔ Beans
- ✔ Fish
- ✔ Poultry
- ✔ Whole grains

Vitamin B_6

You need vitamin B_6, also called pyridoxine, to help with the formation of your structural proteins, red blood cells, and protaglandins. This vitamin is essential for getting energy and nutrients from food. It also helps remove excess homocystine, which can be a major risk factor for heart disease. Lastly, vitamin B_6 plays a supportive role in the production of some of your brain's neurotransmitters, including dopamine, serotonin, and norepinephrine.

If you're low in B_6, expect to have thinking and memory problems.

Good sources of B_6 include:

- ✔ Beans
- ✔ Brussels sprouts
- ✔ Cauliflower
- ✔ Dark green vegetables
- ✔ Eggs
- ✔ Fish
- ✔ Legumes
- ✔ Liver
- ✔ Many raw nuts
- ✔ Milk
- ✔ Whole grains

Vitamin B_{12}

Like B_5 and B_6, you need vitamin B_{12}, also called cobalamin, for the production of your red blood cells.

Vitamin B_{12} also is involved in the methylation process (making the myelin sheaths that coat your neurons), which helps with conduction of firing patterns (see Chapter 3).

If you're low in B_{12}, you're going to be high on confusion.

Good sources of B_{12} include:

- Cheese
- Eggs
- Fish
- Liver
- Milk
- Meat

Folic acid

Folic acid plays a role in DNA synthesis and, during your earliest years, it helped your nervous system develop. Getting enough folic acid in your diet is still critical.

If pregnant women don't get enough folic acid, they may give birth to a child with birth defects, perhaps spina bifida. If you don't get enough folic acid now, chances are you'll experience memory problems and emotional instability, including irritability and even paranoia.

Good sources of folic acid include:

- Asparagus
- Brewer's yeast
- Carrots
- Dark leafy vegetables
- Legumes
- Root vegetables

Choline

Choline is critical in your earliest years and as you grow. If you don't have enough choline, your attention span and memory suffer. Choline takes an active role in your cell membranes and is a precursor to the important memory neurotransmitter, acetylcholine.

Don't shortchange yourself of choline, or you'll shortchange yourself of your memory ability.

Scurvy

Scurvy was a major problem for British sailors, who traveled all over the world. The sailors had limited supplies of fruits and vegetables that contained vitamin C. Sailors suffered from tooth decay, spongy gums, anemia, skin conditions, and memory problems. Eventually, the British Navy got wise and began to remember to carry citrus, especially limes, on board ships. Hence, the slang name for an English person, limey.

Good sources of choline include:

- ✔ Cauliflower
- ✔ Eggs
- ✔ Lettuce
- ✔ Liver
- ✔ Soybeans

Vitamin C — Linus Pauling's wonder

Nobel laureate Linus Pauling brought the public's attention to vitamin C. He claimed that high doses of vitamin C are crucial to good health. Many people initially thought he had become a fanatic. In recent years, however, the numerous benefits of vitamin C have been piling up.

Vitamin C is involved in the production of many neurotransmitters that are crucial for your brain to operate optimally. Vitamin C is versatile: It's a powerful antioxidant and free-radical scavenger. The neurotransmitters acetylcholine, dopamine, and norepinephrine all get help from vitamin C. Without them, your memory ability would barely limp along. (See the related sidebar titled, "Scurvy," later in this chapter.)

Good sources of vitamin C include:

- ✔ Berries
- ✔ Broccoli
- ✔ Brussels sprouts
- ✔ Citrus fruits
- ✔ Green peppers

Vitalizing the fatty areas of your brain

The two chief fat-soluble vitamins are A and E. These vitamins are active in the fat parts of your brain, and they have a lot of room to play out their roles.

Vitamin E

Vitamin E is a great free-radical scavenger. It hunts down those toxic destroyers of your brain and destroys them instead. Vitamin E is the most highly touted antioxidant: It interrupts the oxidative process and protects your fatty cell membranes. It reduces the death of your neurons, as a result of beta amyloid, the protein fragments that form the plaques found in brains of Alzheimer's patients.

Vitamin E has been shown to reduce the damage to your hippocampus if it's injured. Your hippocampus is that structure in your brain that transfers short-term memories into long-term memories (see Chapter 3).

In addition to its great benefits to your brain, vitamin E helps bolster your immune system. Your T cells (part of your immune system) love it, and your entire body loves it because it indirectly helps fight off bacteria, toxins, and viruses that enter your body.

Vitamins: Recommended daily allowance

The National Research Council's Food and Nutritional Board established a list of recommendations for safe amounts for each of the vitamins. These recommended daily allowances (RDAs) appear below:

Vitamin	RDA for women	RDA for men
A	800 mcg	1,000 mcg
B₁ (thiamine)	1.1 mg	1.5 mg
B₂ (riboflavin)	1.3 mg	1.7 mg
B₃ (niacin)	15 mg	19 mg
B₆ (pyrodoxine)	1.6 mg	2.0 mg
B₁₂ (cobalamin)	2.0 mcg	2.0 mcg
C	60 mg	60 mg
E	8 mg	10 mg

Note: mcg=microgram, mg=milligram

Vitamin E is also an anticoagulant, meaning that it thins your blood. Therefore, be wary of using it if you're taking anticoagulant medications such as warfarin sodium (better known as Coumadin).

Good sources of vitamin E include:

- Eggs
- Many raw nuts
- Milk
- Olive oil
- Pumpkin seeds
- Sunflower seeds
- Sweet potatoes
- Wheat germ

Vitamin A

Have you ever heard anyone say carrots are good for your eyes? They're right. Vitamin A is critical for your retina. If you have vitamin A deficiency, you may experience night blindness. Vitamin A also plays a crucial role in your brain by neutralizing "bad" oxygen and shielding cell membranes from injury.

Good sources of vitamin A include:

- Egg yolks (but they are very high in cholesterol)
- Fish liver oil
- Green leafy vegetables

Vitamin A can build up in your tissues. If you consume too much of it, you can get liver toxicity. So, if you supplement your diet with vitamin A, be sure to follow the recommended FDA levels. (See the related sidebar titled, "Vitamins: Recommended daily allowance," later in this chapter.)

Beta carotene is a precursor to vitamin A. Good sources of beta carotene include:

- Broccoli
- Carrots
- Spinach
- Sweet potatoes
- Yellow squash

Taking Advantage of the Chinese Gs

Two Chinese herbs have gained prominence in recent years, ginkgo biloba and ginseng. Both of these herbs are widely used and found not only in most health food stores, but also at many supermarkets. Ginkgo biloba and ginseng have been used for thousands of years in China and have stood the test of time.

Circulating with ginkgo biloba

The first known use of ginkgo biloba goes back 5,000 years. A Chinese medical text describes gingko as a medicine that helps the brain. Ginkgo is now used all over the world as an aid for the brain.

Ginkgo contains flavonoids and terpenoids, which include ginkgolide. (Flavonoids and terpenoids are *phytochemicals,* which are plant chemicals that protect and help prevent disease in the human body.) Ginkgo helps improve the circulation of blood in your brain by causing your small blood vessels (called capillaries) to dilate. Your brain needs an adequate supply of blood to keep your neurons alive and healthy. With advancing age, your capillaries become less able to promote that supply. Ginkgo can help your neurons from becoming oxygen-deprived by getting blood to them.

Ginkgo helps inhibit the actions of a substance known as platelet activating factor (PAF), which causes platelets to clump together. It's for this reason that if you're taking Coumadin or other blood-thinning medications, you need to tell your doctor you're considering taking gingko. Your doctor may suggest that you don't, because the combination of gingko and a blood-thinning medication may cause bleeding in your brain.

Ginkgo received tremendous press as an agent that helped Alzheimer's patients, although it is still unclear as to the degree that ginkgo is helpful in slowing down this horrible disease. It has been shown to be helpful with blood circulation in the brain for some people.

Assuming you aren't taking a blood-thinning medication, ginkgo can help some of the antioxidants, such as vitamin E, protect your brain cells against free-radical damage.

If you take ginkgo after lunch, you may notice that late-afternoon mental tiredness improves.

Buzzing with ginseng

Ginseng is another Chinese herb that can help your memory. Like ginkgo biloba, ginseng has been documented in Chinese medical literature for thousands of years. Ginseng works like a stimulant by helping you concentrate.

Ginseng comes in two main types: Korean ginseng and Siberian ginseng. Korean ginseng (also called panax ginseng — *panax* meaning all-healing) has ginsenosides that act on your brain's hypothalamus and pituitary gland, and on your adrenal glands to help you deal with stress, boost your immune system, and decrease free-radical damage.

Ginseng seems to stimulate the production of epinephrine, also called adrenaline. In doing so, it helps lower the stress hormone, cortisol. This herb also seems to help increase acetylcholine, the neurotransmitter involved with your memory.

Because ginseng is a stimulant, it's not hard to get too much of it in your system. Insomnia, jitteriness, and heart palpitations are a few of the side effects.

If you use ginseng, use it in moderation.

Using Your Herbal Cornucopia

If you go to any health food store — and even some grocery stores nowadays — you'll see ads decorating the vitamin and herb section with grandiose claims. "Turn your mind into a memory machine," says one. Another says, "Supermind." Be wary!

Herbal supplements aren't regulated by the Food and Drug Administration (FDA), which means that you can never be sure what is in the jar. You may think there's nothing wrong with that. You may even have the opinion that the FDA is just one more government agency that makes life difficult. The truth is that the FDA goes through a meticulous process of evaluating drugs and vitamins to ensure that products are safe. Yes, the agency is often slow to approve new products, but I'd rather be safe than sorry.

The potency of the herbal supplement you buy may be something much different than what's written on the label. You may not be getting a good quality product or even not be getting the actual herb that you intended to purchase.

A friend of mine who runs an herb wholesale business told me that he travels the globe making sure that he purchases herbs that are pure and of good quality. It's not uncommon for many herbs to be packaged with dirt and weeds. Some herbs are grown in environmentally toxic areas, high in heavy metals or pesticides. What a sad irony for a person who is hoping to be natural and organic only to be taking in toxins unknowingly.

Just because herbs are largely from plant products doesn't mean they're safe and can be taken whenever you want. Herbs contain elements that create chemical changes in your body and can be toxic if taken inappropriately. In addition, if you're taking other medications, there is a high chance that the interaction between the medication and the herb may put your health at risk. Be an informed consumer, and let your doctor know everything you intend to take.

Make sure that you know what you're buying. I do this by buying only from legitimate companies that have reputations to protect.

When you're considering taking herbal supplements, observe the following guidelines:

- ✔ If you're taking other drugs prescribed by your doctor, let her know that you're considering using a specific herb. Some herbs are toxic or counterproductive when used in conjunction with various medications.

- ✔ If you're taking one herb, don't pile a bunch of other herbs into your system. Some herbs in combination can be toxic and can cause serious medical problems.

- ✔ Make sure you know what you're getting. Buy from reputable companies.

Charging by Hormones

Hormones are chemicals made by your body to help it function. Some of these hormones directly affect your memory.

DHEA

In recent years, many health food stores have advertised the fact that they carry DHEA (dehydroepiandrosterone). DHEA is a steroid hormone produced by your adrenal glands.

DHEA has been touted as an aid to people experiencing stress. It's also reported to help with memory. Its actual effectiveness and safety are still under study.

DHEA is converted to testosterone. Women who take it have been reported to grow facial hair. Men with prostate cancer need to avoid it.

Pregnenolone

One of the naturally produced hormones that's highly involved in your memory ability is called pregnenolone, another steroid hormone. It's produced in your brain, spinal cord, and by your adrenal glands by synthesizing cholesterol. It affects various neurotransmitters that affect memory, including acetylcholine, GABA, and aspartate. Patients who've been given a prescription of pregnenolone have reported to have a general improvement in their memory capacity.

Estrogen

Estrogen is a crucial hormone for women and memory. Menopause is marked by a drop in estrogen, and, with it, changes in memory and mood.

Many postmenopausal women have taken estrogen replacements and have noticed a big improvement in not only mood but also memory. For women not vulnerable to breast cancer, estrogen replacement after menopause can serve many purposes.

The hormone estrogen

- ✔ Helps the cholinergic cells grow and stay alive longer.
- ✔ Appears to have an antioxidant quality.
- ✔ Improves the clarity of thoughts, because estrogen enhances the production of acetylcholine.
- ✔ Helps stimulate nerve growth factor, which protects neurons from free radical damage.

If you have a family history of breast cancer, it may not be advisable to take estrogen replacement.

Falling asleep with hormone help

Getting enough sleep is critical for healthy memory (see Chapter 7). Melatonin is a hormone that your pineal gland secretes to help you get to sleep. You pineal gland is at the center of your brain, but it gets messages via your retina as to whether it's light outside or dark. If it's dark, your pineal gland tells the rest of your brain it's time to go to sleep by its release of melatonin.

Unfortunately, as you age, your pineal gland doesn't do the job it used to do and your melatonin levels go down. In addition, if you work at night, your pineal gland doesn't get the signals it needs, because you try to sleep when it's light outside. Your brain doesn't know if it's day or night.

Recently, melatonin has become popular as a sleep aid. People who experience jet lag use it to readjust to the new time pattern. People who suffer from insomnia periodically take it to get to sleep and stay asleep.

Melatonin is also a good antioxidant and hunts down free radicals from their destructive rampage. Nevertheless, note that taking too much melatonin can hurt some people, so moderation and occasional use is advisable.

If you supplement with melatonin, I recommend not going over 2 milligrams because you may run the risk of contributing to depression. This is because melatonin competes with the neurotransmitter serotonin. Low serotonin is associated with depression. In addition, some researchers report that if you take it too often, your brain will stop producing it naturally.

If you use melatonin as a sleep aid, don't take it every night, and never go over 2 milligrams.

Bathing in Minerals

Some minerals are crucial for your brain and your memory skills. Magnesium and zinc, for example, play a role in your brain's ability to remember.

Magnesium is important for numerous functions, but most important to memory are its energy, sleep, and cardiovascular benefits.

Many people take magnesium as a supplement along with calcium. These two minerals need to be taken together to ensure that you don't get a buildup of too much calcium, which can be harmful. Taking a "cal-mag" tablet before going to bed can aid you in relaxation and better sleep.

Zinc is important for your brain's ability to function properly and to be able to remember. Studies have shown that elderly people with low zinc levels are often disoriented and have memory problems. When they're supplied with an adequate dose of zinc, these memory problems subside. (See the related sidebar titled, "Mind your PS and Q_{10}," later in this chapter.

Mind your PS and Q₁₀

The nutritional supplement called phosphatidylserine, referred to as PS, has been reported to have a mild memory-boosting and stimulant-like effect.

A little-known vitamin called coenzyme Q₁₀ is also involved in your brain's ability to remember.

It's involved in energy production at your cellular level. Inside each of your cells, the mitochondria act as energy units producing ATP. Coenzyme Q₁₀ helps get this all started. Without it, you're going to be thinking like a snail, dull and slow.

One of the best and easiest ways to supplement with zinc is by ensuring that your multiple vitamin contains zinc.

Making Less More

No nutritional supplement is a replacement for a good, balanced diet. Many of the vitamins, minerals, and trace elements are found in a healthy diet. Vitamin and mineral supplements are just that — supplements to your diet.

Because many nutritional supplements have been only recently investigated, be conservative in their use. Some can have destructive and even toxic effects if you take too much or combine them with medications or other compounds.

You should follow the maxim that less is more. Choose your supplements wisely. Take a good look at your diet and decide what you are deficient in and then supplement to balance. If your diet is deficient in a particular vitamin group because you don't particularly like the foods that contain it, learn to like those foods. Supplement only in those elements you can't practically buy in your local store.

Chapter 6

Avoiding the Memory Suppressors

*Y*our mind is a priceless collection of memories, and it depends on a healthy brain. Your brain can lose its memory ability, however, by the way you treat it. In other words, your lifestyle has a direct effect on your brain.

In this chapter, you discover how to avoid damaging your brain. Your brain's ability to remember can erode — you find out how you can either prevent or minimize the loss.

Keeping your brain healthy is easier than you think. All you need to do is

✔ Maintain a healthy diet.

✔ Minimize exposure to toxic chemicals.

✔ Avoid alcohol.

✔ Keep away from smoking.

✔ Exercise.

These five principles can help slow down the dementias and serious medical conditions that bog down your brain and your memory ability.

Minimizing Subtle Brain Rot

Your brain is so sensitive that you risk damaging it in ways that are so subtle that you may not have thought it possible. You can avoid many of these damaging effects (or at least minimize them) if you watch your diet, make sure you aren't exposed to toxins, and pay close attention to what medications you do or don't take.

Dealing with free radicals

One of the subtle destructive effects on the brain occurs through what has been called *free-radical* damage. Free radicals aren't peace-loving, anti-war protesters from the 1960s. They're actually warmongers that attack your brain, and there's nothing peace-loving about them. (See the related sidebar titled, "Free radicals on the prowl," later in this chapter.)

Many fat cells in your brain are support cells, which help neurons do their job, and they are particularly vulnerable to damage. Damage to the mitochondria, the energy-producing factory in your cells, impairs DNA and messenger RNA (a type of nucleic acid that participates in the expression of genes).

Your body produces its own antioxidants to battle the free radicals and the damage they produce. Unfortunately, as you age, these free-radical scavengers subside. In addition, if you're doing things that neutralize these naturally produced antioxidants and if you're maintaining a lifestyle that increases free radicals, then your brain is going to more than resent the double-whammy to its cells.

Many lifestyle choices increase free-radical activity, such as:

- ✔ Smoking
- ✔ Eating fatty foods
- ✔ Being exposed to environmental toxins

You can fight back the free radicals by:

- ✔ Eating a diet rich in antioxidants (see Chapter 4).
- ✔ Taking vitamin supplements such as vitamins C and E, which help break down the bad oxygen and neutralize free radicals (see Chapter 5).

Keeping your detox system A-OK

When your body needs detoxifying, it uses a number of mechanisms, one of which is *methylation*. However, as you age, your body's ability to detoxify breaks down, especially if you have a poor diet.

TECHNICAL STUFF

Free radicals on the prowl

Free radicals develop at the molecular level when an atom carries with it an unpaired electron. The negative electrical charge triggers destruction of your cells. Unfortunately, this process occurs all the time.

Free radicals are the by-products of one of the ways your cells metabolize. Free radicals form during metabolism as highly reactive atoms that bind to and destroy your healthy cells. This *oxidative* process occurs as you breathe, and

your cells take energy from the food you eat. There's no escape from free radicals!

Some cells are particularly vulnerable to free-radical attack. These susceptible cells are fat cells and the energy-producing part of cells called mitochondria. Since we are all fatheads (see Chapter 3) and your brain is composed of 60 percent fat, free-radical damage can be extensive.

One of the destructive compounds that methylation normally cleans out is called *homocystine,* which is a regular by-product of amino acid metabolism. When homocystine builds up, however, it slows down your blood circulation by encouraging blood platelets to stick together.

As if this effect isn't bad enough, homocystine also contributes to free-radical damage and a number of other major problems including atherosclerosis, cancer, DNA damage, and Alzheimer's disease.

WARNING!

A bad diet can cause defects in your methylation system. For example, if your diet is deficient in foods containing vitamin B_{12} and folic acid, you'll not only have defects in methylation, but also in your memory.

TIP

Make sure you have a balanced diet by including foods that support methylation:

- For vitamin B_{12}, eat eggs, liver, and milk (see Chapter 4).
- For folic acid, eat carrots, dark leafy vegetables, and whole wheat.
- Take supplements in both (see Chapter 5).

Bringing inflammation under control

Inflammation can damage your brain subtly and not so subtly. Inflammation occurs normally when you are injured or when your cells have been under attack by bacteria. The area around your injured cells is put into an alarm state so that repair and healing can happen. Blood vessels dilate to bring in supplies. Swelling often occurs, however, as blood vessels leak fluid. Immune system cells come to the rescue, and blood-clotting agents form.

Unfortunately, as you age, the inflammation that's so helpful to healing doesn't bounce back as quickly as when you were younger. This slowdown occurs because your circulatory system can get sluggish as plaque builds up on your artery walls. In addition, your immune system may misidentify your healthy cells for unhealthy ones because the signaling mechanism can break down. If all this happens, you run the risk of chronic inflammation.

Chronic inflammation occurs with several serious diseases, including cardio-vascular disease and arthritis. Recently, it has been found as a major factor in Alzheimer's disease.

Because inflammation has been so strongly associated with brain impairment, many doctors recommend a moderate use of anti-inflammatory drugs.

Anti-inflammatory drugs come in two classes, steroidal and non-steroidal. Because steroids can also damage your hippocampus, many doctors recommend non-steroidal, anti-inflammatory drugs such as acetylsalicylic acid (aspirin) or ibuprofen (Motrin).

Minimize inflammation in your brain by:

- Maintaining a diet free of artery-clogging fats (see Chapter 4).
- Taking a low dose of a non-steroidal, anti-inflammatory drug as you get older.

Keeping Clear of Neurotoxins

Many years ago when I was studying neuropsychology, my professor said that neurotoxins would become notorious in the years to come. He was right, they have.

Now, neuropsychologists are called in to give tests to people who have been exposed to environmental toxins in their office buildings, factories, and even in their neighborhoods. These workers often have been exposed to solvents, heavy metals, herbicides, pesticides, or cleaning agents. One of the symptoms that neuropsychological tests identify is a memory problem.

Neurotoxins are found all around. Heavy metals, such as lead, were used in paint and are still found in old buildings. Lead is also present in lead-soldered pipes, lead-based ceramic cookware, and even crystal cups.

Aluminum is another neurotoxin. This metal is in some types of cookware, in cans, antiperspirants, and even drinking water. Autopsies of people who had Alzheimer's disease have been shown to have an uncanny amount of aluminum in their brains. It's difficult to say whether the aluminum was the cause of the disease or the result of it.

Carbon monoxide can also contribute to memory loss, because it displaces oxygen in your hemoglobin. As a result, less oxygen goes to your blood. Carbon monoxide can really mess with your hippocampus and its ability to transfer short-term memories into long-term memory (see Chapter 3).

Minimize your exposure to neurotoxins by following these guidelines:

✔ If you work near toxic chemicals, make sure you get proper ventilation.

✔ Avoid exposure to pesticides and herbicides.

✔ If you work close to or are exposed to car fumes on a regular basis, get proper ventilation.

Saying No to Certain Food Additives

Processed foods are everywhere. We want convenience besides nutrition, but too often, health goes by the wayside. You may not know that many of the processed foods we all eat contain food additives that are not good for your brain and, therefore, your memory ability.

Aspartame

Two of the most common food additives are the artificial sweetener, aspartame (such as NutraSweet), and monosodium glutamate (MSG). You can find aspartame in literally thousands of foods. Aspartame is not nutritious, as some brand names imply. Don't fall for that corporate advertising ploy. When you pick up a diet soft drink because you're conscious of weight, your intentions are good but, unfortunately, the results aren't good.

When you consume large quantities of aspartame, you run the risk of over-exciting your brain's neurons and damaging them in the process. The aspartame you consume breaks down into toxic chemicals, including methanol (wood alcohol). Scores of people have complained of memory problems, headaches, and dizziness after consuming aspartame. You don't have to be one of them.

Don't buy into the need to have everything sweet. Instead, learn to appreciate and savor foods and drinks that aren't overly sweet. Your brain will appreciate it.

Monosodium glutamate

Monosodium glutamate (MSG) is a flavor enhancer, but it's the opposite of a brain enhancer. You'd be surprised how many of the foods you eat contain it. If you eat snack chips, seasoning, bouillon, canned broth, and a whole host of other foods, you're getting a big hit of MSG.

By consuming MSG, you make your brain overfire neurons so much so that some neurons can become overly exhausted and die. This exhaustion occurs because MSG spikes up the neurotransmitter glutamate and your brain becomes overwhelmed. Many people complain of a mild headache after eating foods laced with MSG. That's the mild effect. Some people react more severely. As with aspartame, the bottom line is that MSG isn't good for anyone's brain and is not good for your memory.

If you want your brain to work at tiptop shape and be able to remember as much as possible, then:

✔ Stay away from aspartame.

✔ Stay away from MSG.

Saying "No, Thanks" to Alcohol and Marijuana

If you use alcohol or marijuana as a way to relax, and if you are serious about improving your memory, you need to find a new way to relax. The effects of drugs and alcohol impair your concentration, memory, and energy level for days after you last use them. Although you may not think you abuse alcohol or marijuana, your memory can suffer anyway if you use them.

Sobering up to remember more

What feels good to you may not be good for your brain. If you drink, it's probably because it makes you feel relaxed or uninhibited, but alcohol is destructive to your brain.

Because alcohol has been around for thousands of years, we've unfortunately built up many myths about its benefits. If you accept one or more of these myths as truth, expect multiple problems if you drink it to excess.

Some of the main myths about drinking alcohol are that it

- Decreases your stress
- Lifts you out of depression
- Decreases your anxiety
- Helps you sleep

The facts are that if you use alcohol you'll

- Have more difficulty dealing with stress
- Feel depressed after your last drink
- Feel anxiety or even panic attacks
- Have sleep problems

For several years, I taught a seminar in psychological and neuropsychological testing to Ph.D. psychology interns. One of the rules about testing people who have consumed alcohol on a regular basis is that you "don't test a wet brain." We require that they be sober for at least three to six months. The reason for this time requirement is people who drink on a regular basis have a variety of deficits in their ability to think.

People who drink alcohol regularly display decreased

- Performance on memory tests of visual and spatial perception
- Visual and spatial learning ability
- Ability to make fine motor movements
- Adaptive abilities
- Short-term memory
- Non-verbal abstract learning
- Abstract thinking ability
- Conceptual thinking ability

If you drink alcohol, you can take in up to 50 percent of your total daily caloric intake and, in the process, restrict the normal consumption of macronutrients — fats, carbohydrates, and proteins. In other words, by drinking, you suppress your body's ability to make full use of the food you eat. (See the related sidebar titled, "The red wine debate," later in this chapter.)

If you drink large amounts of alcohol, you run the risk of developing a memory disorder called Korsakoff's syndrome. Korsakoff's syndrome so badly damages your brain that you become psychotic and have severe short- and long-term memory loss and major damage to your hippocampus.

The red wine debate

A lot has been said recently about the pros and cons of drinking red wine. This debate is far from being settled. However, if you drink two to three glasses of wine each night and have done so for years, it's time to reconsider this habit.

Memory researchers, such as Dr. D. P. Dvanard of Columbia University, state clearly that consuming two to three glasses of wine daily causes brain toxicity as you age. Withering memory ability is but one subtle symptom.

You may become defensive and wonder if I'm some kind of prohibitionist. Hey, I drink wine too. In fact, I live in the wine country of Northern California. Some of my neighbors own wineries. Yet, I don't drink wine on a regular basis because I want to preserve what few brain cells I have.

Alcohol can cause liver damage. Well before cirrhosis of the liver sets in, you'll experience thiamine (vitamin B_1) deficiency. Low thiamine causes you to have problems utilizing glucose. Because your brain is the highest glucose consumer in your body, drinking alcohol deprives it of fuel for your memory.

The low B_1 level causes those parts of your brain centrally involved in memory to deteriorate. Your hippocampus and amygdala will suffer and your ability to transfer short-term memory into long-term memory will suffer, too. In addition, your ability to remember the appropriate emotional context to memories will whither away. You'll have a tendency to misread emotional cues.

I've evaluated literally hundreds of people over the years who drank too much. By the time they got to me, they had hit their bottom. Significant people in their lives had abandoned them or threaten to. They consistently reported they were accused of forgetting how to communicate to others with sensitivity.

Clearing the cloudy memories: Marijuana

You may be one of those people who feel that a few tokes of marijuana are what you need to mellow out after a stressful day. If so, it's time to reconsider the facts.

It was my generation, which came to age during the 1960s, that promoted marijuana as a safe and even healthy alternative to the most popular drug of our parent's generation, alcohol. To this day, some people still argue that it is just an herb. To complicate matters, researchers from my generation hesitated to do serious research on the harmful effects of marijuana until recently.

Just as considerable evidence about marijuana's destructive effects finally did come to light, the "medical marijuana" debate broke out. Soon, patients suffering from cancer, glaucoma, and chronic pain were seeking a "prescription of marijuana." Medical marijuana initiatives emerged on state ballots. When I try to explain to patients who use marijuana how it clouds their memory, they sometimes say, "Yeah, sure, then why are doctors prescribing it?" I explain that some cancer patients are using it to increase their appetite during chemotherapy, or glaucoma patients take it because of the buildup of pressure in their eyes, but that marijuana doesn't spare their memory.

Marijuana is notorious for causing short-term memory deficits and difficulty in maintaining attention. People who smoke marijuana regularly have a great deal of trouble maintaining clarity of their thought. They experience cloudy, confused, and often befuddled memories.

If you smoke marijuana on a regular basis, chances are you'll become irritable, mildly depressed, and prone to lack initiative and motivation. Each of these problems fuels the other. As your motivation drops, you gain fewer rewards from your actions and you find few reasons to feel good about yourself and become depressed.

Over the years, I have seen many people who wish to be tested for attention-deficit disorder (ADD). The ability to pay attention is a key component of forming a memory. During my initial interview with patients, too often I find that they smoke marijuana on a regular basis. I tell them that marijuana causes the very symptoms that they are complaining about. Often, they don't believe me and feel threatened that I am taking away their way of relaxing.

> They say, "I've done this for years."
>
> I ask, "How long?"
>
> "Since I was 17."
>
> "And how long do you think you've had ADD?"
>
> "Well — ah — since my late teens."
>
> "I rest my case."

If you smoke marijuana, quit. A word of caution, however: THC *(tetrahydrocannibanol),* the primary active ingredient in marijuana, is stored in your fat cells and will take weeks to leach out. Therefore, you won't experience relief from the symptoms until weeks after quitting. Some people make the mistake of saying to themselves, "Well, I quit and I still have the same problems, so I may as well go back to smoking." You need to give yourself the time for your entire body to clear out the THC that you've stored up. (See the related sidebar titled, "THC and exquisite doorknobs," later in this chapter.)

THC and exquisite doorknobs

The chemical found in marijuana, referred to as *THC (tetrahydrocannibanol),* mimics a chemical in your brain called *anandamide.* Unlike neurotransmitters that affect brain cells directly, anandamide is a *neuromodulator.* It orchestrates the activity of several neurotransmitters at the same time.

If your brain is flooded with THC, the anandamide effect will temporarily "enhance" (or distort) your perception. This virtual novelty may make a simple doorknob seem like the most exquisite doorknob you have ever seen. You'll look at that same doorknob several hours later and wonder why you thought it was so special (that is, if you even remember thinking about it).

To make matters worse, many of the neurotransmitters that enable you to think clearly and feel good aren't as readily available. The neurotransmitters got "down-produced," meaning your brain produces less. With less serotonin, GABA, dopamine, and norepinephrine, you'll feel more depressed and stressed, have less motivation, and find that your short-term memory is clouded.

THC also lowers the level of acetylcholine in your brain. Acetylcholine is centrally involved in your ability to maintain attention and to remember (see Chapter 3).

Getting Clear on the Side Effects of R_x

We all go to a doctor for treatment for specific medical problems, but sometimes, the treatment causes other problems. Despite the great advances in medicine over the past hundred years and the hard work of our physicians, many of the medicines used aren't magic bullets. Most medications have side effects. They cause more than their intended effects. The side effects of many medicines may include memory problems. In most cases, these side effects are not permanent. When you're off the medication, the memory-depressing side effects fade away.

Calcium channel blockers, beta blockers, painkillers, and antihistamines are but a few of the medicines that have memory-depressing side effects. The following list shows types of medications that have been known to cause memory problems.

- Antihistamines
- Antipsychotics
- Barbiturates
- Beta blockers

- ✔ Calcium channel blockers
- ✔ Digitalis
- ✔ Glaucoma eye drops
- ✔ Incontinence medications
- ✔ Painkillers
- ✔ Sleeping pills

Steroids

Steroids, such as prednisone and hydrocortisone (which are used to treat autoimmune diseases such as arthritis, lupus, and asthma), can cause memory problems even at mild doses. In large doses, these steroids can cause confusion and even psychosis.

I'm certainly not advocating that you avoid the medications in the preceding list. They're very useful treatments for a variety of diseases. Yet, I want you to be aware that a problem with your memory may be but one of the side effects of the medications you are taking.

Recently, I've seen increased numbers of patients who are prescribed Benadryl or even self-prescribe a form of it as a sleep aid. Benadryl does contribute to sedation, but the depth of the sleep you get is rather shallow. One of the nuisance side effects of Benadryl is difficulty concentrating the next day and poor short-term memory.

Acetylcholine blockers

Many drugs that have *anticholinergic* side effects can cause memory problems. To be anticholinergic means to block acetylcholine, the crucial neurotransmitter associated with your memory (see Chapter 3).

Among medications that have anticholinergic side effects are

- ✔ **Tricyclic antidepressants.** These old-line antidepressants, such as Elavil (amitriptyline) and Tofranil (imipramine), are now given as sleep aids in addition to their antidepressant effects.
- ✔ **Some antipsychotic medications.** Thorazine (chlorpromazine) and the relatively new Zyprexa (olanzapine), are anticholinergic.

"Doctor, I'd like to try something else"

You may have gone to your primary care physician and complained that you're stressed out and need medication to "calm" you down. In the era of managed-care, primary care physicians are overworked and may feel compelled to prescribe something quick without fully assessing your problems. The type of medication your doctor will probably prescribe will be one of the benzodiazepines. The "benzos" include Valium, Librium, Ativan, and Xanax. They're the most prescribed and the most addicting drugs in the United States.

These drugs act on the neurotransmitter GABA, which serves to inhibit specific neurons from firing. This is why they're referred to as minor tranquilizers or anti-anxiety agents.

In addition to the anti-anxiety effects, benzos have a number of negative side effects. They have a tendency to make people depressed. You don't want to treat your anxiety by replacing it with depression. Benzodiazepines also have a tendency to contribute to deficits in clarity of thought and dampen short-term memory.

Unfortunately, too many physicians continue to prescribe these medications for too long. I've seen patients who have been on benzos for years. They wake up feeling less rested, more cloudy headed, and depressed, and almost always complain of memory problems.

For all these reasons, I seriously caution people to hesitate before asking their primary care physician for a prescription of a benzodiazepine. Avoid taking them until you've tried all dietary and psychological methods to deal with stress (see Chapter 7).

A word of caution, however, when you quit: Don't go cold turkey. Withdraw gradually and with your doctor's supervision. In worst-case scenarios, people have had seizures during withdrawal off benzos.

The more medications with memory-depressing side effects that you take, the greater chance that they'll not only double but quadruple the memory-depressing effect. This increase makes it even more important for you to work with your doctor to minimize unnecessary medications and make sure that she knows all of the ones you're taking.

An added word of caution for the elderly: Your liver and other organ systems don't metabolize medications as efficiently as when you were younger. Toxic effects can occur even at lower doses than when you were younger.

If you've experienced a sudden loss of memory, you need to take a good look at what factors have changed since the decline. After ruling out any causes of major memory loss due to strokes or something of that magnitude, ask yourself if you've begun to take any new medications or changed the doses of the medications you were taking.

Work with your doctor to minimize unnecessary medications and go to the lowest effective dose of the medications you're already taking.

Suffocating your brain in smoke

Smoking increases LDL (bad) cholesterol and decreases HDL (good) cholesterol. High LDL cholesterol increases the risk of cardio-vascular problems such as high blood pressure, which can contribute to low stress tolerance and eventually memory problems.

Smoking causes restricted blood flow and starves the brain of oxygen. If you smoke just one cigarette, it will take eight hours for your blood oxygen levels to return to normal. Because your brain is such a high oxygen consumer, you starve it of one of its most critical ways to stay healthy and alive.

Stamping Out the Butt

Most smokers know that nicotine is a stimulant. They say that after smoking a cigarette, they feel like they're better able to concentrate and remember. This effect stems partly from nicotine, which aids acetylcholine (the neuro-transmitter involved in memory and learning).

What feels like help from nicotine comes at extremely high costs. Smoking not only causes cancer but a wide range of other very serious problems. Nicotine actually increases breathing rate, heart rate, brain waves, and stress hormones (including cortisol). When you smoke, you're drawing in heavy metals, such as cadmium, which are toxic for your brain.

In addition to cancer and emphysema, smoking can cause cardiovascular ill-nesses. Because of the restricted and interrupted blood flow, smokers run the risk of having mini and major strokes that can cause devastating memory loss. (See the related sidebar titled, "Suffocating your brain in smoke."

If you're addicted to nicotine, you're frequently craving the next smoke. During extended periods of not smoking, you may often get anxious. This is one of the reasons why you may have poor sleep. Because you can't get a fix while you're sleeping, your brain begins to crave the next fix. You may even have more trouble getting to sleep than non-smokers. If your sleep is poor, then your memory abilities will be poor, too. You'll be less likely to focus and pay attention to the world around you the next day. If that's not bad enough, you'll be prone to more accidents than non-smokers.

Nicotine is one of the most addictive substances available. If you're a smoker, you probably know how hard it is to quit. You need a wide range of tools to use at the same time.

To stop smoking, do all of the following:

- ✔ Enroll in a smoking cessation program.
- ✔ Exercise.
- ✔ Minimize caffeine and sugar use.
- ✔ Don't make any major life changes while you are in withdrawal.

Slowing the Dementias

One of the most devastating illnesses that anyone can endure is to have a brain-wasting disease. Brain-wasting diseases are generally referred to as *dementias*. With most of these dementias, memory is the first to go. Dementias come in a wide variety, and the most notorious is Alzheimer's disease. (See the related sidebar titled, "That's demented," later in this chapter.)

Stalling Alzheimer's disease

The number one fear among many people is that they'll suffer from Alzheimer's disease. Losing your mind to such a horrible brain-wasting disease is a nightmare. With it comes losing oneself and, so, one's memory. In short, it's a disease that causes memory problems at best and a loss of self at worse.

The hallmark of Alzheimer's disease is the presence of plaques and tangles in the brain. The plaques have a protein core called beta amyloid, which is surrounded by dying or already dead cells. The tangles, sometimes called neurofibrillary tangles, are knotty filaments that kill cells from the inside.

TECHNICAL STUFF

That's demented!

The term *dementia* had many meanings through the centuries. In the seventeenth century, it meant delirium. Eventually it came to mean insanity. In fact, at the beginning of the twentieth century, it was used in the term *Dementia Praecox*, which was the early term for schizophrenia. Today we use the term dementia to describe the organic deterioration of the brain leading to memory loss. But teenagers also use the term, as in, "Dude, that's a demented thing to do!"

President Reagan

When former President Ronald Reagan was being deposed for a trial related to the Iran-Contra scandal, he was asked if he could identify a man sitting at the defendant's table. It was his former National Security Advisor, John Poindexter, a man he met with previously on a regular basis. President Reagan responded by saying, in effect, "No, I don't think I recognize him."

That's not perjury. That's dementia.

Some pundits say that during the 1984 Presidential debates, Reagan showed signs of memory problems. Overwhelmed by the details of policies, he eventually said, "Facts are stupid things." We may never know when he really began showing signs of Alzheimer's disease, but we do know that it's a humbling and devastating disease. It's tragic to see anyone else go through this disease.

The neurotransmitter acetylcholine and an enzyme that supports it are drastically reduced in Alzheimer's disease. Particularly vulnerable to this devastation are the hippocampus and amygdala (see Chapter 3).

Alzheimer's disease has several early symptoms. Far before the dramatic loss of memory, including being able to recognize family members, the afflicted person may experience problems with smell, difficulty naming objects, difficulty with spatial perception, and getting lost. (See the related sidebar titled, "President Reagan," in this chapter.) Later, when the disease progresses, the person may find himself getting lost in areas that were once familiar.

Recently, anti-inflammatory drugs have been administered to Alzheimer's patients to moderate success. Although there is no cure for Alzheimer's disease, these drugs slow the inflammation that speeds the decline in functioning.

Although you may not be able to sidestep Alzheimer's disease if you're genetically predisposed, you may be able to slow the onset of Alzheimer's by following the lifestyle advice I offer elsewhere in this chapter.

Staying clear of strokes

Strokes occur when an artery to your brain gets clogged or bursts and the area of the brain that it feeds gets starved of blood and then dies. You're probably quite aware that a major stroke can cause severe brain damage.

But most people suffer minor strokes, sometimes called ministrokes or *transient ischemic attacks* (TIAs). TIAs occur with partial blocking or a spasm of a blood vessel in your brain.

Aphasia: Difficulty in using language

Most people who have strokes experience left-side or right-side weakness, depending on which side of the brain the stroke occurred in (see Chapter 3). Because the right hemisphere controls the left side of the body and the left hemisphere controls the right side of the body, we say that the stroke occurred *contralateral* to the side of the body that has been weakened.

Because all righthanders and 80 percent of left-handers store their language abilities in their left hemisphere, a left-hemisphere stroke can

result in *aphasia*. Aphasia means difficulty using and remembering language.

If the stroke is in the left frontal lobe in Broca's area, the victim can have *expressive phasia* (see Chapter 3). The person knows what she wants to say but can't seem to find the right words. If the stroke occurred in the posterior parts of the left temporal lobe, affecting Wernicke's area, she may have trouble understanding what's being told to her. In such a case, she has *associative aphasia*.

TIAs are difficult to detect, which is why they're sometimes called hidden. Yet, if you find yourself having an acute change to your senses such as pain, touch, heat, or vision, it may be a cluster of symptoms of a TIA. Those symptoms, combined with a simultaneous weakness in one of your major limbs and feeling unusually confused with gaps in your memory, are the warning signs of a TIA or stroke. You need to call the paramedics and go to the emergency room immediately! (See the related sidebar titled, "Aphasia: Difficulty in using language.")

People who suffer from atherosclerosis, the thickening and hardening of the arteries, are at great risk for TIAs. In addition, people with high blood pressure are at risk for TIAs. To minimize the risk of atherosclerosis and high blood pressure, minimize saturated fats in your diet and exercise regularly. This practice will go a long way toward minimizing the risk of both strokes and TIAs.

You can avoid strokes by changing your lifestyle. Reduce the risk factors to a stroke by observing the following:

✔ If you smoke, quit.

✔ If you're obese, get into a program to lose weight.

✔ If you have diabetes, manage your diet meticulously.

✔ If you have high cholesterol, lower it.

✔ If you have high blood pressure, manage it and bring it down.

Keeping Your Thyroid and Pancreas from Causing Memory-Drift

It may sound far-fetched to say that if one of your major organs besides your brain isn't working well, your memory will suffer. Nevertheless, it's true. Problems with the thyroid and pancreas can reduce your memory power.

Thyroid

If your thyroid gland isn't working properly, you may experience memory problems indirectly. *Hyperthyroidism,* which occurs with an overactive thyroid, may not lead only to anxiety but also to difficulty concentrating and, as a result, problems with short-term memory.

The opposite of hyperthyroidism is *hypothyroidism.* This condition occurs when your thyroid is underactive and not providing enough thyroxin. If you have untreated hypothyroidism, you may have noticed a marked weight gain, lethargy, a swollen neck, puffy eyes, oversensitivity to the cold, depression, and memory loss.

If you feel that there is a chance you may be suffering from either hypothyroidism or hyperthyroidism, ask your doctor to check your thyroid level. Treatment is easy and effective.

Pancreas

Your pancreas helps balance the level of glucose in our body. It does this by producing insulin. If you have either diabetes Type I (insulin dependent) or Type II (non-insulin dependent), you run the risk of being either hyperglycemic or hypoglycemic. Because glucose is so critical to how your brain functions, any disruption or imbalance of glucose in your brain can have a very negative effect on your memory.

Hypoglycemia occurs when you have very low blood sugar. Your hippocampus is especially vulnerable to low levels of glucose. Because the hippocampus depends highly on a constant and balanced blood/glucose flow, cells within it can be damaged when it's deprived, and you'll experience memory loss.

Diabetes can also lead to TIAs (see the section "Staying clear of strokes," earlier in this chapter) and damage to the capillaries in your brain. The capillaries are those very small blood vessels that carry blood to your neurons. When the capillaries are damaged, the cells that were fed by them can die. TIAs can put a major damper on your brain's ability to remember.

If you suffer from diabetes, manage it well so you can minimize memory loss. Follow these guidelines:

✔ **Make sure that you eat on a regular basis** and watch your sugar intake religiously.

✔ **Take advantage of indirect memory-saving opportunities.** For example, many medical centers offer very good courses on how to manage your diabetes.

✔ **Don't take a lackadaisical attitude toward any serious medical problem.** Act now before it's too late. Your health and memory is in your hands.

Chapter 7

Balancing Your Mind for Memories

. . . .

In This Chapter

▶ Relaxing to remember

▶ Getting out of the dumps

▶ Sleeping to remember

. . . .

*H*ave you ever shaken a snow globe and watched the snow swirl around the town scene? You can hardly see anything until the snow settles. Imagine your mind and anxiety in the same way. Recalling memories is next to impossible until all the anxiety settles.

In this chapter, you discover how to defuse stress, calm your mind, and get enough sleep. With a balanced mind, you'll be able to build the memory skills you expect of yourself.

Defusing Stress

You have to be prepared to remember. Your mind must be receptive to new information for it to have an impression on you.

If you're unbalanced because of stress, depression, or lack of sleep, your mind is less receptive to forming new memories.

Your anxiety can be a double-edged sword. When you have too much angst, you'll probably have a hard time remembering anything useful for an exam or presentation. Your test anxiety may be so overwhelming that you create a self-fulfilling prophecy and allow your worst nightmare to happen — namely, that you'll do poorly on the exam.

On the other extreme, if you go into the exam with a lazy attitude, seemingly not caring if you pass the exam, you may not pass it. If you aren't the least bit anxious, you probably can't stay alert enough to remember information you need for the exam. In this case, your anxiety is analogous to fuel, and you're running on empty. Anxiety isn't bad in itself. You just don't want too much or too little of it. You need a balance. You need to be focused and motivated, but not overloaded with stress.

If you feel a great deal of stress, you're probably making absentminded mistakes, such as forgetting your keys or turning down the wrong street on the way to work.

Not only can stress hamper your attention and, as a result, your short-term memory, but it can also damage your brain. A stress hormone called cortisol can be very rough on your *hippocampus,* the part of your brain that transfers short-term memory into long-term memories (see Chapter 3).

Negative emotions and preoccupations with personal problems can very easily distract you, making recalling memories extremely difficult. If you're suffering from severe stress stemming a major life event, such as divorce or the loss of a loved one or even the loss of your job, you can be so overwhelmed that paying attention to your surroundings is the farthest thing from your mind.

After you deal with the grief and sadness of your loss, your memory improves because you're freed up from the distractions of your loss.

Well, that's easier said than done, you probably think. Actually, a here-and-now focus helps lay the foundation for a clear mind in preparation for learning and recollecting memories.

When you're overwhelmed with anxiety, don't bog yourself down with needless worries that you're losing your memory. You aren't. You're too preoccupied to remember or form new memories. Deal with your preoccupation by:

✔ Seeking the support of friends or family members

✔ Getting help from a mental-health professional

✔ Joining a support group

✔ Making sure that you don't do anything that contributes to depression and/or anxiety, such as using alcohol or drugs

Don't withdraw from your social support network. This is the time to tap into it, even though you don't feel like it.

Shifting to the Relaxation Response

Imagine that you're standing up in front of a large group of people to recite a poem or give a presentation. You're so concerned with all those people looking at you that you can't focus on the details of your presentation. Your heart is racing, you're beginning to sweat, and your breathing becomes more shallow. You feel so nervous that you forget what you're going to say. All you can think about is getting out of there! Sound familiar? (See the related sidebar titled, "Fight or flight," in this chapter.)

This example about public speaking describes a major reaction to stage fright, which borders on a panic attack. Many people suffer from the fear of speaking in front of groups of people. Some people react to an extreme degree, whereas others react less intensely. The degree to which you feel overwhelmed by anxiety probably dictates the degree to which you have trouble remembering what you are going to say.

You may wonder, "If I'm so nervous, why can't I just spit it out and get out of there?" Your racing thoughts not only bypass those memories, but they narrow down the open mind you need to recall. Your thoughts are minimized to nuisance distractions like your racing heart, your rapid breath, and your profuse sweating.

Fortunately, your body has a *relaxation response,* a built-in capacity to relax. You need to tap into this ability. I describe how you can do that in a moment, but first I want to describe what it is.

Just as your body has a fight-or-flight response that fuels your anxiety, it also has a relaxation response to defuse anxiety. The fight-or-flight response is connected to a part of your nervous system called the *sympathetic nervous system,* whereas the relaxation response is part of your *parasympathetic nervous system. Para* means *beyond* and, in this case, it means in addition to the sympathetic nervous system or as a complement to it. (For the full scoop on the human body, check out *Anatomy & Physiology For Dummies,* by Donna Rae Siegfried, published by Wiley.)

You need to tap into your parasympathetic nervous system's ability to calm down and get focused. Whereas the fight-or-flight response raises your heart rate, the relaxation response lowers it, as shown in the following minitable.

Fight or Flight	*How Your Body Reacts*	*Relaxation Response*
↑	Heart rate	↓
↑	Blood pressure	↓
↑	Metabolism	↓
↑	Muscle tension	↓
↑	Breathing rate	↓
↑	Mental arousal	↓

Fight or flight

The fight-or-flight response is an evolutionary instinct that served our ancestors well. If your ancestor came across a dangerous creature or a violent person, his body prepared to fight it or escape in flight. In preparation, adrenaline shot through his body, readying it to move quickly. His attention narrowed so he had to focus only on the danger at hand. His sweat glands pumped so that his body could remain cool. His heart beat faster, and his breath became rapid to insure that he could fight or flee quickly.

Fortunately, most of us don't have to deal with immediately violent danger. Nowadays, your fight-or-flight response clicks in when you experience stress. In addition, if you're experiencing chronic stress, your memory skills are bound to suffer. Not only are you distracted, which makes your absentmindedness increase, but over time, the chronic stress wears you down.

Stress hormones circulate through your body and brain. They begin to take their toll; they're destructive to your brain and cause more memory problems.

The cortisol attacks your hippocampus, making it less able to transfer short-term memories that you want to remember later. Even free radicals are given carte blanche. They run rampant in your brain.

The fight-or-flight reaction prevents you from remembering your lines. You need a way to defuse it, to calm yourself and get focused.

Relaxing to Charge Up Your Memory

You can induce the relaxation response by a variety of techniques. Most relaxation techniques that you can use involve letting go of sympathetic nervous system arousal by shifting your attention away from the anxiety provoking aspects of your situation.

Don't try too hard to relax, because you'll tense up instead.

I often illustrate this fact with patients by asking them to try not to think of their right index finger. I ask, "It's out of your mind, isn't it?" They often say, "No, now it's more in my head than ever."

By bringing the finger up for attention, it's hard to get it out of their mind. But after we go on to another subject, I come back to the subject and ask, "Well, my guess is that during the last ten minutes, you haven't been thinking of your right index finger."

They say, "Well no, I haven't. We've been talking about other things."

I say, "That's just the point. As you refocus your attention, instead of trying hard not to think of that difficult event, you'll be able to move on."

Because trying "too hard" to relax actually makes you more stressed, letting go allows your body's ability (through the parasympathetic nervous system) to calm down. Letting go can be counterintuitive. If you try to relax, you'll probably stay tense.

As you let go and focus on something else other than what is making you anxious, you become less anxious.

Letting go is a passive process. By *allowing* yourself to relax instead of *trying* to relax, you take the pressure off yourself. For example, try not to think of pink elephants. By forcing yourself to keep pink elephants out of your mind, you fight with yourself and invariably think of pink elephants. Now focus on something else, such as blue kangaroos. Tell yourself if pink elephants pop into your mind, so be it. You probably won't think about pink elephants now, because your attention has shifted and you let go of the pressure that you put on yourself to keep pink elephants out of your mind. Similarly, if you try not to be tense, you'll probably make yourself tenser. By focusing on relaxation, your tension can melt away because you have shifted your attention away from what was making you anxious.

To achieve relaxation, you can employ any of the following techniques. These techniques involve shifting attention and letting go, and they're generally referred to as relaxation techniques:

- Progressive relaxation
- Self-hypnosis
- Visual imagery
- Meditation and prayer

All these techniques involve a focus on breathing, and I discuss them later in this chapter.

Breathing

Your breathing does more than just keep you alive. Breathing right is the gateway to the relaxation response.

Don't take the importance of breathing for granted. If you breathe at different rates, you'll experience different emotional states. Your breathing rate naturally speeds up when you're experiencing stress — the muscles in your abdomen tighten up, and your chest cavity is constricted.

Because you have a *cardiovascular system,* meaning a system in which your respiratory system and circulatory system are connected, rapid breathing makes your heart rate speed up and thus makes you more anxious. On the other hand, if you slow down your breathing, your heart rate generally becomes more relaxed.

Most people breathe from 9 to 16 breaths per minute when they're at rest. Panic attacks often involve as many as 27 breaths per minute. Accelerating breathing alone can cause anyone to experience many of the symptoms associated with a panic attack, including numbness, tingling, dry mouth, light-headedness, and short-term memory problems.

Breathing too fast is referred to as *hyperventilation,* or overbreathing. If you over-breathe, you pull in too much oxygen, forcing down the carbon dioxide level in your blood stream. Carbon dioxide helps maintain the critical acid base (pH) level in your blood. By lowering your pH level, your nerve cells become more excitable, making it more likely that you feel anxiety or have a panic attack.

If you feel anxious, stop and watch your breath, and then slow it down. By breathing deeply, you relax by shifting from the fight-or-flight response to the relaxation response, from the sympathetic to the parasympathetic nervous system.

Slow down your breathing rate by breathing "abdominally," and notice that your belly rises with your inhale and drops with your exhale. This is because as you breathe abdominally, the large dome-shaped muscle that divides your thoracic cavity from the abdominal cavity below expands and contracts. When you exhale, your diaphragm moves upward and your abdominal muscles contract, helping get rid of stale air or carbon dioxide. When you inhale, your diaphragm contracts, pulling it down, and your abdominal muscles relax. This allows for the expansion of your lower lungs.

Your abdominal/diaphragmatic breathing allows you to get more oxygen in and more carbon dioxide out. Because the entire process of breathing is to oxygenate your blood and expel waste air (carbon dioxide), diaphragmatic breathing allows you to get more fuel (oxygen) to each organ, especially your brain. Try abdominal breathing the next time you feel anxious. Notice how your anxiety drifts away and your short-term memory returns.

Sighing with relief

A quick and easy way to let go of tension is to breathe in deeply and then exhale a deep sigh, like "Ahhh. . . ." Letting go of tension with a sigh gives you a quick fix of relief. You can practice the sigh of relief to release tension several times throughout the day.

Relaxing from the bottom up

One of the most popular relaxation techniques is referred to as *progressive relaxation.* When you use this method, your task is to tense and release a particular muscle group, such as your fingers or toes, while simultaneously breathing deeply.

Start with your feet by splaying your toes and keeping your muscles in your feet tense while you count to ten. Then release the muscles and notice and enjoy the flow of relaxation for at least 10 seconds. Tense and relax three times.

Move up your body, tensing and relaxing each body part. Follow these steps:

1. **Splay your toes, breathe deeply, and then let go after 10 seconds.**

2. **Tense your ankles and heels; then let go.**

3. **Tense your calves; then let go.**

4. **Tense your knees; then let go.**

5. **Tense your thighs; then let go.**

6. **Tense your entire pelvic area; then let go.**

7. **Tense your abdomen; then let go.**

8. **Tense your chest and shoulders; then let go.**

9. **Tense your neck; then let go.**

10. **Tense your face and scalp; then let go.**

Try to remember not to tense too hard but just enough to feel the tension. Make this a meditative exercise. Don't rush through the exercise. It's not an aerobic exercise.

After you complete the exercise, breathe easily and pay close attention to how the muscles in your body become limp and relaxed. Imagine them being heavy while you notice that your mind becomes light and airy.

After you finish this exercise, notice how you feel more at ease and relaxed. These feelings will carry over into the next hour, and whatever you may be engaged in (like going to work, studying at school, or even going to the store) will be done in a more relaxed state. You'll not only be calmer, but also more alert and better able to use your memory skills effectively.

Imaging memories

Your imagination can be harnessed to clear your mind and free it up so you can better use your memory skills. You can use your imagination to become more relaxed, preparing yourself to be more receptive to the world around you and recall memories.

Visual imagery is a relaxation technique that has gained popularity over the past 20 years. You can use it to clear your mind. You visualize being in a tranquil place that gives you a sense of peace. For example, imagine yourself in a mountain meadow with the sun shining on your back or at the beach watching the waves roll in, one after the other. Imagine the vivid details of a mountain meadow or beach. Concentrate on all of the visual and tactile sensations.

Concentrate on the sound of the surf ebbing and flowing, just like your breath. Concentrate on the bird sitting on a branch on a tree. The bird looks at you and then gracefully flies away. Feel the sun on your back gently warming you.

Imagery takes you away on a break from all the stress of the day. If you fully absorb yourself in the scenes that you imagine, you'll feel refreshed and better able to clear your mind in preparation to use your memory skills.

You're hypnotizing yourself: 10, 9, 8, 7 . . .

Hypnosis is a form of relaxation that utilizes both breathing and imagery. Hypnosis is much easier to do than you may think. First, you have to dispel the myths that have developed about hypnosis.

Hypnosis, like relaxation and meditation training, is a form of concentration, focused attention, and increased receptivity to suggestion and direction. Hypnosis is a method of focused relaxation.

Self-hypnosis is essentially the same thing as hypnosis only without the hypnotist as an aid. The type of self-hypnosis that I teach people involves focused breathing and counting from 10 to 1. While decreasing in numbers, you can imagine particular parts of your body relaxing on every exhale.

Try the following steps, counting backward while saying the phrases:

10. **I am allowing the tension to leave my body with every exhale.**

9. **I am feeling my body become heavy.**

8. **Sounds, physical sensations, and thoughts are occurring around my external self, all way up on the surface. I am deep within myself.**

7. **I feel like I am descending deeper within myself, as if I am going down an escalator.**

6. **I don't need to fight the relaxation. I can visualize myself drifting with the current down the river. I don't need to swim up stream.**

5. **I am falling deep within myself and gently swaying like a feather that slowly moves back and forth as it falls to the ground.**

4. **I am deep within myself without worry and time.**

3. **I am letting go of the external world.**

2. **Relaxation and I are one.**

1. **I am at peace with myself.**

While you're going through this exercise, you want to remind yourself to "step out of the way" so your body can relax itself. This point is important to remember because you can unknowingly keep yourself tense throughout the day. Allow your body a chance to do what is natural for it, stepping out of the way so the process of relaxation can happen.

Meditating and praying

You may wonder why I include meditation and prayer in this chapter. In fact, perhaps you're thinking, "Is he suggesting that I pray for better memory?"

The practice of meditation and prayer have much in common with relaxation techniques and hypnosis. Although these methods have religious connotations, the result is the same. You feel refreshed and more able to focus on the world around you with clarity and better memory skills.

When you meditate, you clear your mind and focus on your breathing. Clear your mind by concentrating on a few words or sounds called a mantra, such as Ommm or Sat Nam. Concentrating on the mantra neutralizes all other thoughts. By concentrating on your breathing, you can clear your mind and relax.

You want to include four common elements in most forms of meditation:

- **Point focus:** You focus on a single word, such as a mantra, and your breathing
- **Quiet environment:** You want to be free from distractions
- **Passive and accepting attitude:** You let yourself simply be
- **Relaxed posture:** You want to be comfortable

Whatever type of relaxation technique you practice, regard it as important as eating or sleeping. It allows you to clear your mind so you can boost your memory skills.

Begin to structure relaxation into part of your day. Ritualize the process of relaxation by picking a particular time, say 10 to 40 minutes before or after a shower. Make relaxation as important as sitting down for dinner.

Not all relaxation exercises need to be lengthy in time. Take a few moments throughout each day to slow down your breathing and drop your shoulders. You can remind yourself to do this by placing a blue dot on your computer monitor or wristwatch. When you see the dot, stop for five seconds and breathe deeply. You'll probably find that your memory skills improve just by slowing down to relax for only a few seconds throughout each day.

A worldwide tradition

Meditation and prayer are practiced worldwide. Most religions have literature, including manuals, on meditation and prayer. Within Hinduism, Buddhism, Islam, Judaism, and Christianity, meditation has a long tradition and has been practiced for thousands of years. It was not until late in the twentieth century that the effects of meditation and prayer were thoroughly researched. In the United States, meditation grew in popularity in the late 1960s with Transcendental Meditation, often referred to as TM, a method of meditation based on such Hindu techniques as frequent repetition of a personal mantra.

Because meditation and prayer are practices embraced by all religious traditions, there is an attempt to lose a sense of self-identifying awareness. That is, there is an attempt to appreciate a wider sense of consciousness by circumventing sensory awareness or filters of cultural conditioning. These traditions promote the methods of prayer and meditation to aid people in losing their selfish, ego-oriented focus and gain an appreciation of God or a higher being.

During the past 30 years, researchers have demonstrated that prayer and meditation help people achieve deep relaxation and clarity of mind. Much of the early research on meditation was based on people practicing TM. From the beginning, researchers found that, like prayer, TM promoted calming effects.

In addition, both meditation and prayer can do the following:

✔ Help release tension

✔ Promote insight into one's personal process by taking a step back

✔ Increase the expectation that something will happen, such as a spiritual awakening

Pulling Out of the Dumps

If you're down in the dumps and depressed, your memory skills become depressed. When you're preoccupied with your own pain, you're less present to form new memories or recall memories formed before you were depressed.

When giving people memory tests, psychologists always take into account the degree to which those people may be depressed. Usually, psychologists give non-memory tests, such as the Minnesota Multiphasic Personality Inventory, to rule out depression.

The reason for ruling out depression is that if you're depressed, your memory scores will be depressed. Psychologists like me have to be sure that the person has a true memory problem and not a hidden symptom of depression. Because depression itself causes problems with memory, treating depression usually increases a person's memory ability, but how much isn't clear until depression is alleviated.

Think of depression as a drag on all your cognitive abilities. If you're depressed, you're less able to concentrate and pay attention to important information, and you're less motivated, less energized, and more prone to absentmindedness.

What's more, you run the risk of distorting your memories by putting a negative spin on all of your experiences. Your colleague who isn't depressed may regard what you remember as an unfortunate incident at work as nothing of importance. But for you, the supposed unfortunate incident, much of it fabricated by the negative spin, sticks with you as if you've stepped on gum.

If you're depressed, you may have a great deal of trouble disregarding negative memories that are better overshadowed by more recent and positive experiences.

When you try to suppress rather than recollect disturbing memories, paradoxically, you think of them more often. By trying hard not to think of those memories, you actively put a greater charge to them. Try instead to create new memories that do not necessarily block the old but overshadow them. These new memories gain prominence the more often they're remembered. Try any or all of the following:

✔ Adopt new hobbies

✔ Meet new people

✔ Take a trip

✔ Switch jobs

In short, get out of the rut; give yourself something new to focus on.

If you're depressed, there's a way out. It involves:

✔ **Broadening and opening up your life again:** Instead of isolating yourself and doing little, you need to connect with other people and do more.

✔ **Avoiding old memories that play like broken records:** You need to move on with your life, not stew in your regrets.

✔ **Avoiding alcohol and drugs:** Alcohol and most drugs cause depression.

✔ **Eating three meals a day:** If you're not getting proper nutrition, this alone could cause depression.

✔ **Exercising:** Study after study has shown that people who exercise get a boost, sometimes completely out of depression with no other intervention.

Getting a Move On

This may sound far-fetched, but exercise is good for your memory. It helps your brain receive the nutrients that it needs. Every time you exercise, you increase your respiratory rate, your metabolism, and your energy level. Exercise not only calms you, but it also helps you be more alert.

Your brain, in comparison to the rest of your body, is a high-end consumer of glucose and oxygen (see Chapter 3). By exercising, you increase your blood flow, which contains the glucose and oxygen you need to stay healthy and focused.

If you bog down your system by being a couch potato, you deprive your brain of the optimum level of support it needs, so you can't expect your memory ability to be what it can be.

Exercise maintains healthy organ systems that support your brain, such as your heart, arteries, and lungs. These systems need to be in good shape to support the constant demands of your gluttonous brain.

By exercising over an extended period, you can reduce the buildup of cholesterol related plaques. This clearing benefit is not an excuse for a poor diet. Don't think that you can automatically have a steak and eggs for breakfast everyday. The combination of regular exercise and a good diet can reduce your chances of stroke and heart disease tenfold.

Your cardiovascular system is called that for a reason, meaning your heart and blood vessels working together. As your breathing capacity increases, so does your heart capacity. They're connected. Better circulation means better blood flow to your brain. If you exercise regularly, you feel more invigorated and alert.

This isn't just because of the more efficient blood flow; it's also because of the rich nutrients your blood brings to your brain. Exercise changes your brain's chemistry that's so critical to how it communicates within itself. It stimulates the release and absorption of several neurotransmitters (see Chapter 3).

You may be familiar with a "runner's high," an endorphin rush resulting from your brain's ability to medicate and reward itself. Endorphins are *neurotransmitters,* which are like opium without all the addictive and destructive consequences. They enable you to feel calmer and better able to concentrate for hours after you exercise. Better concentration means better ability to remember.

Aerobic exercise not only has a calming and antidepressant effect, but also helps your sleep. To get the best sedative effect, exercise 3 to 6 hours prior to sleep. This time gap allows your body temperature to drop well before you go to sleep.

Avoiding sleep suppressors

A wide range of factors have been found to contribute to insomnia, including aging, medical conditions, and drugs. For example, as you age, the quality of your sleep deteriorates. You wake up more and spend more time in light sleep. To complicate this problem, many older people spend time indoors and are exposed to less light. Thus, their circadian rhythm is thrown off. In addition, when people wake up at odd times or lose social cues, such as eating dinner at set times, their sleep cycles have a stronger chance of becoming disrupted.

Caffeine causes insomnia because it blockades adenosine receptors in the brain. *Adenosine* is a sleep promoter. Because caffeine suppresses adenosine, it also suppresses sleep. Moreover, adenosine is responsible for promoting slow-wave sleep. Researchers at Stanford University report that because of this caffeine/adenosine antagonism, caffeine suppresses slow-wave sleep.

Many people try to improve their sleep by using techniques that actually exacerbate their sleep problems. For example, although you may feel sedated after drinking a nightcap, alcohol can create a sleep problem. Alcohol contributes to a reduction of stage-4 sleep (the deepest stage of sleep) and Rapid Eye Movement (REM) sleep. Alcohol can also contribute to midsleep cycle awakening because the alcohol is wearing off during your sleep.

Ten percent of all sleep maintenance problems are caused by alcohol. Therefore, you shouldn't consume more than one drink per day, and you should ensure that you consume the drink several hours before bedtime.

If you drink a nightcap, you'll have a more shallow sleep than you would have otherwise. Alcohol depresses stage-4 sleep, which is when you get the most rest and your immune system is recharged. Alcohol also dampens REM sleep. Therefore, drinking tonight may not only result in losing the opportunity to get some deep sleep, but it can also distort your dreams and may even cause you to wake up in the middle of the night. This midsleep cycle awakening occurs because the effects of alcohol begin to wear off and leave you with more anxiety and tension than you had before drinking.

Exercise also stimulates the *nerve growth factor* (NGF). NGF helps your dendrites reach out and make contact with other neurons. Your dendrites receive information from other neurons (see Chapter 3). The more connections that each of your neurons has with other neurons, the richer and more varied are your thoughts and memories. Bottom line: The more input, the better the memory.

Therefore, you and I have no excuse but laziness stopping us from exercising For advice and inspiration, take a look at these other books published by Wiley: *Fitness For Dummies, 2nd Edition,* by Liz Neporent and Suzanne Schlosberg; *Fit Over 40 For Dummies,* by Betsy Nagelsen McCormack; and *Mind-Body Fitness For Dummies,* by Therese Iknoian.

Getting Some Sleep So You Can Remember

Too little sleep can set you up for a pack of memory problems — faulty short-term memory, lack of clarity of mind, and general slowing of your ability to think.

If you practice all the following methods, you can improve your sleep:

- ✔ **Don't do anything in your bed other than sleep (except for sex).** Don't eat, watch television, balance your checkbook, discuss finances with your spouse, or argue in bed. Make your bed carry only one association — sleep.

- ✔ **Don't try too hard to go to sleep.** You end up frustrating yourself and having more difficulty sleeping. If you can't sleep and you find yourself tossing and turning, get up and go to another room.

- ✔ **Don't drink large quantities of liquid at night.** This lowers the sleep threshold and causes you to wake up to go to the bathroom.

- ✔ **Don't work on the computer into the late evening or use any other source of bright light.** (I explain why in a technical note later in this chapter.)

- ✔ **Do all planning for the next day before you get into bed.** If you think of something you need to remember, get up and write it down. Tell yourself that you'll postpone thinking or worrying about anything until the next day.

- ✔ **Avoid all daytime naps.** Think of naps as a way to steal sleep from the nighttime.

- ✔ **Try eating a light snack with complex carbohydrates before bed.** Eat foods rich with tryptophan. Don't eat anything with sugar or salt before bed. (I offer eating suggestions later in this section.)

- ✔ **Avoid protein snacks at night.** Protein blocks the synthesis of serotonin and, as a result, promotes alertness.

- ✔ **Exercise 3 to 6 hours before you go to bed.**

- ✔ **Use earplugs if noise bothers you.**

- ✔ **Don't drink alcohol before going to bed.**

- ✔ **Try the sleep scheduling technique if you're experiencing chronic insomnia.** See the sidebar, "The Harvard sleep scheduling program," later in this chapter, for more details.

- ✔ **Try relaxation exercises to help you fall asleep and/or go back to sleep if you wake-up during the night.** See the section "Relaxing to Charge Up Your Memory," earlier in this chapter, for more information.

Asleep on my feet

I remember the time after my first son was born. My wife and I had him sleep in our room during the first six weeks. He woke up throughout the night because, as you may know, babies don't know the difference between night and day. He was hungry and let us know with a loud cry.

My wife was breast-feeding, so she thought that the least I could do was to go pick him up and bring him to her. During an extensive period of sleep deprivation, I became less and less effective at work.

During that time, I was the director of three-day treatment programs for mentally ill adults. One of the programs served the most severely mentally ill, 60 people at once. On one of my

sleep-deprived days, I met a new client in the program, a nice young man suffering from schizophrenia.

I said, "Hello, my name is John. What's your name?"

He responded politely by saying, "Oh, it's Steve."

I said, "Good to meet you, John."

He said, "No, I'm Steve, you're John. Hey, Doc, you been getting enough sleep?"

Don't wait until you make a fool out of yourself to get more sleep. Make sure that you do what you can to get the sleep you need.

Sedating your insomnia

If you experience insomnia, you're not alone. Approximately 95 percent of people report that they've had insomnia at least once in their lives. Approximately 50 percent of people report that they have trouble sleeping once a week, and about 15 percent of people report that they've had trouble sleeping two nights a week.

Your sleep is very much tied to the light of the day and the dark of night. Light is taken in through your eyes, and your retina sends the information to your pineal gland, which is positioned in the middle of your brain. Your pineal gland suppresses the production of melatonin, thereby convincing your brain that it's daytime and not time to become sedated. In contrast, when it's dark outside, your retina sends information to your pineal gland that it's night outside and that it should produce melatonin to induce sedation.

Watch the amount of light you're exposed to during the daytime because it affects your sleep. If you maximize your bright light exposure during the daytime, you set your body clock to match the natural day/night cycle of the world around you. If you've had trouble getting to sleep, expose yourself to bright light in the early morning. This way, you ensure that your melatonin production is low throughout the day and that your body temperature is the lowest when you sleep.

Boomerang sedation

If you're one of the millions of people who treat your insomnia with over-the-counter sleep drugs or physician-prescribed benzodiazepines, it's time to reconsider this bad habit. Benzodiazepines aren't an effective long-term treatment of insomnia. If you take them on a regular basis, you'll experience daytime grogginess and shallow sleep, and you'll suffer from withdrawals when you try sleeping without them, making it even harder to sleep.

Over the years, I've seen numerous people who've complained of having short-term memory problems. As I gather more information,

I discover that they had been using a benzo as a sleep aid.

You should only consider benzodiazepines as a short-term treatment for acute insomnia. However, if you're looking for a solution beyond a few nights sleep, don't take the drug. In fact, one of the key goals of the Harvard University Insomnia Program is to withdraw from all sleep medications. If you're taking sleep medication, don't abruptly withdraw off of them. Your withdrawal should be a gradual tapering process that is self-paced but monitored by your doctor.

Exercising 3 to 6 hours before bedtime can also help you sleep better, because you push your heart rate up and still allow enough time for it to drop before you sleep. Even more importantly, you raise your body temperature and allow it to fall in time for bedtime.

If you suffer from insomnia, don't use your computer in the late evening, because it worsens your inability to sleep. When you look at the computer screen for extended periods, you're essentially looking straight at light. This light tricks your brain into adjusting to a daytime pattern because it suppresses your pineal gland's ability to secrete melatonin, which is needed to be able to go to sleep.

Chilling out

If you have insomnia, you may have difficulty regulating your body temperature. You may unknowingly make your body temperature increase rather than decrease at night by being less physically active in the daytime. If you don't get any exercise during the day, don't expect much of a dip in body temperature at night.

To correct these problems, do the following:

- ✓ Keep your room cool during bedtime.
- ✓ Exercise 3 to 6 hours before bedtime.
- ✓ Make sure that you move around when you get up in the morning so your body can adjust to the correct body-temperature cycle.

Thinking about sleep

Don't worry if you can't get to sleep during the first several minutes of attempting to sleep. Few people can get to sleep within 15 minutes. In fact, researchers in sleep labs usually regard the person who can get to sleep in under 15 minutes as sleep deprived. In such cases, this shortened "sleep latency" time is the result of a rebound effect, making up for sleep lost the previous night.

The most severe effect of sleep loss is drowsiness. Moderate sleep loss has generally been shown to negatively affect mood. However, sleep loss doesn't affect mood in the same way in all people. If you find yourself becoming angry and concerned about sleep loss, the negative affect on mood will be greater than if you take it in stride. Parents remember well the sleep loss associated with having a newborn in the house. But they're focused on the newborn, not the sleep loss. In contrast, insomniacs overreact and overestimate their sleep loss.

If you're a shift worker, try to eat frequent small meals and get regular exercise before work. When you get home, go right to sleep. Don't make the mistake of going to sleep in a lighted room. The exposure to light delays your ability to sleep because melatonin production is low. Make sure that the room is completely dark. Also, try to get exposure to full-spectrum light as soon as you wake up.

Eating to sleep

Diet also has a major effect on sleep. Some foods sedate you and some foods can keep you from going to sleep.

Try to avoid eating simple carbohydrates, such as white bread, before going to bed. Simple carbohydrates increase insulin, which in turn increases *tryptophan,* an amino acid that converts to serotonin. This may sound good, but this conversion takes place on a short-term basis. As a result, your blood glucose rises, and you may wake up.

Try to eat complex carbohydrates, such as whole-wheat bread. When you eat complex carbohydrates, you trigger a serotonin conversion on a long-term basis, resulting in a slow and sustained rise in glucose. If you eat foods rich in tryptophan, you become sleepy.

Good sources of tryptophan include:

- Milk
- Turkey
- Complex carbohydrates (like whole-wheat bread)

The Harvard sleep-scheduling program

If you have chronic insomnia, your sleep cycle isn't easily corrected. Hopefully, you aren't like many people who suffer from chronic insomnia. Do you "catch up" on sleep because you never feel rested? Do you try to sleep longer in the morning only to find it more difficult to sleep the next night?

Don't try too hard to go to sleep. By trying to fall asleep, you release *neurotransmitters,* such as epinephrine and norepinephrine, which are activators that increase muscle tension, heart rate, blood pressure, and stress hormones. In a recent study, participants who were told that they'd receive a prize if they went to sleep fast actually had more trouble falling asleep than those who weren't trying too hard.

If you have a difficult time falling asleep, try the sleep scheduling approach. Get up at the same time each morning despite how much sleep you managed the previous night. Instead of going to bed earlier, go to bed later. Now you may think, "But I need to allow myself as much time to sleep as possible, even if I toss and turn." Not true. The point is to get rid of the toss and turn time and use your time in bed only to sleep.

Calculate how many hours you actually do sleep on average and add one more hour. Use this formula to schedule how much sleep time you allow yourself. For example, if you were averaging 5½ hours of sleep for the past month, despite staying in bed 8½ hours, allow yourself 6½ hours of potential sleep time. If your normal wake-up time has been 6:00 a.m., go to bed at 11:30 p.m. Calculate backwards 6½ hours from your normal wake-up time. Do this for at least four weeks. Your goal will be to fill up most of that bedtime with sleep. Eventually, your body temperature adjusts, and the sleep pressure builds up so you can make another adjustment, adding another hour for 7½ hours of sleep.

Vitamins can also affect your sleep. Deficiencies of B vitamins, calcium, and magnesium may inhibit sleep.

Take a calcium-magnesium tablet at night, and you'll probably find that you'll be more relaxed. It may also help with the restless leg syndrome (that odd sensation of tension in your legs).

Hush-h-h-h-h

Your brain is primed to pay attention to novel stimuli, so you want to eliminate sounds that grab your attention. Don't keep the television on at night, because it can wake you up. On the other hand, *white noise* (a blend of sounds distributed equally over the range of the frequency band) is boring and monotonous and serves as a good screen for other noises, such as barking dogs. If you need to block out noises while you sleep, try the following:

✔ Keep a fan on all night long to provide white noise.

✔ Use good-quality earplugs to filter out noises.

Part III
Preserving Your Memory

The 5th Wave   By Rich Tennant

"Oh, now I remember! Each of your names is associated with your appearance and personality. You must be Creepy and Sleazy and Moron and Zit Face and BO..."

In this part . . .

Some people seem to remember everything. Other people are not so quick on the draw. The difference may have less to do with sheer brain power and much more to do with simply paying close attention to items you want to remember — such as names, numbers, places, and shopping lists. This part introduces you to general habits that can improve your memory and little tricks you can use to help recall specific memories. I devote a whole chapter to the special topic of keeping memory strong as you grow older.

Chapter 8

Tricking Yourself into Remembering

*Y*our memory skills are as wide and strong as the memory techniques you use. If you don't use any techniques, chances are that your memory isn't what it could be. If you use a variety of memory techniques, your memory skills can increase tenfold.

In this chapter, I talk about some of the most commonly used memory techniques: You discover how to use specific words to lock in memories. These words, called pegs, do just that — they peg a memory. You find out how to use a location in a room to remind you of memories. This Loci system will help you locate your memories. You figure out how to wrap up memories in a story so that when you tell the story later, your memories will unfold. Finally, you find out how specific sounds can cue you into memories you want to recall.

Introducing Mnemonics, Your Memory Sidekick

You've probably heard people say that they've learned memory tricks called *mnemonics* (nee-MON-iks) to get around a poor memory. To call mnemonics merely tricks demeans their importance. Mnemonics aren't just tricks, they're cues or links — almost like the hyperlinks that you click on when surfing the Internet. Click a link, and another page pops up on your screen.

Memory mnemonics are simple techniques to help you remember what you want to remember. A mnemonic is as easy as, "One two, buckle my shoe; three four, shut the door; five six, pick up sticks." Many people learned that simple number rhyme before they ever heard the word mnemonic, yet, it's an example of a mnemonic.

To use a mnemonic, all you have to do is

✔ Decide what you want to remember

✔ Match what you want to remember with an image or word cue

✔ Refer to the cue to recall your memory

Think of mnemonics as a way for you to organize information so you can later recall it more easily. The word mnemonic actually means, "aiding memory." You can structure or package your memories so they are easily available to you. A mnemonic is like a thread that, when you pull it, has a whole string of memories attached.

 Twice a year, in April and October, most people change their clocks by one hour. Almost everyone forgets if the time needs to move forward or move backward. If you use the simple mnemonic, "Spring forward, fall back," you won't have to find out the hard way that you forgot to change your clock. This timely mnemonic links the season with the action of the same name: In the spring, the time springs forward by an hour. In the fall, time falls back by an hour.

If you mistakenly move your clock backward instead of forward in the spring, you may arrive at work not just one hour late but two! Your boss is probably not going to buy your excuse. On the other hand, if you move the clock ahead one hour and show up for work two hours early, you're going to kick yourself. Not only have you lost two hours of sleep, but you may also stumble groggily through the day wishing that you had learned the simple mnemonic, Spring forward, fall back.

Hanging Memories on Pegs

Word pegs are so named because you do just that — you peg a word to another word or number that is easier to remember. Pegs are "hooks" that you can use to capture the word you are trying to remember. Thinking of the peg word leads you to think of the word you wanted to remember. For example, if you need to remember the word _shoe_, then use the children's rhyme "One two, buckle my shoe." The peg word, two, attaches to shoe.

To put the peg system of mnemonics into action, try the following brain workout. The goal is to remember a list of ten words, in order. Sound hard? Don't worry, here's a hint: The pegs for remembering the words are the numbers one through ten.

The words you need to recall appear in the following list. Slowly read through the list just one time, and, as you do, think one, two, three, . . . through ten (as in _one sun, two due_):

Sun

Due

Sea

Door

Hive

Stick

Heaven

Gate

Tine

Hen

Now, quick — cover up the list! Can you repeat the words in order? (No peeking!) I bet you can. The pegged word ties to the number. All you have to do is run through the numbers to remember the words. If you don't want to run through each word and want only "gate," go directly to eight.

Pegs in schools

Various segments of the student population have used the peg system successfully. For example, learning-disabled junior high school and high school students learned the hardness levels of minerals, while eighth-grade learning-disabled students got to know all about dinosaurs. Sixth-grade general mainstream students learned recipe ingredients, and eighth graders concentrated on the names of the presidents of the United States.

Sure, I stacked the deck in that example, but you get the point: Peg words attach easily to the words you want to remember. Making the peg word rhyme with the target word makes this mnemonic technique even easier to use.

By rhyming with the number peg, the tie is easy to remember. For example, in "eight gate," the tie doesn't lie in the number alone, but also in the sound of the word *gate* that gives you the clue you need.

You can also use alphabet pegs to tie letters to words. The letter of the alphabet can be either a rhyme or just contain the letter within it. For example:

A-acorn	N-nut
B-bee	O-oh
C-sea	P-pea
D-dog	Q-cue
E-eel	R-ray
F-frog	S-star
G-goat	T-tea
H-hut	U-umbrella
I-eye	V-volt
J-jay	W-wheel
K-cake	X-axe
L-elf	Y-why
M-mate	Z-zebra

You can use letter pegs without having to use the entire alphabet. Just tie your memory to the first letter of a word. A first-letter mnemonic is quite economical because it narrows your search down to a letter. All you have to do is associate the first letter of a word with what you are trying to-remember.

For example, perhaps you want to remember the day you were stung by a bee at the beach. In that case, you would need to remember only B.

Putting Memories into Familiar Places

Realtors are fond of saying that the three most important factors to remember when buying property are location, location, location. Location is also the most important element in the mnemonic technique called *Loci* (LO-sigh). (See the related sidebar titled, "Old but not forgotten," in this chapter.)

Old, but not forgotten

Twenty-six hundred years ago, Mnemosyne, the Greek goddess of memory, was said to know everything — the past, the present, and what will be in the future. Storytellers, called bards, learned how to remember long poems and epic tales by relying on Mnemosyne. The truth is, they used a mnemonic technique later to be called Loci.

Loci is plural for *locus,* which is Latin for place or location. Sometimes, the Loci system is referred to as the topical system. *Topo* (as in topography) is Greek for location.

Like many aspects of Roman culture, the Loci technique originated in Greece. Building on the Greek use of location, orators and performers memorized locations to help them remember their lines without having to rely on notes. The speakers would walk past or look at specific locations, and the line that was associated with that location would come to mind.

Unbeknownst to the audience, the storyteller or orator purposefully walked around the room in a dramatic fashion to jog his own memory. The audience found these movements stirring, not distracting, and had no idea that the speaker was using an ingenious technique to remember.

Imagine the ancient Roman orator Cicero rousing the audience with his eloquence and provocative phrases. The audience assumed all of the impromptu poetry came from his heart and not from his memory.

Cicero told a story of how important location was to the Roman method of remembering. He described how the early Greek poet Simonides was at a large banquet, chanting a lyrical poem that extolled the exploits of the host, Scopas, king of Thessaly. However, Simonides included a passage with praise for the gods Castor and Pollux. Scopas became angry that the spotlight strayed from him. The king refused to pay Simonides the full fee, saying that he could obtain the balance from Castor and Pollux. A messenger summoned Simonides and told him two young men waited outside and needed to talk to him immediately. Simonides complied with this request. When he went outside to meet the men, they were nowhere to be seen. In the meantime, the building collapsed, killing all the occupants inside.

As the cleanup and rescue effort got under way, no one could identify the bodies of the victims. No one but Simonides, who identified each person by where he or she was sitting at the time he (Simonides) was summoned outside. Or so the story goes.

The Loci system was the most dominant memory system used throughout Western Civilization until the Peg and Phonetic systems were developed 400 years ago. The Loci system was how the great storytellers remembered their lines. Just because some people abandoned the Loci system as a way to remember doesn't mean you won't find it useful. This system has been around for the past few thousand years because it's simple to learn.

The Loci system has two main steps:

1. **Commit to memory several locations of a familiar place in the order you want to remember them.**

2. **Associate the things you want to remember with the various locations.**

By taking these two simple steps, you can recall what you're trying to remember by looking at the location (the living room, for example), walking by it, or simply picturing it in your mind.

Skeptical? Give it a try. Suppose you want to memorize a poem or speech. When rehearsing your lines, walk around your living room and make specific associations to the various objects or locations. At your coffee table, remember the first part. Then go to the lamp, china cabinet, couch, and so on, remembering a new part for each location.

As you rehearse, walk around the room and time your presentation to match the locations with each part. Next, stand in one spot and look at each location as you go through the presentation again, matching each part with each location. Next, leave the room physically, but re-enter it mentally, going through your presentation and again making the same matches.

Say that you want to remember part of the poem by Robert Hass entitled, *"Monticello."*

> *Snow is falling*
>
> *On the edge of reason, on Thomas Jefferson's*
>
> *Little hill and on the edge of sensibility.*

When you look out the window think of "Snow is falling." Then, when you look at the TV monitor think of "on the edge of reason." Then look at your bookshelf and think of "on Thomas Jefferson's." Look at the desk and think of "little hill." Finally, look at the mirror, and think of "and on the edge of sensibility."

By the time you need to present your speech, you can skip the crib notes. You'll be able to go to the room in your imagination and make the presentation by seeing each location and remembering what it was associated with.

Telling Yourself a Story to Link Memories

Almost everyone loves a good story. People gather around storytellers, read good novels, and enjoy movies. Stories are a part of the fabric of our culture. You use stories as a way to learn, teach, and pass the time. You can also use stories to link information you want to remember.

Remembering a list without paper and pencil

The Link system is a mnemonic technique that helps you link memories of serial type information, such as lists of words. The link, as the name implies, helps you link a chain of information. This system sometimes is called the chained system, because your task is to chain together links on a list.

Suppose that you have to run to the grocery store to buy food for dinner. You frantically look for a pad and pencil in your car, because halfway to the store you realize you forgot your list. Your glove box contains only maps and a lot of junk you should have thrown away long ago.

For a moment, you forget what you decided to make for dinner. Then it comes to you as your stomach growls. You remember that you had decided to make fettuccini with clam sauce. You have to remember to buy olive oil, fettuccini, parsley, garlic, clams, and Parmesan cheese. You decide to chain together the items into some kind of image that you'll be able to remember when you get to the store. A picture comes to mind of Uncle Fred (for "fre-duccini") sitting under an olive tree (olive oil) with grass growing as high as parsley. Uncle Fred is chopping garlic, grating Parmesan, and storing those ingredients in clamshells. As you walk into the market, that picture draws you into the entire chain, which links together your list. Now, all you have to do is remember how to cook it.

Mark Twain, always witty and seemingly a person who had never been short of words, relied on mnemonics to get himself through speeches. Twain wrote that he would often rely on pictures that he had drawn to help him link together elements of his speech. For example, he once drew a haystack with a squiggly line to remind him that he was to talk next about the West. He gazed down again at his sheet of paper and saw two jagged lines to remind him of lightning. In this case, he was trying to remind himself about talking about the weather in San Francisco, its lack of lightning, and its frequent fog in the summer. He went on to quip about San Francisco weather. When I lived in San Francisco, I was fond of quoting Twain's remark: "The coldest winter I ever spent was a summer in San Francisco."

Weaving a story to recall a list

The Story system of mnemonics is similar to the Link system, but a little more elaborate. This technique requires more time than does the Link system. To use it, you develop a story that reminds you of the list or group of words you need to remember. Your story should weave together the items in the order that you want to remember. Those items connect with one another as the story unfolds.

With the Link system, you use primarily visual images, whereas you may not need them with the Story system. If you do have time to develop visual imagery, the story becomes all that more indelible for your memory.

The morning I wrote this page, a furious storm had awakened me. When my wife went downstairs to make breakfast, we noticed that the ceiling just above one of the window frames was leaking. We quickly surmised that the storm, with its near-sideways pounding rain, had torn up some flashing on the roof, allowing some rainwater to seep down into the wall. The water dripped all over the windowsill and onto the carpet. We hastily checked the garage for something we could use to plug the spot, but found nothing suitable.

We hopped into the car to go to the hardware store and drove faster than we should have through the flooded streets. In the car, we thought up a list of items to buy, but we had no pencil and paper. We came up with the following story to take with us into the hardware store:

> Mr. Moosely found that he was out of denture adhesive (caulking), so he used one of his finest steak knives (putty knife) to mince up dinner. But he worried that mashing up the minced food with his gums would result in food dribbling out of his mouth and onto his new shirt. Therefore, he took out a plastic bib (plastic sheet) that was left in his apartment the last time his young grandson was visiting. He realized that the bib was far too small, and he could hardly tie it around his neck. Mr. Moosely knew that if he used this small bib, food would fall onto the table or floor. He managed to find a rectangular container (drip pan) from the cabinet. It was only then that he was able to enjoy his minced meal.

We carried this story into the hardware store and completed the project, in the driving rain, by lunchtime. I looked for a place to put away the items in the garage so that I was sure to find them later. In the place I chose to store the tools, I found most of those same items that were left over from a similar incident! Had I developed a story about finding the tools, I may not have spent my morning at the hardware store.

Choosing the Right Mnemonic at the Right Time

Not all mnemonic systems work the same for everyone. Just as people are unique, so are their needs and preferences. What you find useful may be totally useless to your neighbor and vice versa.

Choose a mnemonic that works for you

Choose the mnemonic that fits best with your personality and familiarity. Doing so can increase your chances of remembering your memory-aid in the future.

To use mnemonic aids effectively, consider the following basic principles.

Make sure the mnemonic:

- ✔ Gets your attention.
- ✔ Contains an easy association.
- ✔ Is organized in such a way that it's easy for you to remember.
- ✔ Is meaningful to you.

Don't rely on a mnemonic technique that you've read about if you already have one that suits you personally. Each person's life experience is different, and people will respond to images in their own way. Consider the image of an onion dome on a Russian Orthodox church. Having spent some time in Eastern Europe over the years, I think about all that the image of the onion dome has absorbed throughout history.

That image of the dome carries with it how the Russians absorbed the culture of the East and picked up Christianity from the Ukrainians after they picked it up from the Byzantine Greeks/Armenians. For me, seeing an image of an onion-dome church initiates this range of associations: I think about the day I walked around the Kremlin during a blizzard in 1974, or the summer day in 2001 when, during an intense thunderstorm, I took refuge in St. Basil's Basilica in Moscow. Another person will not carry the same imagery.

Mnemonics that grab your attention and make remembering fun are always more effective. If your mnemonic is stale and boring, you'll tend to forget it. Make the mnemonic stand out by making it silly, funny, absurd, or even titillating.

Choose a mnemonic that fits the situation

If your mnemonic has little to do with what you're trying to remember, you'll probably forget it. For example, for your biology class, you're trying to remember that the Galapagos Islands off the coast of Ecuador have one of the widest ranges of unique animal species, including aquatic dragon lizards.

You may think of mnemonics like these:

- **The Ecuadorean flag.** A flag image probably won't grab your attention, compared to a more vivid and evocative image.

- **A knight fighting off a dragon just outside a medieval castle.** You're trying to associate the dragon lizards on the Galapagos Islands with the image of castles and knights. Hmm — looks like a tangent to me. Remember, you're trying to recall the Galapagos Islands, not the British Isles.

- **A huge number of gallon containers with dragon lizards crawling out.** With the word *gallon,* you have a link to the word *Galapagos Islands,* and you have added the lizards. You also want to make sure that you organize your imagery in such a way to carry the broader point, namely that not only are there aquatic lizards on the Galapagos Islands, but a wide range of animals. In this case, you may want to envision the gallon containers brimming over with a wide variety of living creatures, in addition to the dragon lizards.

- **Darwin's boat, the Beagle, anchored in the bay, and hundreds of gallons of containers on shore, brimming over with life.** You want to make sure that there's personal meaning to the image you're trying to remember, and for me, an actual image from history works: Darwin's boat. The overall concept of the Galapagos Islands should represent a geographical location so remote that living species have evolved differently from others on the mainland.

Taking shortcuts: They're okay

Although the visual mnemonic route (the Link system) can potentially carry much more than just one image, the lack of time you have could make identifying an image impractical in some situations.

Visual mnemonics take much more time for you to develop than do peg, link, story, or phonetic mnemonics. When you don't have a lot of time and need to develop a quick way to remember something important, using a peg may be wiser.

For example, if you're listening to a lecture and don't have a notepad, then you'll end up in the dust when the lecturer moves on to another subject while you're trying to conjure up a visual image.

One of the advantages the Peg system has over the story, phonetic, or link systems is that you can select individual items from a list. In contrast, the link system relies on a sequence. (For more about the Link system, see the section titled, "Remembering a list without paper and pencil," earlier in this chapter.)

Like the Loci system, which depends on prememorized location-connected links, the Peg system use prememorized word or number links. With the Peg system, that information connects to nouns.

The more complex or abstract the noun, the more vulnerable it may be to association with other words or ideas. The nouns are most useful if they are concrete nouns.

Whatever mnemonic system you use, make sure that it's flexible and meets the demands of what you're trying to remember. Practice using mnemonics so that you'll be versatile in their use. Mnemonics have a long history and have been used all over the world. Make them work for you.

Chapter 9

Troubleshooting Your Forgetfulness

In This Chapter

▶ Avoiding forgetting

▶ Getting it down cold

▶ Organizing your memory

▶ Getting the meaning of your memory

*W*hen your memory engine is humming along nicely, memories get processed and coded for storage in your long-term memory, and you can call them up at will. You hear yourself saying, "I forgot!" less frequently.

But a number of snags and traps lie along the long-term route — annoying things that divert, distort, or even dump your memories. Although some of these roadblocks can be embarrassing when you recognize what they are, none are serious memory problems, and all can be pushed aside if you know what to do.

In this chapter, I show you how to troubleshoot your forgetfulness with some handy, everyday tactics to ensure that your memories get laid down in long-term memory and pop back up at your command.

Cutting through Memory Fog

A lot can happen to foul things up on the way to long-term memory and back into recollection. Sometimes, memories don't get formed when you expect them to. They don't make the journey from short-term to long-term memory (see Chapter 3 for more on how your memories get formed). Sometimes, what you think is a memory problem isn't one at all. Instead, the problem comes from:

✔ Laziness

✔ Fear

✔ Lack of motivation

✔ Having a reason to forget

Repressing your memory of your dentist appointment

People forget for a variety of reasons. One of the first of these reasons to gain popularity was proposed by Sigmund Freud over 100 years ago. He proposed that people forget because they can repress what they don't want to think about. *Repression* means a sort of pushing back out of consciousness those thoughts and feelings that you find overwhelming. From Freud's point of view, you repress memories that you find unacceptable or unpleasant.

Suppose, for example, that you forget a dentist appointment for the third time. Would it be safe to say that you have a serious memory problem? Not necessarily. Perhaps your fear of going to the dentist comes into play. Perhaps you've repressed the memory of the appointment.

Much of what you code into memory and what you recall has to do with your motivation. If you have some reason to be motivated to forget, you may do just that. The fear of going to the dentist and getting that shot of Novocain or feeling that drill grinding away at your tooth certainly can be something you'd be motivated to forget.

In this case, you don't have a memory problem; you have a fear problem. Deal with your fear, and you deal with the problem of forgetting the appointments.

You do have the ability to distort, filter, or selectively forget those memories that you find distasteful. This ability is the concept behind what has been referred to as "repressed memories." However, the entire concept of deep, dark, hidden repressed memories of childhood is unresolved. (For more on childhood memory, see Chapter 2.)

Listening selectively

You tell your teenager to take out the trash. He says, "Yeah, sure," as he drifts through the room on the way to the computer to reply to an e-mail. An hour later, you remind him to take out the trash. He says, "Oh yeah, I forgot."

Did he really forget? Possibly. Possibly not. He may not even have paid attention to your initial request. He may have been operating on automatic pilot when he said, "Oh sure." Attention is critical for memory to form. (For more about the role of attention in short-term memory, see Chapters 2, 3, and 4.)

Maybe your teenager chose to avoid what he assumed was just another request to do even more chores. He focused on something completely different. He was probably composing his e-mail as he drifted through the room. This behavior is *selective attention*.

You probably have a much easier time seeing how selective attention works in the previous example, but seeing how it operates for you may be a bit more difficult. You probably selectively pay attention to other things rather than to questions or comments made by other people, but you likely don't realize that you do it.

Don't condemn yourself to believing that you have a memory problem after a series of selective attention mishaps. Instead, try to recognize any attention, motivation, or laziness problems and deal with them to improve your memory.

Recognizing memory-jams

A variety of interferences can come between what you learn and what you hope to remember. Here are some typical examples:

- A subject that you remember may be too similar to another subject that you're trying to learn, so you confuse the two.
- Learning new information can interfere with your memories.
- Your memories can be manipulated by suggestions from other people.

Mistaking similar memories

Your memory can be distorted by how much time has passed and what has happened since you learned the original information. Perhaps the old information that you learned is similar to the information you're now learning and interferes with it.

This interference can happen with any kind of memory, from what you remember about entertainment to learning a language. For example, you watch your son play basketball and notice that he's pretty good at taking the ball from the opposing team and dribbling it down the court to take a shot. But then he shoots and misses. You think, "Well, I guess he and I could shoot some baskets between games for practice."

Next week, you go to another game. He catches a rebound and dribbles down and shoots successfully. You remember the preceding week and assume that the ball almost went in the basket. In reality, it wasn't even close. You've sort of melded the two instances together to form an inaccurate memory.

This type of distortion is called *retroactive inhibition* (*retro* meaning backwards and *inhibition* meaning that the new memory inhibits the earlier one).

Say that you go to the next game and see him catch a rebound, dribble, and shoot. This time, he misses. Later that night, you report that his shot almost went into the hoop, but the fact is, it didn't. In this case, psychologists call this distortion *proactive inhibition*.

New learning blocking old

Your memories are also distorted by new learning. Suppose that you're traveling from Spain to Italy. Before you leave Spain, you manage to pick up some basic traveler's Spanish to help you find your way around, order at a restaurant, and greet various people you meet.

After spending a little time in Italy, you begin to learn the same level of traveler's Italian as you did with Spanish. The languages have similarities because they're both based on their common Latin core. However, they're not similar enough to reinforce the Spanish that you learned earlier.

Now, you go back to Spain and find that your traveler's Spanish has melted away. Your basic understanding of Italian interfered with your vague memory of Spanish. You say *ciao* instead of *hasta luego* when you tell someone goodbye, and, when you thank someone, you say *grazie* instead of *gracias*. As you walk out of the store, you're not quite sure, but you think that the store clerk swore at you.

When you think that you've been vulnerable to learning new information that interferes with what you learned before, take a little time to review what you learned before. In the case of the previous example, take out the Spanish phrase book and practice with your friend before going to the store.

Outside interference

Your memories can be also distorted by interference from another person. They can be altered by the way that person asks you to recall them.

This type of distortion is well known in the courtroom and is often the basis for one attorney to say, "I object, your Honor! Counsel is leading the witness."

You may have seen this outside interference played out in the movies or on TV. The defense attorney asks a witness, "Tell me if you can remember the shape of the murderer's glasses."

The witness is put on the spot, but she says anyway, "Oh, I don't really remember the shape."

What if the murderer didn't wear glasses? Because the witness was put on the spot, feeling under pressure, she was led to believe that the murderer did wear glasses. Unknowingly, she allowed her memory to be distorted.

The defense attorney may later call up his client, the defendant. Looking slyly at his client, he may ask, "Have you ever worn glasses?"

Looking at the jury for full effect, the client responds with a straight face, "I've never worn glasses."

Just as that witness was led astray from his memory and now is on record as verifying a fact that is untrue, you, too, are subject to constant modifications of your memory. This problem comes up when you use the wrong cue when you're under pressure to recall a memory.

You probably won't have to suffer the stress of being a witness in a court trial. However, you'll periodically be put under pressure, and you may not have time to recall your memories clearly.

Give yourself enough time to clear your thoughts. If someone is pressuring you, say, "Well, I'm not sure. Let me think about it." You'll be able to use the right cues (your own cues) to recollect your memories.

Getting It Down Cold by Overlearning

Have you ever heard anyone say that they have something "down cold?" What they usually mean by this expression is that they've learned the skill or can remember the information so well that they don't have to strain to remember it. This section gives you a selection of techniques for doing the same.

The more time you spend learning a particular subject, the better you'll be able to remember the details later. That's what overlearning means — by doing something over and over again (the right way) you get it down cold. Just like typing this sentence. I didn't have to look at the keyboard because I've overlearned where the keys are and how to type.

Ten years ago, I first learned how to use the Windows operating system on my PC. I was overwhelmed with all the steps I had to go through to perform one task. A friend tried to teach me over the phone.

"Go to the *Start* button," he said.

I looked on the face of the tower case, saw the on-off button, and wondered if I should turn it off. Fortunately, I held back that urge and said, "You mean you want me to turn it off?"

"No, just go to *Programs,* then *Systems Tools.*"

"I have no idea what you're talking about," I said.

"Put your cursor on the *Start* button and click it. Then, another window comes up. Then, you go to *Programs.* Click it. Then, another window comes up. Click *Systems Tools.*"

After that confusing introduction, I'm now able to zip around on my computer almost as if I know what I'm doing (that is, until my teenage son comes by and untangles the mess I've woven).

The point is, I've learned through years of practice how to "move around" within the system, and I've learned how it's organized. Now, after I wait for an hour on one of those phone trees and finally do get to a computer tech person, she can command me to move around and diagnose a problem. When she tells me to go to the *Start* button, I don't have the urge to turn the computer off.

The more you overlearn the material that you want to remember, the more you can be confident that you'll be able to remember it later. Whatever the circumstances, say during an exam or performance, you'll be able to remember what you need to remember.

With your confidence up, your nervousness goes down. You can remember that you have the material down cold. Even if you're distracted by the number of people watching you or by the situation surrounding the exam, you can rest assured that you've gone over the material so many times that it'll just roll off your tongue or onto the paper, almost as if you're operating on automatic pilot. A part of you is recalling the material because it has become an ingrained habit.

Overlearning involves more than just repetition. If you just repeat something over and over again, you're only going to remember it superficially. However, if you want to remember something deeply, you're going to have to do more than repeat it. For instance, if you're learning French, you need to do more than just repeat phrases. You need to know the meanings of those phrases.

The opposite of overlearning is called *cramming.* When you cram, you try to learn all the superficial details as quickly as possible. That's why it's called cramming — because you gorge all at once and naively expect to digest it. In contrast, when you overlearn something, you digest it into memory.

You can maximize what you remember by learning as much as you can about a subject.

For example, suppose that you're trying to remember the five boroughs of New York City for a political science exam. Repeating Bronx, Queens, Brooklyn, Staten Island, and Manhattan over and over again may help a little, but add the dimension of looking at a map and noting the shapes, and you'll know them even more. Then, find out what each borough is like in character, who lives there, and what buildings and monuments are there. Furthermore, if you read a book or article on New York, you add even more dimension. Then you remember that John Lennon used to say, "If you're not in New York, you're hiding." So, go to New York and explore the neighborhoods. You'll really remember the boroughs, then!

Overlearning differs from cramming in many ways (see Chapter 13 for more on these ways). First and foremost, overlearning makes sure that you'll remember what you've learned far beyond the exam. With cramming, assuming that you even remember what you crammed, the information will leave your head as quickly as it came in. The facts will be replaced by a new set of facts, and those new facts will be blown away by yet another superficial set of facts.

You want the facts that you learn to have depth, to grow roots. Those rooted facts may very well form the foundation for other facts and information. Cramming, by contrast, grows no roots. A stiff wind can blow down an entire shallow-rooted tree.

Overlearning lets you cultivate the information, helping it grow in association with other information. Gradually, this information grows into a body of knowledge that you'll remember in depth.

You may ask, "Can I go over information too much? Is there a point where overlearning becomes counterproductive? Would I develop a mental block to the information if I spend too much time with it?" The short answer to all these questions is *no*.

Overlearning deepens the foundation for memory of the information and helps you develop confidence in your knowledge of it.

Think of how a person becomes an expert in a subject area. They don't take a quick course, cram the information for the exam, and walk away with a deep knowledge of the subject.

Think of overlearning as a way to ensure that you'll be resistant to nuisance information that could get you off track. If you're trying to commit to memory subject matter that you know little about, you'll probably be vulnerable to thinking irrelevant information is relevant until you know about it in detail.

Say that you're trying to remember what the environment is like around Flagstaff, Arizona, for a geography exam. Perhaps you've never been there and seen the millions of ponderosa pines and smelled the powerful vanilla-like scent of the pinesap. After you're finished studying for the exam, a friend brings up Tucson in conversation and describes the saguaro cactus that surrounds the city.

Later that day, Flagstaff comes up in class. You comment on how beautiful the saguaro cacti are. Your professor corrects you by saying, "What are you talking about? Flagstaff is at an elevation of 7,000 feet and gets several feet of snow every year! In the summer, the temperature rarely gets above 80 degrees!"

Had you thoroughly researched Flagstaff, looked at maps, pictures, and read about it, you wouldn't have slipped in information about Tucson. You would have built up resistance to nuisance information. Your memory of the information about Flagstaff would have depth because you overlearned.

If you had to have brain surgery next week, would you want your neurosurgeon to have learned his skill in that way? Would you want him to be fresh out of his residency program and for you to be his first patient as an independent practitioner? Chances are, you're like me and would want to know that he has performed this same operation 100 times — not one time. He'd be more confident in his abilities, and so would you.

Getting Organized

How well you remember information often depends on how well it's organized in your mind. The better the information is organized, the easier it'll be for you to remember later.

If you manage to commit to memory information that's disorganized, it'll be harder to recall than organized information. It's as if you filed a piece of paper away in your file cabinet and forgot which drawer you put it in. Think of all the time you'd waste going through all those drawers and files.

Consider your response if someone were to ask you to recite all the states of the United States. You'd probably try to organize your recall in such a way that you wouldn't miss a state — for example, starting on the West Coast and working your way east.

Perhaps you'd start by naming Alaska or Hawaii, so that you can get them out of the way. Then you'd probably try to use geography to organize your recall. Maybe you'd run down north to south, beginning in the Pacific Northwest, and move east. For example: Washington, Oregon, California, Idaho, Nevada, Montana, Utah, Arizona, and so on, until you reach Florida. This way, you'd organize your search and work visually.

If you aren't visually acquainted with the map of the United States, you may try to organize your search by letter pegs. You begin with *A* and remember Alaska, Alabama, and so on until you exhaust the letters and count to 50. (For more about the peg techniques, see Chapter 8.)

If you don't organize your search, you may name the states that come immediately to mind. Maybe you'll first name the state you live in and those bordering it. Then, you may pick them randomly. If you use this disorganized method, you'll probably come back to states you already mentioned, saying, "Did I say Colorado?"

Organize your search. Your recall is always enhanced when you use an organized method of retrieving what you already know.

Serializing

If you're being asked to remember a list of names or numbers, you may find it easier to remember the first few and the last few names or numbers and have greater difficulty with those in the middle — especially if the list is long.

I've seen this problem occur over and over again when giving my patients the brief sub-test called *Digit Span*. Suppose that I ask you to remember a string of numbers, such as the following:

2 5 4 1 3 5 7 9 5 8 3

You'll probably remember the *2 5 4* at the beginning and the *5 8 3* at the end.

If you can detect a pattern in the digits in the middle, you increase your chances of remembering them. With the numbers I give you in the string, you notice that they go up in order by two: *1,3,5,7,9.*

Don't worry if you can't remember a long chain of numbers like this. Very few people can.

If you're asked to name all the presidents of the United States, you'll probably be able to remember the first seven and the last seven and perhaps two (more or less) in the middle.

Yet, recalling the presidents is a more complex task and involves long-term memory, not just short-term memory, as with remembering a string of numbers. You probably would remember some of the presidents in the middle of the string based on fame. Perhaps you'd remember Lincoln and Theodore Roosevelt because of their fame and because their images are sculpted into Mount Rushmore.

Remembering the presidents in the middle is a little more complicated than what you did with the numbers above. In addition to looking for a pattern, make associations between the presidents you remember and those you're trying to remember. For instance, you remember Lincoln, but you may not remember Johnson and Grant, who followed. The Civil War is the key association. Who was vice president during the war? Right — Johnson. And who was the principal general? Right — Grant.

Tagging

Suppose that you're an expecting parent (or better yet, an expecting grandparent) and you know that a girl is on the way. You may spend hours trying to think of a girl's name that everyone can be comfortable with. You may organize the search of your memory of girl names by tagging the names to a cue instead of randomly reciting all the names that pop into your mind.

You'll better be able to structure your recall of names by going through the alphabet. A: Aileen, Amelia, Annabelle, and so on.

Searching your memory this way not only saves you time, but also helps you to recall more names. You're organizing your recall around tagged words Using pegs is kind of like drilling in specific spots, and then pumping out water from your well. Each acquisition allows you much better access to a cavern of water.

You can tag information with cues in a wide variety of ways. People have been doing it for centuries. Performers and speakers have even relied on their surroundings to remind them of what they want to say (see Chapter 8 for a complete description of this technique). They look around a room and remind themselves of their lines or different parts of their speech.

Chunking

Chunking means making digestible, bite-size pieces out of big blobs of data. For example, think of your social security number. When you recall it, you probably don't recite it with all nine digits evenly spaced. For example, if you try to remember *923373452,* you probably have a hard time. It's nine digits long. Even if you have above-average recall, you'll have trouble with that one.

Most people learn to remember their social security number in three chunks — with the first three digits chunked, then the next two chunked, and the final four chunked. When you recall this number throughout your life, you recite it in those chunks.

Take the same number I gave above and put it in three chunks: *923-37-3452*. That number's much easier to remember because it's in bite-size chunks.

The fact that phone numbers in the United States are only seven digits long is no accident. If they were longer, most people would likely forget them.

You may be saying, "Well, what about area codes? That makes ten digits." Most people remember area codes as a separate chunk. In fact, many of the phone numbers you try to remember are in the same area code anyway, so you don't have to worry about it — it's a given.

In the early 1960s, psychologist Dr. George Miller drew attention to how much capacity for information we have in short-term memory. He pointed out that we can remember seven (plus or minus two) pieces of information over the short term before it fades away. The average number of digits people remember is seven. You may remember two more digits than seven or two fewer than seven. If your friend's phone number were more than seven digits, would you remember it before you wrote it down? Maybe. Maybe not.

If you meet a person whom you'd like to get to know better and you get her or his phone number, you have less than 30 seconds to write it down, or you'll probably forget it. If you repeat it over and over again, you'll have a better chance of remembering it. However, if you go on talking before you either write it down or repeat it, you'll probably forget it.

Suppose that you have a poem you want to memorize. You may ask yourself, "Do I try to memorize the entire poem from start to finish, or do I memorize specific stanzas until I've mastered the whole poem?" Of course, the answer to these questions depends on how long the poem is.

If the poem's quite long, breaking the poem up into chunks (stanzas) can help you remember it. On the other hand, if the poem is short, breaking it up needlessly fragments it. When you go to recite it, you may forget how the parts fit together because you were so focused on the fragments.

You want to see how the whole poem works together to grasp its flow. Then you can move to specific stanzas, becoming reasonably comfortable that you've committed each to memory before moving on to the next. Then you can move on to the entire poem as one complete recitation.

Then you need to recite, recite, recite. The more you recite, the easier it's going to be for you to recall it later.

Rhyming Memory

If you detect or impose a pattern upon what you're trying to remember, you have a better chance of remembering it later.

Patterns bring out even the most basic level of meaning. Patterns can include simple and repetitive chunking or rhyming.

Think back when you were trying to recite the alphabet. You probably didn't just say in one long string: *ABCDEFGHIJKLMNOPQRSTUVWXYZ*. For a child, that string would have been quite intimidating.

Your teacher probably led the class through a rhyming singsong recitation that not only chunked the letters but also rhymed them into something like this:

ABCD-EFG-HIJK-LMNOP-QRS-TUV-WX-Y and Z. Now, I know my ABCs, tell me what you think of me.

Not only does this method of learning the alphabet have a distinct and simple pattern, it also has a very basic rhyme to remember.

You can and probably have used rhymes to remember how to spell particularly tricky words that fall into specific patterns such as: *I before E, except after C*. And this history reminder is based on a rhyme: *In fourteen hundred ninety two, Columbus sailed the ocean blue*.

As you're cooking, you probably don't want to have to stop what you're doing to refer to a book of measurements. Even when you're reading a recipe, there's a body of knowledge you're expected to know. For example, suppose that you need to cook some rice. Many packages don't include portions and perhaps, even if they did, you may have done what I've done too often — thrown the package away before reading the directions. It'd be easier to remember the rhyme: *Cooking rice? Water twice*. (The ratio's actually one and a half, not twice. But that's beside the point!)

When thinking of the difference between tablespoons and teaspoons, you can think of the rhyme: *Big T equals teaspoons times three*, to carry home the point that three teaspoons make up one tablespoon.

In the case of an emergency, you can even refer to a rhyme in order to remember how to treat a shock victim. You rhyme: *If his face is red, raise his head. If his face is pale, raise his tail*.

Here, you factor in the information that a red face means that he's getting too much blood to his head. You want to minimize the flow. A pale face means that he's not getting enough blood to his head, and by lifting his feet, you're allowing him to get a greater amount of blood to his head. Because remembering all that information is much harder, remembering the rhyme instead can save a life.

Each of these rhymes carries with it a pattern and information to remember. The pattern, or, in this case, the rhyme pulls the information around it like the gravitational pull the earth has on the moon.

Getting the Meaning of the Memory

If something makes sense to you, chances are, you'll probably remember it easier than something that doesn't have meaning to you. The degree of meaningfulness of what you're trying to remember determines the strength of the memory.

Suppose that you're trying to get to know your VCR before it becomes obsolete to DVD players. You may have read the troubleshooting portion of your manual, but it likely held little meaning because you hadn't encountered any problems yet. Because the manual had no meaning to you, you probably forgot what you read.

As soon as you encounter a problem, however, what you read in the troubleshooting section has far more meaning to you because you're looking for a solution to your problem. (You'll probably remember it better than I. I confess that I often ask one of my sons to solve the VCR problem. I rationalize that he enjoys it. I know I don't, and that's not a rationalization!)

Try to make sense of the information you're trying to remember, even if it's something like the VCR problem. If you read the troubleshooting section of the manual after you figure out what went wrong, try to explain it to yourself to remember the problem and solution.

Feeding Back to Remember

Your memory retention can improve if you get feedback about what you're learning. To begin with, if you're learning something for the first time, you'll want to learn it the right way. You don't want to learn bad techniques that may be hard to forget.

For example, say that you're trying to learn how to ski. If you don't get specific instructions that you can later build on, you'll build up bad habits that you'll later have to forget in order to rebuild basic skills. I've been skiing most of my life and can go down almost any run, including those suicidal double black diamonds. However, I look like a clown doing it. Guts and stupidity are no replacement for feedback.

Receiving feedback can also help you stay focused and interested. Music lessons are great examples of this principle in practice. My wife and I often have a difficult time convincing our sons to practice their instruments. Even though they say, "Why do you keep asking us if we want to play? Of course we do," they don't always demonstrate their interest by practicing. Nevertheless, with music lessons and a class at school, both get feedback on a constant basis. When they receive that feedback, they're focused and interested.

If you're a music student, dancer, athlete, language student, or whatever, getting feedback from your teachers affords you the opportunity to make continual adjustments to your technique and remember how those new adjustments make sense. You've accumulated a "history" of feedback that you can refer back to as you challenge yourself to learn more about your subject.

Getting feedback along the way allows you to approach your goal and to incorporate into memory an ongoing body of knowledge. Ask questions of the person giving you feedback. This will involve you more deeply in the feedback process and increase your memory of it.

Chapter 10

Keeping Your Memory Sharp as You Grow Older

*W*hen you find yourself forgetting what you were going to say, have you ever said that you're "having a senior moment"? This common joke really overplays the reality of aging.

Aging doesn't make you lose your memory as dramatically as you may expect. Although your visual and spatial memory skills generally do decline with age, verbal memories (memory of names, stories, words, and numbers) decline very little — if at all.

Most people do note increasing memory problems as they age, but that doesn't mean that everyone experiences memory loss at the same rate or the same degree. In this chapter, you find out why and how aging can affect your memory skills and what to do about it.

Making Full Use of a Vintage Brain

You don't know less in your old age; you probably know more. During your advanced years, however, your information-processing speed slows down. Don't worry, though — your long-term memory remains intact, and your understanding of what you already know is broader, more thoughtful, and wiser than during your early adulthood.

Here's more good news: You were probably taught in school that, at birth, you have all the brain cells you'll ever have, right? From then on (the lesson continued), you lose about 10,000 brain cells every day — and even more if you drink alcohol.

Well, it turns out that the old wisdom isn't true. The situation isn't that bleak. You *do* have an opportunity for dendrite growth. Dendrites are the part of your neurons that branch out to pick up information from other neurons (see Chapter 3 for more details about the parts of your brain). What you do with your brain determines what happens to it. (I talk more about how to grow dendrites later in this chapter.)

Now, for the not-so-good news: Your brain loses its vitality and size as you age. The levels of neurotransmitters (see Chapter 3 for a description of neurotransmitters) — including various hormones, such as melatonin, testosterone, and estrogen — decline. Your arteries and capillaries grow less flexible and, in some cases, become clogged, hindering the flow of vital oxygen and nutrients to your brain. Uncontrolled stress makes matters only worse.

Reducing stress, keeping the blood flowing

If you're like me, one of your objectives as you age is to retain your power to learn and recall — maybe even get better, if you can. If that's part of your agenda, here are two things to start doing today:

- Reduce your stress level.
- Improve your blood circulation.

Stress kills memory. Hormones, such as cortisol, are destructive to your brain if you stay stressed. As you age, cortisol (a stress hormone) has a particularly destructive effect on your brain's ability to adjust to new learning and memory. Dendritic branching and axonal sprouting (see Chapter 3 for a description of axons and dendrites), which support new memories, get retarded when your body has to deal with stress.

As you age, the blood flow to your brain reduces. This reduction means that your neurons are provided with less life-sustaining support. Your blood brings not only the glucose, which acts as fuel to your brain, but also the amino acids that are synthesized into neurotransmitters. If your diet is high in saturated fats or if you drink alcohol or smoke, count on your blood flow to be slow. (See Chapter 4 for more on how diet influences your memory.)

The reduction in blood flow to your brain doesn't necessarily happen at the same pace as your neighbor down the street who's the same age. You have some control over it. One of the best things you can do to keep your blood flowing is to exercise on a regular basis. You'll not only do your heart a big favor, but you'll also help clear out cholesterol from your arteries and increase the longevity of the elasticity of your arteries and capillaries. You may want to consider taking a modest amount of gingko, which dilates blood vessels.

Don't take gingko if you're also taking a blood-thinning agent such as aspirin. I talk more about gingko and blood thinners in Chapter 5.

To minimize stress and keep the blood flowing:

- ✔ **Exercise.** Take regular walks, swim, bike, or work out in the gym — whatever fits your style.

- ✔ **Join a yoga or meditation class.**

- ✔ **Eat a balanced diet.** Keep the saturated-fat level low.

- ✔ **Minimize consumption of alcohol.**

- ✔ **Don't smoke.**

- ✔ **Consider taking modest doses of gingko** (as long as you're not taking a blood thinning agent).

- ✔ **Avoid high-stress activities** such as working as a trader at the New York Stock Exchange.

- ✔ **Learn relaxation techniques** and use them on a regular basis (see Chapter 7 for more on ways to relax).

Free radicals also begin to take their toll as you age (more on these guys in Chapter 6), because free radicals break down tissue and kill cells.

The main targets of free radicals in your brain are the *myelin sheaths*. The myelin sheaths comprise the oily substance that covers your axons to improve conduction. Axons are the part of your neurons that send information. They help your neurons fire at maximum velocity. When free radicals eat away the myelin, your axons lose their conductivity. This lack of conductivity means that your brain doesn't process information as quickly. Memories are both harder to form and harder to recall.

The other big targets of free radicals are your dendrites. Dendrites are the part of your neurons that receive information from other neurons. Free radicals cause your dendrites to thin out, leaving your brain less able to process information in ways it had before. You find yourself forgetting jokes that you were once able to tell with great punch.

Brain wave slowdown

Your reaction time slows down with age. This slowdown is partly due to a decline in your ability to process information at the same rate as when you were younger. This slowing tendency also contributes to being less able to do several things at once. Unfortunately, multi-tasking has become a way of life in today's society. People talk on cell phones while shopping and answer beepers while sending e-mail.

During your early adulthood, certain brain waves (known as alpha waves) occur at the rate of 11 cycles per second. By the time you reach age 65, they fade to nine cycles per second. By age 80, alpha waves fade to eight cycles per second.

This reduction in alpha waves occurs at the same time that your sleep cycle changes. As

you age, the amount of time you spend in deep sleep decreases. Deep sleep is the most restorative stage of sleep. It's where your immune system is bolstered and you truly achieve relaxation from sleep (see Chapter 7). The lack of restorative sleep can be a drag on you during the day when you're trying to maintain attention and form memories.

All these problems make it more difficult for you to pay attention at the level you could when you were younger.

Resist this decline by staying mentally active. Challenge yourself by taking classes, reading, and going to lectures.

One way to combat free radicals is to consume foods that are rich in antioxidants. You can also supplement your diet with antioxidant vitamins, such as C and E. (See Chapters 4 and 5 for information on antioxidants and vitamins, respectively.)

Compensating for your graying senses

As you pass your prime physically, you may experience some loss of your senses. Most people do — the eyesight fades, the hearing grows less acute, and muscles lose their flex. Sound familiar? These losses are facts of life for older people, and they're all perfectly normal.

Unfortunately, the fading competence of your senses makes it more difficult to pick up the information that warrants attention and remembering. This means you may not get all the information that others get and, therefore, remember less.

With all this sensory dulling and dampening of attention, other people may misread your deficits as a decline in your overall intelligence. Make sure that you do everything you can to keep your eyesight strong, your hearing acute, and your muscles in tone — so that people don't get the wrong idea!

Maximize your sensory ability by compensating for your deficits. For instance:

✔ If your hearing is fading, wear a hearing aid.

✔ If your eyesight is on the blink, wear glasses.

Mental Gymnastics: Inflating a Shrinking Brain

Starting at age 50, your 3-pound brain gradually loses its volume in weight, so that, by age 75, it weighs roughly 2.6 pounds. A lot of the shrinkage in your brain is from a loss of water.

Different parts of your brain lose their volume at different rates. Your *frontal lobes* — which serve as your executive control center, giving you your sense of judgment and allowing you to avoid blurting out rude and inappropriate comments — show the greatest amount of shrinkage compared to any other part of your cortex (see Chapter 3 for more on the cortex and other parts of the brain). The frontal lobes can shrink up to 30 percent from the time you turn 50 to the time you turn 90. Looked at another way, your frontal lobes lose 0.55 percent of their volume every year after age 50. As the frontal lobes shrink, you lose some of your capacity to be in control. (Now, perhaps, you won't be as surprised by some of the rude comments that come out of your grandfather's mouth.)

Your frontal lobes also play a big role in your ability to pay attention long enough to form short-term memories. If your frontal lobes do an inadequate job, they can make you prone to absentmindedness. As you age, you may become more apt to forget where you placed your keys or forget why you walked into a room.

Your *temporal lobes,* which help you remember the gist of an experience, shrink up to 20 percent as you age. This means that your ability to remember what you hear and say falter as you get older. Your temporal lobes also have to try to interpret inadequate information coming in if your hearing is failing.

To combat this shrinkage of your temporal lobes, you need to push them to be more active. To keep those lobes sharp:

- ✔ Engage in debate — participate in a political campaign or join a community group.
- ✔ Listen to lectures and discuss them afterward.
- ✔ Engage in discussion with your spouse, partner, and lifelong friends about memories you both hold.

Intellectual activity like that has the same beneficial effect on the temporal lobes as pumping iron has on the biceps. (But don't worry — your head won't bulge.)

As you age, your *hippocampus* also shrinks. Between the ages of 50 and 90, it loses up to 20 percent of its volume. The levels of the neurotransmitter *acetylcholine* — critical for memory and active in your hippocampus — fall as you age and as your hippocampus shrinks. Your hippocampus is centrally involved in moving your short-term memories into long-term memories

The loss in volume of your hippocampus means that acquiring new memories can be a little more difficult, compared to earlier in your life. However, the situation is far from hopeless. Your brain is highly affected by changes in your nutrition, so your job is to make sure that you have the best nutrition possible. Eat three balanced meals a day.

Each meal should include a:

- ✔ Complex carbohydrate
- ✔ Fruit or vegetable
- ✔ Protein

New neurons?

The recent discovery called *neurogenesis* has shaken the filed of neuroscience. Doctors and scientists have always assumed that we grow no new neurons after our infancy. To the contrary, neuroscientists have discovered that some nerve cells, under special conditions, *can* reproduce. Although more research and explanation are still needed, these findings have brought hope to victims of spinal cord injuries and to the rest of us who fear a waning brain in our later years.

See Chapter 4 for details on nutrition.

Your *occipital lobes* — commonly referred to as the *visual cortex* — lose mass, too. The occipital lobes' ability to process visual information falters, but like your temporal lobes, they have to deal with inadequate information coming in. This lack of information to process is largely due to the deterioration of your optic nerve and retina.

To keep your occipital lobes functioning well:

- ✔ Attend art and photo exhibits.
- ✔ Go on sightseeing trips.
- ✔ Share your pictures with friends and relatives.
- ✔ Use eyeglasses if you have them.

Because the occipital lobes are responsible for interpreting visual information, doing things that demand visual memory provides a good workout for the lobes.

Keeping your neurons from shrinking

The shrinking in your brain isn't due only to the loss of water. Your *dendrites* shrink, too. Your dendrites form the part of your neurons that reach out to other neurons and draw in information. The fewer dendrites, the less opportunity to think and form memories from multiple channels.

This problem explains the tendency of some older people to lose track of conversations or complex sections in books. Their *dendritic connections* have decreased, limiting the complexity of each thought and each memory.

The more you challenge yourself intellectually, the more your brain grows new dendritic connections with other neurons. I come back to this point repeatedly: *Your brain can make new dendritic connections throughout your life despite your age.* One great way to fight the trend of memory loss is to learn new information, challenge yourself to branch out, and think in ways you haven't before.

Keeping pleasure in your life

One effect of aging is that pleasant memories hold less joy for you as you age. A related effect is that you may blurt out things you later regret. (Is that familiar behavior among your elderly relatives?) In both cases, the cause is well understood, and you can do some things to slow or reverse the trend.

Your *synapses* are the connections between your neurons. They decrease in number as you age. You need these synapses to form and access memories because the degree of strength of your synaptic connections determines the relative strength of particular memories. However, as you age, the density of these synaptic connections thins out. This thinning out means that connectivity of your thoughts and memories thins out, as well.

The neurotransmitter *dopamine,* so strongly associated with feelings of pleasure, loses receptors as you age. Receptors are on the receiving end in your synapses. As early as age 20, you begin to lose dopamine receptors, and every decade thereafter you lose 6 percent of your dopamine receptors. That's how the decline in pleasurable memories occurs.

Dopamine is particularly active in your frontal lobes (I discuss the frontal lobes earlier in this chapter). The decrease of dopamine activity in your frontal lobes makes you more prone to absentmindedness and short-term memory problems and reduces your sense of emotional regulation — that's where the blurting out comes in. When you're absentminded, it is because of attention, and your frontal lobes regulate attention.

Reverse this trend. Expand your range of pleasurable activities:

- ✔ Push yourself to do things that other people say are fun.
- ✔ Go see movies that are comedies.
- ✔ Read books that have a comic flair.
- ✔ Share jokes with your friends.
- ✔ Do things that you remember were fun to you in the past.

Closing the window on your NMDA receptors

You have a receptor called *N-methyl-D-asparate* (NMDA) that makes protein for one of the neural gateways for your memory. Your NMDA receptors lie at the synaptic level, and they stay open when they receive different signals at the same time. They help orchestrate the flow of information from one neuron to another through your synapses. When they're activated, they help groups of neurons fire together to form memories. As you age, these NMDA receptors stay open for shorter periods; hence, your memories may become more simplistic. Instead of remembering all the details of an event, you'll remember the basics.

Avoiding those patchy-memory scams

Unfortunately, con artists often seek out the elderly to scam. These unscrupulous types prey on aging people's patchy memories. For example, in Cleveland, Ohio, seniors were warned of a scam called, "Where's the check?"

The con artists called seniors and, in the course of conversation, surreptitiously picked up as much personal information as possible. After a day or two, they called again, knowing that the seniors had a vague familiarity with them but

probably weren't able to identify who they were. Then the con artists said, "We received your $1,500 check, but you sent too much. You were only supposed to send in a check for $1,000. Why don't we tear up the one we have? Please send us one for the right amount." The con artists, of course, didn't have their original checks, but they soon did receive the new checks.

Becoming an Old Dog Who Remembers New Tricks

The old adage that you can't teach old dogs new tricks doesn't have to apply to you. Old dogs become so by relying on *old* tricks.

The problem with some people in their advanced years is that they misuse memory techniques. They may try to remember everything in the same way. They may say to themselves, "This is the way I've always done it, and I'm not about to change now." Or, "It's worked for me all my life, and you want me to change when I'm almost ready to cash in my chips?"

If you learn new tricks as you age, you won't have the syndrome of the old dog.

Stay young by not retiring from life. Don't think of yourself as over the hill. Don't use phrases like, "Back in my day. . . ." Today is still your day if you want it to be.

Branching out of routine

Many of the memory problems older adults complain about relate to experiences that fall outside of a routine. You probably rarely forget to brush your teeth or take a shower. You do those things every day, so they become habits. You don't have to think about them or make plans to do them.

Slips in your memory occur when you have to remember to do something that's not part of your routine.

If you're elderly, you must get out of the mindset of thinking that you're too old to use your mind in a new way. You have your routines perfected down to the exact time each day. However, you may have memory problems when you have to do something outside of your routine. Breaking out of routine and trying something new keeps you alert and activated mentally. Otherwise, you are flying on automatic pilot.

As you age, you may have the tendency not to scrutinize your memories. You may jump to conclusions and actually "remember" something that, in fact, didn't occur. You're especially at risk of remembering incorrectly if the activity or occurrence was outside of your routine.

For instance, suppose that you waved to a friend as you drove into the supermarket parking lot while she was driving out. Later that day, another friend mentions that she saw Betty at the supermarket. You know that you often see Betty shopping there, too. You say, "Oh yes, I saw her, too." The fact was, you saw a friend at the supermarket, but it wasn't Betty. That friend was actually Marjorie, but that fact slips your mind.

The point here isn't that routines are bad; they're useful and help us get things done. But to keep young, you need to engage in behaviors that go beyond routine. Doing so is good for your brain and good for your memory ability.

Following people as they age

Psychologists have found that the elderly possess a rich and varied knowledge base and either can match or outperform their younger counterparts in many skills.

Since 1958, researchers from Johns Hopkins University Medical Center have closely followed normal, healthy adults as they've aged. These adults were evaluated every two years in a variety of ways, including medical and psychological tests. Despite popular belief, people didn't lose their mental abilities. Their vocabularies continued to expand, and their reasoning skills were enhanced. The only ways that they did apparently decline were in reaction time, attention span, and short-term memory. Long-term memory remained intact.

The education edge

Studies have shown that 70-year-olds with college and graduate degrees outscore younger high-school dropouts on many measures of cognitive ability. In addition, depending on the health of the 70-year-olds, they sometimes outscore middle-aged people who graduated from high school.

Study after study has shown that people who stay active intellectually in their later years build up resistance to cognitive decline. Think of it this way: If you're so unfortunate as to suffer one of the tragic brain-wasting diseases, such as Alzheimer's disease, you'll have far more reserve intellectual ability to lose than someone whose intellectual activity is composed of watching television all day or stewing over what went wrong at the store the last time they shopped. To put it simply: The more intellectual abilities you have, the more you'll have in reserve to compensate for any future loss.

For this reason, when using psychological tests, I have greater difficulty detecting signs of cognitive decline among those who were very bright before the testing. If a person would've scored in the superior range before and he now scores in the high average range, that's a decline. But what if I didn't know that he scored so highly before? I might misinterpret his current high score as a sign that he's still doing well. This problem is why other psychologists and I always have to know "the previous level of functioning."

Numerous studies have shown that people who have the greatest degree of education experience the least memory decline. This result works on the principle that the more you expand your mind, the better you'll be able to use it — even during declines.

You're never too old to become more educated. In fact, you're actually becoming more educated right now, by reading this book. Don't stop with this one!

You need to stay alert to the world around you. Try to do the following:

✔ Vary your activities.

✔ Choose different routines.

✔ Take daily walks, but vary the route.

Educating your memory skills

The more educated you are, the less susceptible you are to memory loss. No one is quite sure why, but experts generally believe that a greater degree of education allows you to use your brain in a variety of ways.

Choosing your company in old age

Experts know that people who lead full and varied lives in old age suffer less from degenerative brain diseases. They stay young longer. You can, too.

I've met several people in my life who personify staying young in old age. Twenty-five years ago, I had the thrill of meeting one of the twentieth century's most famous psychological theorists, Eric Erickson. He was an elder statesman at the San Francisco Psychoanalytic Institute because of his contribution to our understanding of how people develop psychologically as they age.

In the last few years of his life, Erickson and his wife chose to live in a house with young people. He pointed out that he wanted to keep his mind young and challenged. He dreaded taking up a life of routine and mental retirement. By staying with young people, he made sure that he'd be challenged, be on his mental toes, and stay sharp.

The more you think in novel ways, the greater the number of connections between your neurons. In other words, although you may not have any more neurons than your less-educated counterpart, you'll provide yourself with many more connections between your neurons.

These connections provide you with many more ways to code and recall memories. As you advance in age, those more numerous connections allow you to resist the decline in memory and cognitive abilities experienced by your less-educated counterparts.

Getting artsy

Many people in their advanced years begin to cultivate an aesthetic sense. You can be one of them. Like those people, you can take art classes, go to concerts, garden, or do whatever pleases your sense of aesthetics.

My father, now close to 80, wasn't an artist earlier in his life (he was a judge and prosecuting attorney), but he now takes art classes on a regular basis. He's a frequent visitor to art museums and has season tickets to three different symphony orchestras in three different cities.

He has been an inspiration. He's still taking college classes and has covered everything from geology to advanced painting. Every year, he travels from Asia to Europe by himself. He's proud that now, on his fourth trip to Paris where he stays for three weeks, he knows the city like his own.

Many colleges and universities are finding that people in retirement can be some of the best students. They're in school because they want to be there. They attend to learn for the sake of learning, whereas some of their younger fellow students are going to school as a means to get a good job later.

Several colleges and universities throughout the United States have tuition-reduction programs, and some even spend money on providing seniors with special housing. Take advantage of these opportunities; give your memory the education edge. The advantages are:

- ✔ You think about things from more angles.
- ✔ Your perspective enlarges; you see the bigger picture.
- ✔ Your memories have more dimensions — more associations.

Start a new to-do list with these items:

- ✔ Take classes
- ✔ Go to concerts
- ✔ Travel
- ✔ Turn off the television

Part IV
Exercising Your Memory Every Day

The 5th Wave   By Rich Tennant

"There's only one item on this list I actually need. But who'd remember to look at a list with only one item on it?"

In this part . . .

In Part IV, I accompany you on your daily rounds at school, at work, or on the social scene; and I show you how to maximize your memory in everyday situations. Do you have an exam coming up? Take a look at Chapter 13 for time-tested tactics you can employ to do better on exams. Do you sometimes feel your memory is unraveling in the speed of this postmodern age? Chapter 16 contains advice for slowing down and remembering more information. In short, Part IV covers the territory. Welcome aboard!

Chapter 11

Schooling Memory

- -

In This Chapter

▶ Organizing your learning

▶ Figuring out how to remember deeply

▶ Searching for the meaning of the subject

▶ Taking notes that you can remember

- -

*H*ow you study is very different from *how much* you study. This difference is the same as the difference between quantity and quality. Simply studying "hard" or "a lot" can be like spinning your wheels if you don't do it correctly.

Instead of spinning, you want your wheels to make traction. The traction here is your memory of what you've studied. How you study determines whether you spin your wheels or make traction. Choosing the right techniques can improve the quality of your studying and make sure that you don't spin your wheels by wasting time.

In this chapter, you discover how to make the most of your time and how to ensure that you remember what you learn.

Organizing Your Recall

Organizing your studies is not something that you do only if you're obsessive-compulsive. It's something that good students do. Organized learners remember more, and the bottom line is that's what learning is all about.

Your recall of important information depends more on *how* you organize information in your mind than on *how much* material you've memorized.

Think of loading files on your computer. If you simply save the material on your hard drive with no organization to where you put it, you may have a great deal of difficulty trying to access the information later. You've not only wasted time accumulating random pieces of information, but now you don't know where to find it.

Think how much easier it would be to retrieve the information if you had placed it in clearly marked files along with related material.

REMEMBER

When preparing to remember important information, you must ask yourself the following questions:

- ✔ How is this information organized? (For example, is the information a poem, a mathematical equation, a speech?)
- ✔ How will I be required to recall the information? (For example, will I have to stand in front of a class and recite it, answer a question on an exam?)

These questions have a bearing on what method you use to learn the information. The way you learn the information prepares you for the way you recall it.

For example, if you want to remember a series of events that are described in your history book, you'd be wise to understand the *context* in which the events took place.

Recognition: The police line-up of memory

You remember in many ways. Sometimes, you don't have to search your mind to recall a memory. It's right in front of you to recognize.

Recognition is much easier than recalling a memory. If you can't remember through free recall, recognition allows you one more chance to remember.

A multiple-choice exam is a type of recognition method. For example, if you're asked:

What is the most demanding way to remember information?

a) Free recall

b) Recognition

c) Standing on your head

d) True or false question

You'll recognize that the right answer is *a) Free recall.*

Another form of recognition is the police line-up. Often, six or seven individuals are lined up, and a witness is asked which one of those people standing in the line-up they saw at the crime scene. The idea is that the simple presence of the prime suspect is meant to jog the witness's memory into recognizing him.

Yet, this form of recognition is now controversial in criminal justice because it's a forced-choice question. In an exam at school, the teacher knows for sure that the right answer is offered among the four possibilities. However, in a police line-up, no one really knows if the prime suspect is the one who deserves that forced-choice recognition.

Suppose that you're trying to remember the creation of the Works Projects Administration (WPA). If you understand the context in which it was created — the massive unemployment and the poor shape of our public works — it might hang in your memory longer. Also, if you think about the full context of the Great Depression, the WPA makes more sense because you understand the context in which it was created.

You may even want to use mnemonic devices to remember names and dates. The initials themselves *W* and *P* help code the memory, and you can remember that people were **w**orking on **p**rojects. (Turn to Chapter 8 for more on mnemonic devices.)

Stretching out your learning

Procrastination and laziness are two reasons why you may wait until the night before to study for an exam. (Head to Chapter 13 for details on remembering for an exam.) Another reason is that you may think that doing so is a good way to study, believing that studying at the last minute will keep the information fresh in your mind.

This method of studying is called *cramming*. Cramming is a way to forget, not remember.

Cramming may be marginally useful if you're going to be tested right after the cramming session. However, its usefulness also depends on the material you learn. The material needs to be relatively superficial information, such as name recognition. It the information gets more complex than that, don't cram. You'll remember very little.

Another frequent mistake that many students make is to stay up late burning the midnight oil the night before the exam. Not only does this late-night cramming contribute to poor memory, but the sleep deprivation makes your mind less able to concentrate enough to recall that superficial information (see Chapter 7 for details on the role of sleep in memory).

Make sure that you get enough sleep the night before an exam. Even superficial knowledge can be accessed more easily if you're well rested.

Because cramming is such an ineffective learning method, it's just a waste of your time. Sure, you may remember a little for the test the next morning, but you should ask yourself why you didn't take the time to actually learn the material.

Economize your time. If you've been told that you need 20 hours of studying on a particular subject, don't spend all those hours in a concentrated period. Spread those hours out over the days and even weeks before the exam.

Think of the information as seeds needing fertile ground to grow in. You won't harvest much of a crop unless the seeds are tended. You want to be picking up the fruit and vegetables from that garden for years to come.

As you spread out your studying of a subject, you'd be wise to do a quick review of what you learned the previous session — not only to tune yourself up for more information, but also to be able to build on top of it. Most subject areas are cumulative. That is, to master the subject, you need to build on each lesson.

Follow these steps:

1. **Study at first study session (sowing the seeds).**

2. **Review (letting the rain fall on the crops).**

3. **Study again (fertilize).**

4. **Review (let the sun shine on the crop).**

When organizing your required time to study, don't thin out your time too much. You don't want each session to be so brief that you barely allow yourself to get a whiff of the material before closing the book.

If you use the 20-hour allotment that I identify earlier in this chapter, the best way to divide your time would be to spread your 20 hours over the next ten weeks, two hours per week. If you study daily for ten weeks, you'll study ten minutes per day. That's not enough! Instead of barely sitting down before you close the book, you need to allow yourself time to absorb the information.

On the other extreme, if you concentrate your studying time to four five-hour blocks, you should anticipate becoming tired and needing a break. If you don't take a break, you may waste time daydreaming or thinking about something completely irrelevant to the subject that you're trying to concentrate on.

Taking a break not only allows your mind time to rest up but also allows you to integrate and absorb the information.

Sectioning learning

Unless you're taking just one subject at school, you'll have a lot to study. What do you do if you have many subjects to study in one night?

If you go from one subject to another without a break between studying each subject, you run the risk of not allowing yourself the transition. That transition is critical because you want to be ready to absorb new information.

You can separate your study time for biology and math by taking a break or even going to a different room. Here, you're controlling the context in which you're learning the information. You may even want to use a different pen for each subject or write notes for one subject and use the computer for another.

If possible, segregate the times you spend on each subject. Maybe biology is before dinner, and math is after dinner.

Learning deeply

Not only do you need to make sure that the information you're committing to memory is well organized and learned over time, but you also need to know the *context* of that information — how this information relates to other information you remember.

You also need to build a body of information that can grow over time. You need to know how it applies to other information that you've learned.

For example, when learning a foreign language, you need to be able to conjugate verbs, learn vocabulary, string together a sentence, and respond conversationally to someone in the context in which you're meeting them.

If you sputter out a crude, "You were okay?" in a foreign language instead of "How are you?" the person you're meeting may be pleased by your making an effort to speak her language, but she's probably not going to go beyond saying, "Fine. And you?" She's noticed your poor sentence construction and inappropriate verb usage.

Speaking a new language requires more than learning a few words. You need to learn the many facets of the language. If you try to take in a brief Berlitz tape before a trip to France, you'll remember much less than if you were to take an immersion course, live in France, or read a copy of *French For Dummies,* by Dodi-Katrin Schmidt, *et al.*, published by Wiley.

In this way, the body of information that you learn forms the basis for more learning. Without forming this body, you wouldn't allow yourself the opportunity to interlink new information and probably would forget it.

Relearning

Another way to make sure that you remember is to *relearn* the subject matter. Relearning is almost like dusting off an old bookshelf. By the second and third time, you learn the information; the previous memories are freshened up. Relearning, or freshening up, memories deepens your knowledge of the subject.

A good example of relearning is taking a course in a specific language over again. I've taken Spanish several times throughout my life. Each time I take it, I get a little better, and understanding and speaking becomes a bit easier. (You may be saying, "Well, I would hope so! Are you dense?")

I'll sidestep that question to go on with my point. Learning a language requires *practice*. Because I get little chance to practice Spanish outside of my infrequent trips to Latin America and Spain, I need to relearn my Spanish-speaking skills.

Yet my friend is much more able to speak Spanish. Every time he relearned Spanish, his knowledge of it deepened. The key is that he began taking Spanish earlier and more consistently, whereas I jumped from language to language, barely skimming the surface.

Putting relearning and direct recall together

Relearning by taking a course a second time (or a third time) is a luxurious way to improve your memory, I admit, and I know that, most of the time, you don't have that option. You have to take the shorter, harder route of *direct recall*. The big problem with direct recall is that it's open-ended, kind of like staring into space and hoping that you spot a shooting star of a memory.

You can make direct recall work better if you box it in with some relearning techniques. Suppose that you're asked to name the capitals of all the states on the East Coast of the United States, recalling a lesson from the past. When you begin thinking, you may decide to use the *cued recall* approach, using the state name to remind you of the capital city name, like this:

Maine: _____

New Hampshire: _____

Massachusetts: _____

Rhode Island: _____

Connecticut: _____

New York: _____

New Jersey: _____

Maryland: _____

Delaware: _____

Virginia: _____

North Carolina: _____

South Carolina: _____

Georgia: _____

Florida: _____

If your teacher sees you sweating bullets and is tenderhearted, he may offer an additional cue to help you make an association — the first letter of each capital city:

Maine: A_____

New Hampshire: C_____

Massachusetts: B_____

Rhode Island: P_____

Connecticut: H_____

New York: A_____

New Jersey: T_____

Maryland: A_____

Delaware: D_____

Virginia: R_____

North Carolina: R_____

South Carolina: C_____

Georgia: A_____

Florida: T_____

I use this example because it's information that you've probably encountered before, and when you went over the list, you probably challenged yourself to remember the capitals again. You relearned the material.

What if you were to relearn the list of the presidents of the United States? If I asked you to list them in order, you'd be performing a *serial recall task*. (A serial recall task is one in which you remember information, such as the list of presidents in historical order.)

Suppose that I ask you to list the first 12 and give you only the first letter of each of the last names:

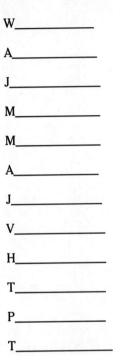

W_____

A_____

J_____

M_____

M_____

A_____

J_____

V_____

H_____

T_____

P_____

T_____

In this case, you were relearning information by using a *peg first-letter cue* in a serial arrangement. As you can see, the peg technique cues your recall by using the first letters of the presidents' surnames in historical order (see Chapter 8 for details on pegs and Chapter 9 for more on serial techniques). By requiring yourself to use a peg cue to recall information you learned previously (such as the previous example), you'll probably remember it well into the future.

Striving for Meaning Instead of Rote

Rote learning is the regurgitation of unattached and meaningless facts. These facts are prone to be forgotten because you haven't incorporated them into a body of knowledge.

Unfortunately, still too much of what's required in school is based on rote learning. Your job is to deepen the meaning of what you learn, so that you'll be able to remember it later.

To have knowledge means that you understand the meaning of facts, how they're organized, and how they fit into what you already know about a particular subject area. Because the meaningfulness of information determines how well you remember it, rote memorization isn't exactly the best method and is probably a setup that's best forgotten. (Maybe schools will someday realize this truth, too.)

An example of rote learning would be to try to memorize the list of presidents I highlighted in the last section without any association or memory cues.

When you try to remember the list by factoring in meaning, you may consider, for example, that George Washington was the principal general who helped the colonies gain independence from England. In addition, the three presidents to follow were major contributors to the Declaration of Independence and the Constitution.

How well the information that you're trying to remember is organized has a lot to do with the degree of its meaningfulness. So, the more meaningful the information is, the more likely you are to remember it.

Having some interest in the subject matter that you're trying to commit to memory is helpful. This interest forms part of the meaning that you can attach to the information to help you remember it.

For example, many people complain that they have little interest in mathematics, yet they're required to learn it nevertheless. You may say, "I'm no good at math." Because of either your lack of interest or your self-paralyzing fear of math, you create a self-fulfilling prophecy — you don't retain what you learn.

My wife has described how much difficulty she had with math in grade school, college, and graduate school. She said that she "didn't have that type of mind." I knew differently. I knew that if she applied herself to it, she would master the subject.

Before her comprehensive exams for her master's degree, she was worried that she'd forget the math related to the statistics she was required to know. (Believe it or not, math, in the form of statistics, was part of the comprehensive exams for a degree in art education!)

To help my wife, I did a few hypnotic sessions with her to try to help her get over the fear and percolate some interest in the subject. I gave her posthypnotic suggestions that she would find the math as easy as tying her shoes. She was the only one that year to pass her comprehensive exams with distinction.

Prior to taking my licensing exam for my practice of psychology, I knew that I had to learn math-related statistics inside and out. Although I managed to get through statistics classes during college with little trouble, I had little interest in the subject and was worried that I wouldn't remember what I'd learned. Nevertheless, I knew that in order to get my license, I had to pass an exam that 64 percent of the test-takers would fail.

I knew that my only hope was to develop an interest in the subject. The more I studied it, the better appreciation I had for the subject matter. I began to reflect on the broad meaning of the mathematical equations. I found myself actually enjoying it after a while. Statistics became a language that I was beginning to understand.

Now, I have a confession to make that illustrates another fact about memory. I recognize formulas from statistics but can't remember what they mean anymore. However, if I take time to relearn statistics, I will probably manage to learn it at a quicker rate than I had originally and will remember it longer. The key word is *if*. I think I'll pass now and enjoy writing about memory instead.

If you're trying to remember something, you can always *think around it*.

For example, suppose that you're trying to remember who was president of the United States after Abraham Lincoln. If you think around the question, perhaps you'll touch on Reconstruction and then move back to Lincoln. Perhaps you'll move back to the Civil War and then to the surrender at Appomattox. You begin to wonder which two generals were present. Robert E. Lee for the South, of course, and Ulysses S. Grant for the North. Hey, wasn't Grant later elected president?

This chain of associations is like a series of links that you may click as you surf the Internet. As you read about the Civil War on one page, you click on the blue hypertext word *Appomattox*. Then at that page, you click on the word *generals*. These links are associations. They each focus on one topic, but they link and relate to similar topics and give you a broader knowledge base.

Taking Notes and Remembering What You Heard at Lectures

More than 25 years ago, I gave a series of lectures on note taking at Northern Arizona University. At that time, I was a teaching assistant and a graduate assistant — cheap labor, basically. The fact was, I knew very little about note taking besides what I taught myself.

So I gave a lecture to my students on the Middle East, where I had spent the previous six months. I told them to watch for inflections in my voice and pauses punctuated by short stares. These, I pointed out, mean that the lecturer wants to highlight a point. If he looks at your notepaper, he expects that you take down what he just said. Unfortunately, my lecture focused too much on watching the lecturer and not enough on listening to the content of the lecture.

You're often going to be slightly familiar with some of the information presented during a lecture. For example, my students knew a little about the Middle East, but not much. Your task is to link up the new information that you're not familiar with to what you already know and perhaps modify that preexisting knowledge base, making associations and links.

Some people take notes during a lecture and never read them over again. Don't be one of those people! Although you probably *will* remember *some* main points if you only take notes and never go over them, think of all the information you're throwing away. Your notes provide a condensed outline of what the lecture was about from your perspective, which can be very useful for learning the material in a meaningful way to ensure that you'll remember it well.

Try to go over your notes soon after the lecture while everything is still fresh in your mind. Doing so can help you code the information more thoroughly into memory.

As you go over your notes, you can highlight, scratch out, or add to what you have written down. You'll have a better picture of the subject matter and of how all the elements of information are integrated into a whole body of knowledge.

Highlighting is a great way to bring out the major points. Some people underline; others use a highlighter. Either way, you're making your next glance at your notes more productive because those highlighted points form the essentials of what you need to remember. From this perspective, you can look back at your notes and make better links between points and what you already knew about the information.

Use diagrams and visual props in your notes whenever possible. The use of visual images can help anchor concepts into memory. These visual images also serve to boil down or connect subjects. For example, if you write words like short-term, long-term, recall, recognition, and so on, and draw arrows to the word "memory," you'll know that they're all related to or part of memory.

When going over the notes, you also want to look for gaps. Ask a peer who was with you at the lecture if he or she "got what the lecturer said about. . . ."

You allow yourself to fill in the gaps of information you missed (which is typical because lecturers often go over material faster than most people can integrate it).

An even better way to fill the gaps in your notes is to go up to the lecturer after class and ask her to fill in the parts you didn't quite get. She'll most likely elaborate and provide you with additional useful information that you can integrate into your long-term memory.

If you can't catch her after the lecture, go early to the next class and ask for clarification on the areas you're still hazy on. You may be better able to formulate a good question, having gone over your notes and read the text. She'll respond by not only answering your questions but maybe even beginning the next lecture in such a way that she integrates what she said previously. She'll also probably think that other students need more clarification as well.

Don't be afraid to approach the lecturer in these ways. The lecturer won't take it as a sign that you're dumb or that you shouldn't be in the class. Rather she'll take it as a sign that you're motivated, interested, and attentive.

I can tell you from the perspective of a lecturer that I appreciate it when students approach me. It gives me an opportunity to tune in better to where the students are and understand my own inadequacies in presenting the information. Without that feedback, I could go on thinking that I was reaching everyone when, in fact, I wasn't. Do yourself and the lecturer a favor — ask questions.

One of the most important prerequisites for memory is attention. If you attend a lecture and only your body is in attendance, you probably won't remember anything. Make sure that your mind's there, too — no matter how boring the lecture may be.

Challenge yourself to see beyond the lecturer's inadequacies and the social scene. Think of the content of the lecture as a destination you must travel as you're blasted by a dust storm. Try to forge ahead with your goggles on and your head tucked. You can see where the lecturer is weakly pointing. Go there and meet the information, even if it's badly presented.

Remembering What You Read

If you're like most people, you've had the experience of reading an entire page and then realizing that you weren't paying attention. Your mind was off daydreaming about what you plan to do on the weekend or what you should've said to that rude store clerk.

Reading retention is a big issue in educational circles. Having the ability to read a sentence, pronounce all the words fluently, and have a vocabulary wide enough that doesn't necessitate referring to a dictionary is one thing. But having the ability to remember what you read is something else entirely. If you can't remember what you read, why read at all?

If you want to make sure that you retain what you read, try to use one or part of the various study systems developed by educators. Along with psychologists, they've been studying how people retain what they read for more than 50 years.

One of the oldest such systems is called *SQ3R*. (Many of these systems have names that make them appear more complicated than they really are.) The SQ3R system works like this:

S = **S**urvey the book.

Q = **Q**uestion. Generate questions based on your survey.

R = **R**ead the book.

R = **R**ecite the material.

R = **R**eview.

To begin with, consider what you do when you open a textbook or nonfiction book that you hope to be able to remember after you've completed it. If you simply barrel into reading it without looking it over, you may find yourself wondering what's coming up or not understanding how the body of knowledge is organized.

Survey the book

The first step in remembering what you read is to survey the material. Scan the book cover to cover. Read the dust jacket (if it has one), the preface, and even the acknowledgments section to get an idea of what the author went through to write the book, who he or she was influenced by, and who made significant contributions.

Scan the table of contents to see how the book is organized and how the chapters present the information. Read the chapter summaries and look at the graphs, pictures, and diagrams. This way, you'll learn a great deal about the subject before you actually read the book. In many ways, you've begun to grasp a glimpse of the big picture that the book offers.

Develop questions

Generate questions based on what you saw in your scan of the book. These questions can provoke other thoughts about what you may expect when reading. Later, during the actual reading (and, remember, you haven't even begun reading yet), some of these questions may be answered as you begin to master the subject matter.

Read the book

The third step in the SQ3R system is to read everything. Don't skim. I'm particularly fond of underlining. For this reason, I rarely borrow someone else's books. If I do borrow one and find that I want to read it, I give it back and buy my own, so I can underline.

I don't just underline. I use a simple system of underlining the main points, leaving out many of the redundant or excess phrases. When I go over the book later, I want those underlined sections to stand out.

Don't underline too much. Not everything you read is intended to be a kernel of truth or the heart of the subject matter. When you go over the material later, you don't want to sift through page after page of over-underlined sentences, wondering why you went crazy with your pen.

In addition to underlining, use vertical lines to the right or left of the text to indicate particular sections that are important. These sections elaborate upon the sections that you underline above or below the vertical lines. Use a double line to indicate that the section is particularly important.

Many people do their underlining on the second reading to ensure that they don't underline points that really aren't that important.

If you don't have time for two readings, you can underline as you do your one read through the material. (Just don't let your highlighter get carried away and underline every word as you read it!) Because I'm a busy person and don't have the time to commit to two readings, that's what I do. Then, I go over what I've underlined.

Recite the material

After you finish reading the entire book, you can now move to the next step of the SQ3R system — reciting. Reciting the material can help you integrate, understand at a deeper level, and pull everything together. If you can explain the material to another person, you really do understand it.

One of the reasons I like to teach is that I'm forced to really get to know the material. I've always said that teaching is learning.

Spend as much time as possible on the material that you weren't quite sure about. As you do, you'll bring it into focus with the material you already understand and deepen your memory of it.

Review main points and notes

Your job isn't completely done yet. The next task is to review. Here's your chance to go over it all again. Make use of your underlined passages and review your notes. In fact, incorporating review into your reading process is always a good idea. After you read each section, review the main points in that section.

Because most forgetting occurs soon after information is read, the reviewing step allows you the opportunity to really lay down those memories in a comprehensive way.

Remembering How to Spell

Spelling can be a stumbling block for many people. English is a smorgasbord of many languages, so many words are spelled in counter-intuitive ways.

Spelling mnemonics are quite useful. Mnemonics are tricks that you can use to remember (see Chapter 8 for details on mnemonics). Look at these examples:

She screamed — emphasizing the three "EEEs" to remember the word *cemetery.*

For letters, you use stationery.

We all have trouble with grammar from time to time, and we often can't spell it, mistakenly spelling it "grammer:"

Gramma *knows her* **grammar.**

Or,

You'll **mar** *your composition with bad grammar.*

You can remember many words by remembering a catchy little sentence such as:

*The Ni**le** Valley is fertile.*

*You can't **tell** an int**ell**ectual anything.*

*The queen **ant** is domin**ant**.*

Chapter 12

Taking a Powerhouse Memory to Work

*U*ntil retirement, most adults spend the majority of their waking hours at work. Your memory is in high demand at work. If you're having any problems with memory, they're sure to show up there.

Your ability to remember can be the difference between being hired and getting fired. Your memory can also be taxed heavily if you're experiencing job stress. Four major factors can affect your memory skills as you face your workday:

- ✔ Attitude
- ✔ Coping skills
- ✔ Effort
- ✔ Focus

In this chapter, I describe practical, everyday suggestions to improve your memory at work and how to apply these four factors to your job. You discover how to keep your memory skills sharp while searching for work, retaining your memory while experiencing job stress, and improving your memory to improve the quality of your work experience.

Interviewing for the Job

You're nervous about an upcoming interview. You really want the job, but you're worried that when you sit down, your mind will go blank. You want to remember to explain details of your skills and how they fit with the company.

You decide that you must look knowledgeable and experienced, so that the interviewers will know that you're prepared to work for them. You also want to make sure that you can anticipate the job demands before they ask you about your skills.

If you're confident about your interview presentation, you can focus on the details of the company that you'll be learning about during the interview. More importantly, if your memory is strong, you can be free to be friendly and engaging and convey a sense of teamwork during this give-and-take session. You want your interviewers to remember you as a complete person, not an automaton. However, the only way you can present this image is to not have to concentrate too hard on remembering what you want to say.

You need to put a memory cue to use to boost your self-confidence. You may want to use a mnemonic device such as a peg. Pegs are cues that aid you in remembering (see Chapter 8 for more on pegs). You may want to use a first letter peg to remind you about the key points that you want to remember during the interview.

For example, if the company produces quality semiconductors for less money than its competitors, that may be easy enough to remember by itself. However, if they have a good research and development program that they've invested millions of dollars in and are seen as being on the cutting edge in the business, you have more to remember.

In this example, make up a word, using the first letters of the points you want to make during the interview. Use the first letter in **Super Cheap Conductors Of** the Future — **SCCOF.** All you need to do is go into the interview and remember that the company isn't anything that you can "sccof" at.

So much of what's on the line in an interview is making a connection with the people who are interviewing you. This connection can be a tall order, especially because you're probably meeting them for the first time. In addition, because you're being evaluated on whether you have the skills to assume the position, focusing on the interviewers can be hard when you're trying to highlight your skills.

The trick to presenting your skills *plus* focusing on the interviewer is to listen very carefully to each interviewer's question to you. Listen for the special spin or slant that you hear in the question. The emphasis and slant that the interviewer attaches to her question reveals how she expects you to answer. When you reply, look directly at the person and try to give your answer the same slant.

For example, you're interviewing for a customer service representative position, and one of the interviewers asks whether you're able to convey concern to a customer while resolving a problem. You can tap into memories of when you empathized with a customer while, at the same time, remaining in a problem-solving mode.

Until the other interviewers show their cards, you don't know their beliefs and opinions. You'll be best served by communicating without conveying any biases. In this case, you want to make sure that you remember how to balance the needs of the customer within the constraints of the company.

You also want to demonstrate that you're personable. To do that, you have to maintain a connection with each of the interviewers, even after you've answered their respective questions. The best way to accomplish this connection is to remember each of their names and use those names during and after the interview. That courtesy shows them that you're a considerate person who pays attention to important details.

One of the problems that some people encounter when using the interviewers' names is to overuse the names. If you repeat someone's name too often, you sound phony.

One of the ways you can use the interviewers' names is to refer to a question by attaching one of their names to it. For example, you may say, "Earlier, when I answered Jack's question about the layaway plan, I forgot to mention that I . . . ."

However, what if you have a hard time remembering people's names in stressful circumstances, such as an interview? You may want to use a few of the techniques for remembering names, such as the following:

- **Repeat the person's name more than once just after you meet him.** This action is subtle, but it gets the name in your mind. When you meet the person, as you shake his hand, say something like, "Jack . . . nice to meet you, Jack."

- **Associate that name with a unique facial characteristic.** When associating a person's name with a unique facial characteristic, look for a prominent feature (see Chapter 14 for more on how to use this trick). For example, perhaps Jack has a crooked nose. You may think to yourself it almost looks as if it's jack-knifed. As you try not to stare at Jack's nose, you code his name in your memory as, "jack-knifed nose Jack."

- **Associate the name with the question they ask.** Perhaps old Jack is throwing some tough questions your way. You may think to yourself that Jack's hacking at you with his questions. Perhaps, you find him to be as irritating as a jackhammer, and you wish that someone else would take over the questions. (Or, Jack may come across as a total jackass, but that may be too risky.)

Remembering How to Pass Political Probation

Getting through probation can be the most difficult period of anyone's job. Not only do you have to figure out how to perform the job with precision, you also have to figure out how to remember all the procedures that this new job entails. What's more, you have a completely new cast of characters to remember — new co-workers, supervisors, and the overall organizational structure. There's a lot to remember during this six-month period when you're put to the test.

You're well aware that those individuals who'll decide whether you stay on the job are evaluating your performance. If you appear to be unable to catch on, you're at risk of being let go.

The person who's evaluating you is your supervisor. However, you may not have as much contact with her as you do with your co-workers. These people are measuring you up and forming opinions of you during the first few months, trying to see whether they like you and whether you're a competent colleague. You want to try to get to know these people and develop a good rapport with them, but be careful. As is often the case in most work environments, you'll soon encounter office politics. Your office may be full of cliques and factions, some of which are in opposition to your supervisor. As you adapt to this new social environment, you may run the risk of over-identifying with one of these groups that has gotten under your supervisor's skin. Don't forget that you're still on probation. Right now, you can't afford to get on the boss' bad side.

Suppose that you want to remind yourself not to get sucked into any factions. Olivia, Tina, and Henry represent such a faction. Rearrange the names and use the first letter of each name to come up with the word **HOT** from **H**enry, **O**livia, and **T**ina. When you think of the word **HOT,** you'll be reminded of how getting too close to them can be dangerous.

Because you're often overwhelmed with meeting new people and learning new procedures while you're at work, remembering this cast of characters can be quite difficult. To make sure that you're catching on to who's who, periodically try to describe the social scene to your spouse or a friend when you get home in the evening. When you describe the scene, make sure that you make note of your supervisor's expectations. This step can help you remember what you need to do to meet your supervisor's expectations while you're simultaneously swimming around in the social stew of office politics.

While you're in the midst of trying to get to know your co-workers, you may need to remind yourself that your future with the company depends on your supervisor's opinion of you. You may want to schedule periodic meetings with her to track your progress and get a feel for how she feels you're doing so far.

Dealing with Passwords and Procedures

Your workplace is probably saturated with a maze of passwords and procedures that you have to wade through before you can even get to your work. Many offices have intensified their security systems, so that just to get in the front door you must not only present your ID but also apply a password. After you sit down to your computer, you still have to follow various procedures and apply another password before you can use it.

In my office, I start my day by getting into my computer via a password, so I can get to my e-mail (which requires another password), the scheduling system (applying another password), and the registration system (with one more password). Then, I go on to my voice mail system to retrieve my phone messages, but I have to apply yet one more password.

This chain of procedures may not be so bad if you only had to learn the passwords once and commit that information to memory. But chances are, your systems are like mine and require that you change your passwords and procedures periodically. You're told that you need rotating passwords to ensure that your identity is secure and that others are locked out of your workstation. In your frustration, you feel that you're the only one locked out.

You need a method that serves as the backbone, so you can easily remember the passwords and procedures. Because you choose your passwords, you have the opportunity to make sure that they cluster around the backbone.

Choose passwords that are both personal and rotating. Recycle your passwords.

If, for example, you and your family have pets, they undoubtedly all have names. Use the names on a rotating basis, but be sure to mix in a numeral or two for further password security. Every time the network administrator decides to torture you with the message that your password has "expired," don't get sidetracked on fantasies of expiring him. Rotate another numbered pet name into the new password slot. Keep the names alphabetized, so that you'll remember them in order.

If you don't have any pets, use the lyrics of a song, such as: *The answer is blowing in the wind.*

Remembering New Technology

You may be one of the millions of people who've found the new technologies that rushed into the workplace to be intimidating. In that case, you may complain of what many people have called *tech stress.*

How I blitzed techblock with a mnemonic

Almost 15 years ago, when I began to work in the Kaiser Permanente System, high-tech gadgetry poured into the healthcare system. Computers were used for scheduling, medical information, and e-mail. Pagers and voice mail were used for on-call duty, and on and on. Just about everything had a password. I not only had to learn an entirely new healthcare system, but also how to use all the high-tech gadgets.

I decided to construct my passwords and my attitude to blitz through the intimidation barrier. I decided to use the word *easy* as a password and a mantra for my adjustment to all the new gadgets. Soon I found it all not only easy but also immensely helpful.

The new computer system, voice mail system, beepers, cell phones, video conferencing, and hand-held planners may all seem like a series of assaults. You may even find that your ability to remember how to turn them off drifts away. You may also find that your memory for other aspects of your job is failing because of having to figure out the new systems.

The high-tech invasion is here to stay. Your resentment of it is only going to contribute to your stress and complicate your memory skills.

Invest the energy you were wasting in resentment into learning the new systems. You'll not only remember more about how to use — and yes, even turn on — these tech devices, but you'll also improve your memory for other aspects of your job because your mind won't be so drained and, as a result, you'll have more energy to focus your attention.

Be knowledgeable and be at the forefront of the use of these tools. Take advantage of any opportunity that presents itself, such as:

- Taking any company or community class on computers, voice mail, and so on

- Joining a staff/management committee that oversees and makes recommendations regarding the deployment of the new technologies in your company

- Making big use of your tech support team (Don't be afraid to ask for tutorials and consultations. They'll be glad to help you figure things out.)

- Learning from your colleagues

Satisfying Customers

Whatever the type of work you perform, your company has probably embraced the new "customer focus" trend. Even the healthcare system where I work, the Kaiser Permanente Medical Centers (the largest HMO in the United States), has reorganized into "Customer Service Areas," or CSAs for short.

You can't call for service in a company without hearing the message, "This call may be monitored for quality assurance." The quality that the canned message refers to is how the person you'll talk to will accommodate you as a "valued" customer.

My wife took a break from her art teaching and coordinating career to sell art in a gallery for one year. She worked hard to remember her customers, many of whom visited the gallery several times. She knew that her pay was tied to her commission from the sales, and those sales increased if she remembered details about her customers.

When you're dealing with customers of whatever type, your memory is going to be taxed. But you can maximize your relationship with a customer if you remember his or her

- Name
- Likes and dislikes
- Buying habits
- Hometown
- Occupation

Trying to combine many of these descriptions of the person into one memory is good practice. For example, when my wife encountered a repeat customer named Paul, she noticed that he was particularly fond of paintings that were neo-cubist. She learned that he worked as a professor at a local university and taught Spanish. She decided that remembering him as Pablo combined his interest in cubist (Picasso) paintings and his local professorial role as a Spanish teacher.

As you tap into your memory of your customers, bring up things you remember about them. With Paul, my wife said, "I thought of you while at a Picasso exhibit this weekend."

Of course, later I asked her why she thought of this man while we were at the Picasso show. She assured me that her thoughts were directed toward increasing sales!

Here's another example. Suppose that you're a dental hygienist. You know that you need to engage in pleasant conversation with your patients as they sit down in the dental chair. If you're not pleasant, they may not come to have you scrape and pick at their teeth.

Bob, a jolly man with a rather large belly, sits down in the chair. You discover that he works for the nearby bakery. As you work, you notice that his teeth reveal that he eats too many sweets. When you let him know that he needs to cut back on the sugar to help his teeth, he tells you that he just loves to eat the jellyrolls that he bakes. You decide to remember him as, "Jolly old Bob who eats too many jelly rolls on the job." That'll work fine as long as you keep that trick your own little secret. After all, Bob's a nice person, and you don't want to hurt his feelings.

Dealing with Deadlines

Your boss gives you a deadline to finish a project, and you cringe. You know that the date he's giving you will make it extremely difficult for you to finish it without setting everything else you have to do aside. You wonder how you're going to do this assignment without pulling out all your hair.

Feeling so overwhelmed with this daunting task, you find yourself not being able to remember even the most basic steps you must take to begin the project. Your memory for the important details blurs with the irrelevant and unimportant details.

To complete this task, you're going to need to develop a way that you can remember what you're doing while you're in the midst of details. You're going to need your memory skills to stay on track.

To deal with the overwhelming pressure of a deadline, use the chunk-and-step-back approach. Start by taking a broad look at the entire project and then break it up in chunks — in mini tasks. Then proceed by taking on one chunk at a time. Step back between chunks to get a perspective to see how the chunks fit into the overall project.

Say that you work at a grocery store, and your boss tells you that you must come up with a plan to reorganize the produce department so that it can be re-opened after the holiday. Of course, the first thing you'll want to do is get over the resentment that you may be counting bananas on Christmas Day.

Next, take a step back and look at the entire project. You realize that you don't have enough time to get everything on paper, so you're going to have to rely on memory and a rough sketch.

After you decide how to break up the fruit and vegetables, you start with chunks of each type of fruit. Organize each chunk by type of fruit — citrus and melons and so on. Then, take a step back to see the whole. Now, you can go count the bananas. The chunk-and-step-back approach helps you avoid mixing apples and oranges.

By using this approach, you allow your memory skills to apply to the task. If you don't use this approach, you'll run the risk of remembering irrelevant details and getting off track. You may meet the deadline, but with the wrong project.

Remembering Your Co-workers

Few jobs exist in isolation. Chances are, your job requires that you work with others. Your collaborative effort is what produces the product or the services for your customers or clients.

Too often, I've heard people say, "I'm good at what I do. If it wasn't for those other people, I'd be able to do an even better job." This kind of self-centered attitude blocks their memory of their interdependence with their co-workers. If you develop the attitude that you're "just there to do the work and can't be bothered by other people," you set yourself up for job stress and, ultimately, memory problems because of it. I help people discover their interdependence with others and maximize their sense of teamwork.

Suppose that you work in a large department store. You may think that just because you're in the bedding department, sheets and comforters have nothing to do with cosmetics and shoes. Sometime in the future, the employees in those departments may have an influence on your potential advancement or longevity in the company. They may influence you directly or indirectly. More importantly, remembering them will make your tenure in the company far more enjoyable.

You can remember your co-workers in a large company by:

✔ Associating their job with a personal characteristic

✔ Connecting their name with a rhyme about their job

✔ Using a facial characteristic to tie in their job

✔ Tying in lyrics to a song to remind you of the person

Use any one of these techniques to remember people at the department store. As is often the case, your first impression of a person may turn out to be not a very good description of the person's personality. However, after you get to know that person better, you won't need the cue anymore. In fact, you may find that your initial impression is totally the opposite of what the person is really like.

Betty works in the shoe department, and you notice that she always wears boots. You hear that she's applying to be a supervisor in your department. You can remember her by a line in a song: *Betty's boots are not going to walk all over me.* She later gets the job and turns out to be a very supportive supervisor.

Fred works in the china department, and you notice that he's a particularly large man. You remember him as a *bull in a china shop.* After you get to know him, you find that he's a very gentle man and anything but bull-like.

Patty works in the cosmetics department, and you notice that she wears a great deal of makeup. In fact, her face almost looks plastic. You remember her as *Plastic Patty.* You get to know her later and find that she's actually a very sweet young woman who happens to be very self-conscious.

You can use your memory skills to improve your collaboration with other people and minimize your job stress. To help facilitate the collaboration, you're going to need to remember a few things about your co-workers. Even those people you have little in common with possess some trait or interest you can relate to, even if it's just the weather or the local baseball team. See beyond the traits that are contrary to yours. Try to remember at least a few of their hobbies or interests.

When you see a co-worker's face, consider it a cue to remember this trait or hobby.

In any team, people have special talents in one area and limitations in others. If you're a supervisor, delegate accordingly. Cue your memories into those talents, so that your team will make the most of their joint effort. Free yourself up from distractions related to their negative traits. Those are easy to find. Look instead for those talents and traits that foster teamwork and collaboration, and you won't have to focus on all those negative memories of an employee's weaknesses.

Invest your efforts into teamwork. By doing so, you take some of the pressure off yourself, and you free up your memory skills to operate at their highest potential.

Stressing Your Memory at Work

Well, you got the job of your dreams, but, sometimes, wish you hadn't. Job stress threatens to put a lock on your memory skills.

When job stress fogs the clarity of your mind, you may find it difficult to focus on the work at hand. Distracted, preoccupied, and overwhelmed with feelings of stress, your memory skills are put on hold.

Working with others is difficult in itself, but assuming you've managed to deal with that, you still have to handle the job itself. Your memory skills can get sidetracked on the job in a variety of ways.

Some of these ways include:

- ✔ Being confused or intimidated by tech stress
- ✔ Being overwhelmed with the workload
- ✔ Being harassed by a supervisor or co-worker

Each of these stressors can serve a body blow to your memory skills. Until you deal with them, your ability to concentrate and maintain a good memory will be sidetracked.

To avoid being sidetracked by these demands, I recommend that you follow these guidelines:

- ✔ Convert your resistance of the new tech workplace into an embrace of it.
- ✔ Consider new assignments as opportunities, not as burdens.
- ✔ When overloaded with the amount of work, compartmentalize the tasks.
- ✔ When harassed, get support from peers, friends, and family. Then, file a grievance and contact upper management.

By following through on these efforts, you'll find that your degree of job stress drops while the integrity of your memory skills rises back up.

I've led a job-stress group for the past seven years. Of the several hundred people I've seen, a very common complaint is a patchy memory. People complain that there are times that they just can't remember where they are and what they're doing there. I help them to defuse that feeling of being so overwhelmed by job stress that they can think of nothing else.

One of the first things I suggest to pull yourself out of the memory lock caused by job stress is to differentiate yourself from your job. In other words, you aren't your job. Your job is your occupation, not your identity.

This step is important because if your sole identity is your job and the job is extraordinarily stressing, you have no break, no time to recuperate. You need to have a life away from work. Your memory (and your sanity) depends on it.

When experiencing job stress, you may have the tendency to think about nothing else but work when you're at home. You need to push yourself to get involved in other activities. Don't sit around and stew in obsessive thoughts about the problems at work.

Follow these guidelines, even if you don't feel like it:

- Increase your social activity.
- Take a class.
- Read.
- Go to lectures.
- Engage in hobbies.

You probably don't feel like doing any of these things because you're over-whelmed with stress, but that's no reason not to do them. In this case, you have to do what you don't feel like doing to get your happiness and your memory skills back.

If you do some of these activities, not only will you gain a sense of differentiation between you and your job, but you will also free yourself up to be alert to the world around you so that you can remember.

Practice good self-care techniques for the sake of your memory skills. Use the following guidelines:

- Exercise on a regular basis.
- Get enough sleep.
- Eat three balanced meals per day.
- Practice relaxation techniques.

I've found that people get through job stress not only by differentiating themselves from their job and practicing good self-care techniques, but also by taking action to deal with the factors that led to the stress. In doing so, you mobilize energy and, therefore, your memory capacity. Try these options:

- Get retrained if you're experiencing job burnout
- If you're in conflict with co-workers, get someone like a supervisor to mediate
- Forgive and let go of petty disagreements
- If you're harassed, file a grievance or take legal action

By taking action, you free yourself up from being distracted by feeling powerless. By mobilizing your energy into solutions, you energize your mind and your memory capacity.

Dealing with a personal attack

Working, at times, can be stressful enough. But if you're experiencing job stress because of your relationships with co-workers, the stress can be so unbearable that your ability to concentrate will be compromised — along with your memory skills.

If you're experiencing job stress because of the way someone at work has treated you, quite possibly your sense of trust for your employer has plummeted. If you're like many people, you may find yourself losing trust in co-workers as well. I work with people to help them regain a sense of trust with "safe" people.

I've seen people who forget that they have allies and friends at work. If you're like many of these people, overwhelmed by harassment from a supervisor, you may globalize your fear. Instead of focusing on that harassing supervisor, you may think that everyone in management is out to get you. You may unintentionally go farther and fear that your co-workers are in cahoots with them. Now, you're in the position of fearing all of THEM. THEY have become a big wall. Your supervisor, management, and your co-workers are part of the same conspiracy. Your memory of your friends and allies is fogged over by the global anxiety about THEM.

Your job is to dissolve your idea of THEM. You need to shift out of black and white thinking and begin to rekindle memories of your friendships.

Don't set yourself up in the trap of wiping out those memories by saying, "Those friendships were all a lie because nobody's rallying to my defense."

As you concentrate on work, you're easily sidetracked by what you think you see in the interactions of others. You forget about all your prior relationships.

Don't allow yourself to get sidetracked by the anger and frustration. As you begin to rekindle the memories of those previous friendships, identify one person whom you felt good about before you started experiencing job stress.

Now for the big challenge: Even though you don't feel terribly trusting of anyone at work and see just a wall of THEM, approach that person you identified and begin to rekindle your friendship. Begin to rebuild your relationships with other people who weren't party to the harassment.

Rekindle your memories of your friendships with them. As you do, the overwhelming wall of THEM will crumble away and what remains will be a clear picture of only those involved in the harassment.

Managing the flood of incoming messages

Imagine yourself arriving at work in the morning to be met by 20 voice mail messages, 26 e-mails (four of which are marked urgent), and 10 old-fashioned paper messages in your mailbox. Whatever do you answer first? Overwhelmed by it all, you begin to sweat, and your breath becomes rapid.

Over the years, I've seen many people who can't seem to close the floodgates of demands. They want to regulate the amount of incoming and outgoing messages and manage their workload, but they get overwhelmed by it all instead. They find their memory failing and wonder if that's why they feel so overwhelmed. The fact is, if they approached the flood and the job duties more reasonably, their memory skills wouldn't be as taxed.

The way to minimize memory problems at work is to regulate the flow of work. You can do this by:

- Prioritizing
- Chunking
- Pacing

You need to decide what task carries the highest priority, the next highest, and so on. All other tasks and phone messages and e-mails take a back seat. Not everyone needs an immediate response.

As you begin to tackle the highest priority assignment, chunk the tasks. *Chunking* involves sectioning off pieces of the job. Only do the amount that's in front of you and needs to be done before the other parts. Don't flood yourself with other tasks. If you do, it's here that your short-term memory will begin to short out.

I've seen scores of people whose jobs have changed dramatically because of corporate downsizing and mergers. Their jobs became the work that two or three people used to perform. I work with them on setting reasonable goals and to bolster their coping skills.

If your job is beyond the capability of one person, your challenge is to do your best but not burn out by trying to do more than you can do. You need to pace yourself. If some work is left undone after you leave that evening, it's not your fault; it's the management's fault for thinking that one person can do it. Talk to your supervisor about your workload and see if the two of you can come up with some sort of solution.

In fact, if you burn the candle at both ends and try to do what you're not capable of doing, management may get the wrong idea. Wearing yourself out by trying to do the job of two people only encourages further downsizing: Management will think that since employees can handle extra-heavy workloads all the time, it becomes expected of them. You're doing them (and yourself) a favor by doing your best, but, at the same time, maintaining a healthy balance between work and your personal life.

By only doing what you can, and doing it to the best of your ability, your memory is left intact, and the quality of your work remains at your highest level. If you try to do more than you can handle, you burn out and dampen your short-term memory because of stress, the quality of work goes down, and you run the risk of being written up for poor work performance. The company loses because the managers think that they just have a poor employee and not a poor reorganization plan.

Surviving the memory of assault

If you were traumatized at work either by harassment that involved a threat of violence or even an assault, you may be so overwhelmed with the experience that you suffer what's called *post traumatic stress disorder (PTSD)*. Your task isn't to forget because you don't want to suppress memories; instead, you want to *de-center* them.

The de-centering of the memories related to the PTSD experience involves working through the feelings of the trauma by talking with people who provide support. The psychotherapeutic work centers on what's called *cognitive reframing*. This approach means that your belief system needs to expand to acknowledge the sad truth that it was, in fact, possible that you experienced an assault outside the range of believable experiences.

By either trying too hard to forget or stewing in the feelings, you end up thinking about and remembering the trauma or harassment as the center of your life. At some point, you need to regroup and go on with your life.

If, on the other hand, you center your work experience on memories of the harassment or assault, you allow no other experience and no other opportunity to develop new memories. You may say, "Well, how can I think about other parts of my work when it's there in front of me all the time?"

If you de-center the memory of the assault, you can see everything that happens to you as not necessarily related to being a victim. You won't over-interpret new experiences as yet another example of being a victim. You won't re-traumatize yourself and will be able to move on with your life.

Doing a to-do list

I've kept a to-do list for 20 years. This list of things to do has not only kept me organized, but also brought me great satisfaction when I can cross off one as *done*.

To-do lists aren't an alternative to developing good memory skills. They're a support for them. Think of the items on your to-do list as cues for your memory. You still have many opportunities to remember details of every item on the list.

Your to-do list must be easy to use and readily available. Abide by the following guidelines when maintaining your list:

- ✔ Avoid clutter by staying with a few words per item.

- ✔ Regularly clean house by re-writing the list after several items have been checked off.

- ✔ Keep only one list because two or more will be redundant and/or disregarded.

- ✔ Prioritize what needs to be done first, second, third, and so on.

Speaking from Memory

Most people try to avoid public speaking. If you're one of them and find yourself delegated the task of giving a presentation at work or in front of the class, your anxiety may shoot up, making your memory ability plummet. High anxiety means short-term memory problems and difficulty retrieving long-term memories (see Chapter 7 for more tips on reducing anxiety).

You can rely on memory aids during the talk. Visual memory aids aren't a cop-out or cheap way to fool the audience into thinking that you know the information. They're a way to enhance the talk.

If the audience has to watch you drone on and on about your subject, you run the risk of having them squirming in their seats. Without something else to look at, you'd have to be incredibly entertaining and prepared to talk with jokes and funny stories. That's just more pressure that you don't need.

What if you don't have the opportunity to make handouts or use high-tech gadgetry? You still need to develop a plan to ensure that you'll remember what you need to say.

To help control your anxiety, go to the room where you'll be giving the presentation. You'll gain confidence as you build associations between elements of your talk and the room itself. If that technique sounds wacky, check out Chapter 8.

You begin to look for cues in the room. Perhaps a particular lamp can jog your memory for some parts of your talk, and the door can be associated with another part.

While practicing the presentation, take note of those cues and the corresponding part of the presentation.

If you don't have access to the room, try to duplicate it as closely as you can. Don't go sit in a hot room to practice your presentation if the room you'll be presenting in is cold.

Try to find a similar room and try to use cues to associate parts of your presentation with windows, doorways, and so on.

In this way, you aren't so rigidly tied to an environment. You can be flexible and adaptive to uncontrollable changing circumstances.

Visually aiding your memory

Your visual aids can serve to offer the condensed high points of your presentation. These points can be provided in diagrams, bullets, or even keywords.

You can present the visual information in a variety of ways. The old way was to write it on a chalkboard or overhead monitor. But that puts pressure on your ability to remember every detail, and you run the risk of presenting a disorganized or even sketchy talk. In addition, if you have handwriting even the slightest bit like mine, it'll be illegible.

A better way to provide yourself and the audience with visual reference points is to have the material already prepared to either hand out or present on the screen.

I'm particularly fond of giving handouts to the people I'm talking to. Handouts can serve as a visual cue for my audience and me, and they can take the information home with them when the presentation is done.

If I also present the same material on an overhead, they can look at their paper or on the screen. Most importantly for me, it provides me with memory cues to keep on track.

In recent years, many people have used numerous computer programs such as Microsoft PowerPoint to present the visual information. These programs are projected onto a screen via your laptop and projector. Every time you move to the next slide or screen or add another point, you click the mouse and the words glide in.

All these visual aids can serve as memory cues — not only for you but also the audience. If they lose themselves in daydreams, they can reconnect with the subject you're presenting by looking back up on the screen or at the paper handout.

Breathing the work

An old Zen Buddhist saying goes, "Zen is not just like chopping wood. Zen *is* chopping wood." This saying means that Zen (meaning the path to enlightenment and clarity of mind) isn't a matter of doing chores or "duty" to get to the clarity, but the entire process of doing the chore is the vehicle to clarity.

Well, that certainly sounds lofty, doesn't it? So what does this have to do with remembering at work? The clarity of mind part is what I want to stress to you. Your short-term memory is fundamentally tied to your ability to pay attention.

Even the most repetitive and seemingly boring type of work is an activity that you can absorb yourself in. You may say to yourself, "But it's so boring that all I can do is watch the clock and count the hours until quitting time." If you do that, you'll probably forget what you're doing and make memory-related mistakes that can come back to haunt you.

For example, a job that sounds extraordinarily boring, such as an assembly line worker in a corn chip factory, can be enriched. Your job is to watch the belt of chips go by and pick out the ones that are burnt or deformed in shape.

As you watch the clock instead of the belt of chips, you fight with yourself and the work. You build up resentment for even being there. Then chips go by that your supervisor notices that

you missed. He approaches you and says, "What's the matter down here? You missed hundreds of orange and wilted ones!" You respond, "Oh, I'm sorry! I forgot that the orange, wilted ones aren't good."

Is this problem a memory problem? Should you get an evaluation done by a psychologist? *No* to both questions. This problem is a focus problem.

Here's the bottom line: Unless you quit, you're going to have to stand in front of that conveyer belt anyway. You may as well get focused on your work. Why not invest while you're there? You really don't have anything to lose, except, perhaps, the illusion that you have a memory problem.

While watching your conveyer belt, make it a game. Try to notice the wide variety of different shapes and colors. Become an expert at noticing the most-exquisite good ones and the most-comical bad ones. If you make it fun, the time will fly by without looking at the clock. Your sharpened focus will stem any complaints that you're having any memory problem.

This approach can decrease your boredom and increase your job satisfaction. Your enhanced clarity of mind will pull in the Zen saying to mean: Zen is not like watching conveyer belts. It *is* watching conveyer belts.

Because mood and state of mind have a great deal of effect on memories, try to replicate that state of mind. If you typically learn the material after drinking coffee, don't set yourself up to go through a caffeine withdrawal at the time of the presentation.

If possible, wear the same or similar clothing. Try to put yourself in a similar mood. During the practice, try to put in your imagination the room you'll be presenting in.

You can even cue yourself with your own body movements. Stand or sit in the same way in which you'll later present your speech. Your posture is a great tool to use as a cue. If you're finding yourself not remembering, go back to the posture to jog your memory.

If possible, have a bottle of water next you. Take a sip now and again just as you had during the time you were learning the information.

The more you can replicate the context of how you learned the material, the better able you'll be to remember it when you actually give your presentation.

Chapter 13

Acing Exams

• •

• •

*O*ne of the rights of passage that you've experienced before and you'll experience again is having your skill and knowledge evaluated by an exam. Whether you're being tested at school or at work or you're taking a driving test, your memory skills are being tested.

You obviously don't want to waste time when you're studying for an exam. You want to make the time you spend studying count. In other words, you need a strategy that allows you to approach the exam with the maximum amount of memory of the test subject so you can recall the information in the right way to fit the demands of the exam.

In this chapter, you discover how to develop an exam strategy, along with some useful study techniques that can help you recall relevant information.

Replacing Your D– Habits with A+ Habits

If you choose the wrong way to study for an exam, you'll likely forget the information you tried to learn. Here are some major studying blunders to avoid:

✔ Cramming the night before the exam or waiting until the last moment to study

✔ Trying to learn the material while you're doing something else, like watching television or listening to loud music

✔ Focusing on irrelevant information, missing the highpoints, and losing perspective of the big picture

✔ Not preparing for the appropriate test format

If you choose any of the preceding ways to study for an exam, you can derail your chances of passing (unless you're extremely lucky). In the following sections, I explain how you can make sure to avoid these bad habits and replace them with memory-enhancing study habits.

To face the challenge of acing an exam, you have to learn the appropriate information thoroughly. That is, you need to shift away from *rote* learning, which involves simple repetition of the information. Learning by rote is superficial learning; it doesn't grow roots. You want your memories to stick, to be integrated into a body of knowledge. You want your memory to be central rather than remote. Avoid the "remoteness" of rote memory, which not only is time-consuming, but also wastes time.

Uncramming

Sometimes, you may procrastinate and wait until the last minute to try to learn the material that you'll be tested on. You may say that you're too busy to study until the date of the exam is upon you. Worse, yet, you may suffer from the misbelief that waiting is better because you'll forget if you study too soon. You may think that if you wait, the information will be "fresh" in your mind and therefore easier to remember when you're taking the exam. These are simply rationalizations for laziness.

Actually, this is the prescription for "unripeness" rather than freshness, because the information has not been developed. In other words, you won't be able to remember the information because you didn't cultivate the ground and grow the support limbs for the information to cling to.

If you really want to remember the information for an exam, follow this strategy:

1. **Start studying early, weeks before the exam if possible (or even months if it's a national exam).**
2. **Study often and spread out the studying time.**
3. **Organize your study time.**
4. **Get feedback on your progress.**

Soon after you find out that you have an exam scheduled, begin studying for it. Think of this early period as an opportunity to build a broad-based foundation.

Starting early permits you enough time not only to build a foundation but also to organize the information into a coherent body of knowledge that you can remember.

The day I learned time management

If you get through your undergraduate years and want to earn a degree that's higher than your bachelor's, you're not through with exams. You've only just begun. First, you have to take an entrance exam (and pass). For graduate school, you need to take the GRE; for law school, the LSAT; and for medical school, the MCAT.

In graduate school, you have to take comprehensive exams for your Masters Degree and then once again if you go on for your Ph.D.

So after you finally finish graduate, law, or medical school, you think that you're finished with exams. No way! You have to pass your licensing exams. For many people, these are the most difficult exams of all. A psychologist (like me) needs to pass the psychology licensing exam; a physician, the medical licensing exam; and a lawyer, the bar exam.

I'll never forget the time I missed passing the licensing exam by two points. I had actually failed to take the exam seriously, even after hearing reports that there was only a 26 percent passage rate the previous year and that much of the exam contained mathematics in the form of statistics and complicated procedures to construct tests.

I deluded myself with the rationalization that my job as administrator of three-day treatment programs prevented me from devoting time to studying. I finally got under way a month before the exam.

When I received my letter indicating that I missed the passing score by two points, I started studying that night. I studied every night for the next six months for the next exam. I aced the exam by 27 points. I learned my lesson, and I hope you can learn from my mistake.

By spreading out your studying time, you allow yourself time to integrate each installment, each layer. You want the information to take root, to be encoded in your long-term memory. Your studying is cumulative and builds on itself.

TIP

You also want to organize your studying to provide structure to the information. You'll remember more if you know how the information fits together, how it relates to itself.

Getting a broad sense of the overall structure permits you to build on top of it. For example, when you're learning a language, you want to know how the language is structured before you can learn phrases and vocabulary. In many of the romance languages (like Spanish), nouns have feminine and masculine forms, so you need to learn how to conjugate verbs before you embark on conversational Spanish.

As you're learning the information, you want to get feedback on how you're doing to see whether you can recall what you've learned. You can do this in a variety of ways, as follows:

> ✔ **Test yourself by using cue cards, notes, or practice exams.**
>
> ✔ **Participate in study groups and test each other.**
>
> ✔ **Ask the teacher or professor (if available)** about anything that you may not completely understand.
>
> ✔ **Take a study course.** Many major national exams from the GRE to the GED have earned enough attention to garner preparation courses.

Getting feedback also allows you to learn from your mistakes and avoid bad habits or misconceptions that can hamper your memory. It helps you modify your study habits and learn what works best so you can form coherent memories to ace the exam.

Ditching distractions

You can't learn if you're distracted from your studies. Your attention is of premium importance if you expect to commit anything to memory (see Chapter 2).

Watching television while studying is a classic example of distraction. Suppose that you're studying for your driver's license renewal. Unless the television show that you're watching is on driving and the latest Department of Motor Vehicles laws, you'll remember more about the television show than what you're studying.

You can't split your attention between what you'd rather be doing and what you expect to remember. If you want to be doing something else, that's what you'll remember.

The two key aspects of your psychological readiness to remember are:

> ✔ Attention
>
> ✔ Motivation

You need to pay complete attention to what you want to remember for it to soak in. Think of your attention as a gate that allows information into your memory. You can keep the gate open to your memory if you pay attention and fully invest yourself in the process of studying.

You also need to take full advantage of your learning effort. If you're resisting the fact that you have to study for an exam, a large part of you isn't receptive to remembering anything. You simply need to be motivated to learn and remember; otherwise, you're just going through the motions.

Think of your motivation as the energy you need in order to remember for the exam. You want a full tank, instead of running on empty, so you can ace the exam and move on with your life.

Getting the big picture — linking new stuff to old stuff

You can increase the chances that you'll remember new information if you can link it with information you already know. That is, you need to associate the new information with memories already laid down to maximize your chances of remembering it for the exam.

Finding links allows you to establish the relevance of the new information. This relevance adds to the bigger picture — namely, how it fits in with the body of knowledge that you're building.

If you can see relevance in the new information, you'll more likely to remember it. You'll know how the new information fits into place with other information, and you'll have a better chance of understanding its meaning.

This whole process is circular and cumulative. You pick up more memories as you increase your effort to study for the exam; the more you know, the better chance you'll have of remembering more information.

Say that you're studying for a history exam on the thirteenth century and you come across St. Thomas Aquinas. You read that he was a strong advocate of Aristotle's philosophy and that he attempted to introduce and integrate it within Christian theology. You also read that Aquinas called Aristotle the "philosopher," thus putting him on a pedestal above all others. Then you realize that Aristotle lived roughly 1,500 years before Aquinas.

Perhaps you're wondering what's going on here. Why would Aquinas have to "introduce" Aristotle? Why didn't anyone acknowledge his greatness during the previous 1,500 years? Well, if you've already learned the full meaning of the Middle Ages, you know that Europe was in a time warp while the Eastern Mediterranean and Arab world flourished in mathematics and philosophy. Knowing this background helps you integrate the information about Aristotle and Aquinas, instead of trying to remember Aquinas and the dates he lived.

How you learn the information has a lot to do with whether or not you actually remember it. Learn the information in the right way, under the right conditions, so you can remember it.

Timing your memory

Your memory will be enhanced if you pay close attention to the timing of your studying. You may think that you've developed a good strategy for learning the material you want to remember for the exam, but if you don't implement the right timing, you may forget more than you'll remember.

When timing your studying, you need to keep in mind three factors:

- ✔ Timing your initial review
- ✔ Pacing
- ✔ Spreading out your learning

Given that your short-term memory is, well, short term, you forget much of what you learn within minutes after you learn it. This means that if you read new information for an exam and put the book down soon after, you'll forget a lot of it by the time you get to the exam.

To maximize your memory while you study for an exam, try to review the information soon after you initially learn it. After you read about a subject that will be on an exam, go over it again, skimming the high points before you put the book down. Or if you attend a lecture in which the information is presented, go over your notes right after the lecture.

Consider the timing of your initial review as an important first step in capturing the information. You want to make sure that the richness of the information gets absorbed in your mind before much of it evaporates.

Pacing your studying effort helps you maximize your mental energy. If you know that the exam is not for two weeks and you pump all your energy into one "super" study session, you won't experience anything too super about it other than exhaustion. For instance, if you go for a long distance run, you know not to start off sprinting, because as you approach the finish line, you'll be too exhausted to keep up with the other runners. By pacing your study time, you're using your energy to its potential.

Spreading out your study time allows you enough time to integrate the information with your memory (see Chapter 11).

Each time you study, you lay down a layer of memory. Think of it like an oil painting you paint in layers — each layer provides the foundation for the next layer. If you paint the color all at once, the colors blend together into a muddy brown or goopy gray.

Start with an overview of the material you're studying for the exam. This broad view is like an outline of the subject matter or like a table of contents in a textbook.

Next, move on to the second layer, which is like the second heading in the table of contents. For example, if you're studying for a geology exam, the first heading in your textbook may be "Rocks," and the second heading may be "Minerals."

With each layer, you move to a deeper level of complexity or detail. Like painting a tree, you first paint the trunk and a few major branches. Next, you move on to the medium-sized branches. Then you move on to the smaller branches. You don't get to the leaves until later. If you go directly to the leaves, you can't know which branch the leaves are connected to.

As you spread out your learning, allocate a similar amount of time to each session. If you find that you can devote roughly seven hours of study time to the exam, considering the other responsibilities you're juggling, you want to spread out the seven hours evenly. Make sure that it's enough time to get something out of the session but not so much time that you'll get bored or exhausted.

If the exam is in, say, two weeks, you may want to devote one hour of study time every other day. This schedule improves your focus better than had you studied half an hour every day or seven hours on one day, and it gives you time to commit the information to memory.

Scouting the exam

You can't maximize your performance on an exam if you don't know what's expected of you. You don't want to arrive for the exam feeling surprised by the format, the conditions of the hall, or the style of questioning.

Knowing the subject matter isn't enough in terms of readiness for an exam. If you don't know how you're going to be asked to recall information, you may find yourself unprepared and so surprised that you'll be too distracted to remember the information. You may be expecting cues that won't come, and as a result, you'll walk away from the exam frustrated because you knew the material but weren't able to demonstrate it.

Gather as much information as you can about how you'll be asked to recall the subject matter. Also, make sure that you know what aspects of the subject matter you'll be required to know. Don't be afraid to do the following:

- ✔ Ask the teacher or instructor about the test format and subject matter.

- ✔ Consult preparatory books if you're preparing for a qualifying exam.

- ✔ Ask people who have taken exams by the teacher or who have taken the national exam about the kinds of "surprises" they experienced.

- ✔ Sign up for a preparation course if you'll soon be taking a national exam. Most of these courses are excellent ways for you to learn the format of the exam as well as go over the subject matter.

- ✔ Take any available practice exams. You get more practice not only with the material but also in the test format. You can also diagnose your weak areas.

- ✔ Look to the instructor for clues about what may be on the exam by what she highlights and emphasizes in her lectures.

Questions, questions, and more questions

Exam questions require different types of memory (see Chapter 3 for details on different types of memory). For example, multiple-choice questions may demand recognition memory, and fill-in-the-blank and essay questions may demand direct-recall memory.

Multiple-choice or true-false questions allow you to use the process of elimination, because you can eliminate possible answers containing elements that make wrong assertions. You can look for what's wrong with some of the possibilities as well as look for what's right in other possibilities.

With open-ended questions that require direct recall, you're required to pull up memories of the subject matter. You have to look for cues embedded in the question itself. You don't have possible answers to eliminate except those that you're carrying around in your mind.

Many direct recall questions are more difficult than recognition-based questions because you're provided fewer clues and no opportunities to eliminate bad answers. Recognition questions, such as multiple-choice questions, can range from quite easy with a few possibilities to even comical, as in this question:

What is the most environmentally sound commuter vehicle?

(a) An electric car

(b) A hybrid car

(c) A gas-guzzling SUV

(d) A Mack truck

Right away, you can eliminate options c and d. They're both presented in extreme and obvious terms. The test maker, me, helped insure that you got the point by not just giving you the options of SUV or truck. I've added gas-guzzling and Mack to drive home the point.

But this question also illustrates how multiple-choice questions can be difficult. Options a and b are attempts to save the environment. You would have to really know your stuff to pick the right one. If the question allowed you two possibilities or even changing option (d) to read "a and b," the question is a slam-dunk. But if required to pick just one, you have to know more about the difference between hybrids and electrical cars. For example, you have to consider how the electricity is made. Is it powered by solar cells? Or is your local electricity source generated by a coal-burning power plant?

Essay questions require not only direct recall but also the ability to express yourself. To further increase the demand on your memory, essay questions on an exam (such as one third of the bar exam) require that you write in clear legalistic jargon. Your answer not only has to hit all the points, such as the fact pattern, but also has to be coherent. Yet in this case, being coherent may be an oxymoron. Who but lawyers can read legalistic jargon?

After you know what to expect, you can shift your efforts to concentrating on the subject matter you're expected to remember.

Underlining with a Rembrandt Touch

When you're studying for an exam, you'll probably have multiple resources available to you. You may have one or more books and notes from lectures to refer to. Although I describe how to make use of this material in Chapter 11, I want to show you how the main points relate to acing an exam.

When you read over your text, you want to see the forest for the trees. That is, you want the main points to stand out when you go over them. You can use two methods to make them stand out visually:

- ✔ Underlining
- ✔ Highlighting

Underlining can draw your attention to points you need to remember. As you leaf through the books, the underlined passages jump out at you. The rest of the text is background material.

You can underline too much or too little. Excessive underlining is "pointless." If you underline almost everything, you won't have the opportunity to see the main points. On the other hand, if you underline too little, you'll have to read everything again to be able to get at the main points.

Highlighting markers have become very popular in the past 25 years. You can combine highlighting and underlining to give you two levels: The highlighted passages can be the general main points, and the underlined key passages can be the main-main points.

You can use the same method with your lecture notes. If your notes aren't like mine — that is, you can actually read them — you can determine the main points to underline. You can even rewrite them again and emphasize the key points and highlight them. Then you can go back over again and underline the main-main points.

Using Your Memory Techniques

As you learn the information you want to remember for the exam, tap into your memory techniques (see Chapters 8 and 9). The more techniques you use, the more easily you'll remember the information at the time of the exam.

Use the following techniques:

- ✔ Coding from different angles
- ✔ Associations
- ✔ Symbolic coding
- ✔ Mnemonics
- ✔ Visualizing
- ✔ Chunking

Taking different slants on the topic

The more ways you code a memory, the higher the chance you'll remember it (see Chapter 3). By coding in different dimensions, you're allowing yourself multiple ways to link up with that information.

For example, if you're studying for a history exam and you need to remember the Napoleonic Wars, you want to understand the events that led up to the rise of Napoleon, who he became, and how he lost popularity.

You learn about the arrogance and abuse of power in the monarchy, along with the violent rage that overthrew it in the French Revolution. You learn how Napoleon's brief conquest of Egypt gained him popularity. Then you find out how many people who had high hopes for him were shocked when he crowned himself emperor. You read that Beethoven's Third Symphony was originally dedicated to Napoleon until the crowning, when Beethoven scratched off in disgust the name Bonaparte, which he had initially written on the first page as a dedication.

Now, when you remember the Napoleonic Wars, you can link your memories by thinking about Beethoven, the French Revolution, Egypt, arrogance, and power.

Making associations

By linking one fact or piece of information to another, you create a system of knowledge that you can tap into like a well. You can drill down in one area and hit a pocket that is connected to the source.

Look for associations that provide easy links to other information you already know. Make those associations link in logical and natural ways.

For example, if you're taking a physiology course and you need to remember the parts of the brain, make associations between the parts of your brain and the behaviors they're associated with. You do this by using the name of the part and what it does. For your frontal lobes, think of how they contribute to putting you "out front." This association fits because your frontal lobes govern your sense of initiative and ambition (see Chapter 3).

Using symbols

Symbolic links can pull in a lot of information to your memory with one image. For example, picture in your mind a cross or a crescent moon. The cross carries the symbolic image of Christianity; and the crescent moon, the symbol of Islam. If you have the opportunity to incorporate what you want to remember for the exam through the use of a symbol, use it. A symbol is one of the most economical ways to code memories.

Employing mnemonics

Use your mnemonic skills whenever possible, so you can carry clusters of information into the exam. Pegs and story links can help you pull together words that may be hard to remember. Peg mnemonics are memory tricks or techniques that help you connect one simple letter or number with the information you want to remember (see Chapter 8).

The easiest mnemonic is the first letter peg. A peg mnemonic allows you to link up the information you want to remember with a letter.

For example, suppose you are trying to remember these four great writers from the nineteenth century:

> John Keats
>
> Washington Irving
>
> Henry Wadsworth Longfellow
>
> Henry David Thoreau

Now take the first letter of each last name and form a word, as follows:

> **K**eats
>
> **I**rving
>
> **L**ongfellow
>
> **T**horeau

You can see that the first letter (in bold) of each name makes the word KILT. When you take the exam, you can easily remember this word, instead of having to search your mind for each writer's name.

Visualizing

Visualizing what you want to remember for the exam can be quite helpful, too (see Chapter 11). One picture can be worth more than a thousand words and can give you just the edge that you need to pass the exam.

You can use all sorts of visual images to carry memories. You can even carry peg mnemonics within the visual image. In the previous example, I give you the peg for the writers (KILT), so you can imagine a man wearing a kilt. Though all the writers wrote in the English language, I'm stretching things a little with the Scottish image. But that's okay! Just make sure that you don't mistakenly remember that Thoreau brought bagpipes out to Walden Pond.

Chunking

Chunking is another memory technique you may want to use to remember information for the exam (see Chapter 8). Chunking allows you to remember bite-size pieces of information that form part of a larger body of information.

Chunking is especially useful if the body of information that you're trying to remember is hard to remember all together. For example, a poem or a string of equations may be easier to learn in chunks first.

By breaking up the information into chunks, you allow yourself to remember the parts before you get to the whole. Then you can take a step back and see how the parts fit into the whole. As soon as you fit the chunks together, you'll be able to appreciate the maxim: *The whole is greater than the sum of its parts.*

Going to the Bathroom and Other Good Ideas

Studying is not enough. You need to be able to think clearly at the time of the exam. Make sure that you do the following:

- ✔ Get a good night's sleep.
- ✔ Eat a balanced meal.
- ✔ Avoid alcohol and other drugs not only the night before the exam, but also during your studying process.
- ✔ Wear comfortable clothing.
- ✔ Drink enough fluids.
- ✔ Avoid sugar or too much caffeine.

This suggestion may sound silly, but it's sometimes overlooked: Make sure that you go to the bathroom right before you enter the exam room. A full bladder will capture your attention and make you squirm in your seat.

You want to have your mind as clear as possible before and during the exam. Make sure that you don't make any major life decisions just before the exam. Don't discuss plans to move, problems with relationships, or even ambivalence about your career choice with your spouse, family, or friends.

You want to have your mind clear of distractions as much as possible. While you wait for the exam to begin, try the following:

✔ Arrive a little early and take a walk.

✔ After or during your walk, try to clear your mind of the exam, its subject matter, and all other concerns.

✔ Try relaxation or meditative exercises (see Chapter 7 for details).

✔ If you see friends who are also there to take the exam, try to avoid substantive conversations. (You don't want to import their anxiety or spike your own.)

When you enter the exam room, try to sit in a place where you'll minimize distractions. Here are some tips on staying away from problem areas:

✔ Don't sit with friends or those who you want to get to know better, because you may be distracted by their presence.

✔ Don't sit near the bathroom or water cooler, because people will be walking past you all the time and standing near you.

✔ Don't sit near the exam proctors, because they often get up.

✔ Don't sit where light or ventilation is poor.

If possible, bring a water bottle with you. This allows you not only to stay hydrated but also to refresh yourself periodically.

If the exam is long, plan to break the exam up in sections by getting up to stretch and going to the bathroom.

I don't know about you, but I find all the noise in the hall and the people shifting around to be distracting. I like to use foam earplugs to muffle out the sounds. Not only do the earplugs screen out and dull nuisance noises, but they give me the feeling that there's a separation between me and what's going on in the hall.

Give yourself every possible edge to recall your memory of the information tested on the exam. You've studied and encoded into memory a body of knowledge, and now it's time to demonstrate that on the exam.

Chapter 14

Remembering People

In This Chapter

▶ Figuring out how to remember faces

▶ Knowing how to remember names

▶ Discovering how to jog your memory for stories

*I*f you're like most people, one of your most frustrating lapses in memory occurs when you meet a person whom you know you've met, but now, can't remember the name. This situation can be especially embarrassing if that person remembers you. Your challenge is to use various techniques to jog your memory.

In this chapter, you discover some useful techniques to remember people you meet. You discover ways to remember faces and names of those you meet. You also discover ways to steer a conversation to tease out clues and cues for your memory of the person who seems to remember you.

So, before you're put on the spot again, start reading and find ways to be ready for these uncomfortable encounters.

Facing a Face to Remember

Some years ago, while attending a conference, I recognized a woman whom I was certain I'd met before. She was staying at the same hotel as I was and seemed to recognize me as well. I nodded and smiled neutrally but was hesitant to say anything because I didn't remember exactly who she was. I wondered whether I should speak to her regarding our prior meeting, but I couldn't recall where it had occurred.

I was also worried that it would be too forward of me to approach her. I was afraid that she'd get the wrong idea if I should walk up to her, saying, "Don't I know you?" and think that I was pursuing her. She was attractive and probably had encountered men approaching her with "lines" sounding similar to my question. On the other hand, I worried that she may be offended if I didn't acknowledge our prior meeting.

Had I been more skilled in my earlier years at attaching faces to stories, I may not have floundered with my poor recognition. Nowadays, I use an association technique to connect a person's face to their name or identity. If you associate a unique characteristic of a person's face with an aspect of their identity, you can recognize faces more easily.

Everyone has a unique appearance. Look for a distinguishing facial characteristic that draws your attention, and then associate it with the person's personality.

Make that facial characteristic stand out by:

- ✔ Exaggerating it
- ✔ Imagining an artist drawing a caricature of the person and highlighting one physical feature
- ✔ Making that facial feature speak to you as though it, by itself, tells you everything you need to know about the person

Patsy

Suppose that you meet Patsy and notice that she's busily moving around the room, talking to everyone. She almost appears to be gossiping as she drifts from one person to another.

Then you notice that she possesses one very distinguishing facial feature. Her ears are slightly larger than average. You zoom in on those ears, imagining them to be much larger than they really are. You imagine that she grew those ears to pick up everything everyone else is saying in hopes of hearing some juicy gossip.

Barry

As you walk into another room, you're very briefly introduced to Barry. Then you're escorted off to meet three more people. On your way across the room, you see Barry being introduced to another person. You struggle to find a distinguishing facial characteristic.

You notice that Barry has particularly heavy eyebrows. The hair between his brows is quite abundant. He also has a very thick mustache. You image how a caricature artist may draw him.

You imagine that Barry's eyebrows are connected, forming a uni-brow. This uni-brow stands out in your mind and appears to duplicate his heavy mustache. In fact, you imagine the drawing depicting him as having two mustaches, one normal one and one in place of his eyebrows.

The next time you see Barry, you may remember him because of the uni-brow or two mustaches.

Fred

At the same social gathering, you meet Fred. He seems to be a mild-mannered fellow. As you watch him, he appears shy and nervous. His eyes shift around out of nervousness, and he seems to fidget ever so slightly. On one of the few occasions that his eyes meet yours, he quickly shifts them to someone else as if his eyes are trying nervously to find a shelter.

You imagine that Fred feels terribly exposed and seems to have moved to the periphery of the people standing around the refreshment table. He has found shelter behind them. You focus on his eyes, still moving, and the next time you see Fred, you'll remember his nervous eyes.

One of most basic ways that you can remember a person is to associate one unique physical characteristic with some aspect of their personality, such as the way the person:

- ✔ Moves
- ✔ Expresses himself
- ✔ Wears his clothes
- ✔ Smiles
- ✔ Frowns

Lisa

Suppose that you meet a young woman named Lisa at a meeting. You notice that she sits back and lets everyone else do the talking.

As you wonder what opinion she may have about what's being discussed, you notice her sad brown eyes. Those eyes seem to say that she has opinions that she wants to express, but her self-consciousness stands in the way. You become sympathetic to her, wanting to somehow facilitate a way for her to feel comfortable enough to express herself.

Weeks later, when you see her again, you know that you've seen her before but can't remember where. Then you see her sad brown eyes, and it all comes back.

Frank

Now, suppose that you meet a man named Frank. You try to code into memory something about him and combine it with his name. You notice that he stands proudly, expressing himself without censor. You see that he seems like a person who expresses himself frankly.

Yet, when you look at his face, he has no major distinguishing characteristics to help you remember him. You decide that you're going to have to rely on his posture and expressive movements as cues to remember him. You'll remember him as Frank just because he expresses himself frankly.

When you meet someone who has few facial characteristics that stand out, look deeper and you'll find something, even if it's only their overly "normal" appearance.

For example, suppose that you were to encounter a person who looks nondescript. Perhaps she has brown hair and brown eyes and is of medium height and medium weight, with no distinguishing facial characteristics.

Then you notice that her hair is tied back, and you know that if she were to untie her hair, it would fall below her shoulders. You also notice that she's relatively quiet compared to the other people in the room. She makes an occasional provocative statement that seems to move the conversation in an unexpected direction.

You can associate her relatively nondescript appearance with her tendency to sit back quietly. You also decide that you can make the same association with the fact that she has tied her hair back. However, what do you do with her apparent ability to make provocative comments?

Her tied-back hair is long, so you can associate the long hair with the potential to be outspoken and expressive.

Now, suppose that you see her later, and her hair isn't tied back. Will you recognize her as the same person? Chances are, it may take you a few moments to associate your memory of her to her tied-back hair, but you'll remember it. As you meet her this time, she'll provide you with another association of how to remember her because she'll be revealing more of her personality as you talk to her and as she interacts with other people.

Because we typically remember what we see longer than what we hear, your problem with remembering faces is a lot easier to resolve than you think.

You have an opportunity to look at a person's face longer than you have to hear a person's name. She may say her name just once, but you'll continue to look at her face as she talks.

Another reason why you may remember a face more easily than you may remember a name is that remembering a face is a recognition task while remembering a name is a recall task. Recognition tasks are much easier than recall tasks (see Chapters 1, 2, and 11 for details on the differences between these tasks).

Putting a Name on a Familiar Face

If you're over the age of 50 and haven't had the experience of forgetting the names of people you're familiar with, you're special. Most people complain of this difficulty.

Interestingly, remembering a person's occupation is easier than remembering his or her name. Names tell you little about a person because they're just superficial tags with no real meaning or connection to the person, but an occupation gives the person depth because it tells you more about the person and allows you to make a connection.

Forgetting a person's name can certainly be embarrassing to you, but think of the feelings of the person whose name you forgot. Maybe he or she thought that the two of you had a special relationship. When you forget his or her name, in a way, you're almost saying, "I don't think we've met before." And worse, you're pretty much saying, "Who you are doesn't matter to me."

In one year's time, I meet hundreds of people. I know their faces, and I know their stories. Nevertheless, I have great difficulty with their names. If people call on the telephone, I often can't remember them by name. I have to run to the chart room and read their charts to get a picture of their stories. If I had them in my office with their faces and stories to match, I could easily bring people into focus.

Lateralizing names and faces

Your brain works as a complex system in which many different parts of your brain are involved in every memory. Yet, some areas of your brain are more specialized than others to deal with particular memories. When you're remembering a person's face, you're probably using your right hemisphere and, more so, your right parietal lobe. When you're remembering words, you're using your left hemisphere and, more so, your left temporal lobe. (See Chapter 3 for more info about the anatomy of the brain.) When you associate a name with a face, you have both hemispheres collaborating nicely.

In order to try to help myself remember names better, I tried the following techniques recommended by many memory experts. They really helped me, and they can help you, too. Use the following five steps to try to remember a name:

- ✔ **Attention:** Make sure that you heard the name clearly.
- ✔ **Meaning:** Make the name meaningful to you.
- ✔ **Appearance:** Make sure that you notice distinctive physical features.
- ✔ **Association:** Make sure that you associate the appearance with the name.
- ✔ **Review:** Make sure that you review your association.

Attention

If you don't hear the person's name or aren't paying close enough attention when a name is given, you can pretty much count on forgetting that name.

Most people forget names because they stumble at the first step. The fact is, they never even get the name in the first place because they're too distracted.

Ask the person to repeat her name and then repeat it to yourself. Try to use her name in your conversation with her. When you repeat the name, you can ensure that you actually did hear it (and hear it correctly) in order to hold it in short-term memory and begin to transfer it into long-term memory.

Repeat the name just enough but not too much. Otherwise, the person may think, "Well, yeah, that's my name. Don't wear it out!" You just want it worn in — to your mind that is.

Meaning

You'll benefit by constructing a meaningful association to a person. For example, say that you met Barbara, but she's hard to get to know. You may imagine barbed wire protecting her.

After you're sure you have the name, try to think about something that makes that name meaningful. People in all cultures have unique and beautiful names. Here's your chance to discover some new names and apply them to people you meet.

Perhaps you find that the person's name has a distinctive philosophical flavor to it, such as Plato or a carefree descendent of a flower child with a name like Sunshine. Maybe the name has a formal style, such as William or Victoria.

Ask whether the person you're being introduced to chose to change his or her name from the original. William and Victoria may refer to themselves as Bill and Vicki. Some people use their formal name in formal situations and their shortened name in informal situations. For instance, my wife, whose name is Victoria/Vicki, uses those names interchangeably, depending upon whom she's talking to.

Appearance

Now that you have the name and you have focused on a meaningful part of that name, focus on the person's face. Try to search for a distinctive feature of her face. Does she have a large nose? Are her ears large? Does she have beautiful eyes? Are her eyebrows full or plucked?

Be careful with what you commit to memory about their faces. Men can and, often, do shave their beards off. Mustaches can come and go like the seasons.

Whatever distinctive features you key into, try to assign some characteristic to it. This exercise is especially useful if you have had a little time to get to know the person in conversation. Perhaps you've been struck by how sincere the person seemed in conversation. Maybe you were also able to take note of that person's wide green eyes.

Association

Your next step is to associate the face with the name. Unfortunately, many names are so generic and common, like mine (John), that you may find it difficult to remember.

Consider the name Smith. Perhaps you're meeting Bill Smith for the first time. Maybe you notice that Bill has large, broad hands and a hearty face. In Bill's case, maybe the best strategy to remember his name is to associate his name with the occupation that his last name was originally derived from. It's quite possible that one of Bill's distant ancestors was a smith, like a blacksmith. You can now associate his face with the image of being a smith and *voilà*, that's his name!

Names usually have some aspect to them that allow you to attach a mnemonic cue. Sometimes, a name may provide an obvious memory link, while other times, you're going to have to search for it.

For example, if you meet someone who's named Michael Smothers, you'll probably try to use his last name rather than his first name because Michael is a very common name. You notice that he's almost clinging to his wife. You watch as she tries to talk to another person at the party, but he seems to smother her. You remember his name easily as Michael Smothers because he smothers his wife.

If you meet a very tall, lanky man named Larry Linker, you may simply take his last name and remember him as Lanky Larry Linker. (Just don't call him that to his face.)

At work, you get introduced to the new employee, Patrick Shaley. Within a very short period, he seems to be striking up friendly conversations with you and your peers. He even pats people on the back. You decide to work on remembering his first name before moving to his last. You'll remember him as Pat because of all the patting on the back.

Resorting to trickery

Remembering a person's name well after you meet again and are halfway through a conversation presents a challenge. Don't worry! You still have time to dig out the memory of that person's name or trick her into telling you without asking her. To accomplish this Houdini trick, you may have to resort to these tactics:

- Leading her into telling you by example

- Tricking her into showing you something with her name printed on it

- Introducing her to someone else

Now, I must warn you. Each one of these ploys to jog your memory or have her reveal her name is wrought with embarrassing risks. But what do you have to lose? If she finds out that you don't remember her name, so what? She was probably going to find that out anyway.

You can lead her into telling you her name by doing it yourself. You can do it at any time in the conversation. You may start the conversation with a: "Hi! I'm John. We met at the last meeting."

She may say, "Oh hi, John. Yes, I remember. I'm Peggy."

Then you're off the hook.

But she may respond by saying, "Oh hi, John. How are you?" At least she remembers you. However, she left you with nothing to go on.

While you're at the meeting together, make note of the handouts that both of you were given. You could say that you didn't receive a particular paper and ask to see hers. In the process, you may come across her name on the front of her folder. If you can't see it, ask for her card, so that you can connect her with someone you work with that she may network with.

You could introduce her to your colleagues but omit her name. Say to her: "Oh, I'd like to introduce you to someone I work with. This is Jim. He's in our accounting office."

She'll be hard pressed not to offer her name as she extends her hand. She'll probably add, "Good to meet you, Jim. My name is Barbara."

(*Don't* then say, "Barbara? I wasn't even close!")

Of course, Jim could always blow your cover, too, by first saying, "Now John! Aren't you going to introduce me?"

Review your associations

To ensure that you have all the names straight in your head, you need to review all your associations. *Overlearning* and *repeating* ensure a better memory of information (see Chapter 9 for more on these memory techniques). Therefore, the next time you see Bill, you can notice his hearty face, the face of a smith. Oh yeah! His name is Bill Smith.

Using Conversation to Unzip the Person Within

You can remember people that you meet at a deeper level than their names, faces, and a few characteristics if you really try to get to know them. This opportunity presents itself when you're engaged in conversation with the person.

Though we all usually have to engage in a forest of pleasantries when we first meet someone, hopefully you'll take the opportunity to get down to the real person. Take advantage of the opportunity to get to know more about her by:

- ✔ Asking *open-ended* questions, which leave open the possibility of lengthy and leading answers

- ✔ Avoiding *closed-ended* questions, which tend to be answered with one word

- ✔ Using every response as a potential clue about who she is and as an opportunity to ask more

Look for an opening to move the conversation beyond the pleasantries. The person may be more tentative than you, though. If so, it's up to you to segue in and take one of their cues as a prompt to ask a good question.

These cues may be ever so slight, but take them as a sign of cracks in her defensive armor. She's signaling to you that it may be okay to get a little closer and to move away from pleasantries and talk about her real life.

For example, she says, "It's nice that the rain has stopped. I was able to get my son to his soccer game."

You can take the easy way out and say, "Oh yes, it's nice to see blue sky." If you take this route, you lose your opportunity to know and remember more about her. You also run the risk of subtly giving her the impression that you really aren't interested in her.

On the other hand, you could respond to her comment by asking, "Oh, you have a son who plays soccer?" You've just asked a closed-ended question. Now, of course, at the very least she'll respond by saying, "Yes." However, if you ask an open-ended question such as, "Soccer must be a big part of his life," she may even go further and say, "He's 12 years old and soccer is." Chances are, she'll say more. If so, you'll have an opportunity to remember her as the mother of a 12-year-old who plays soccer. Next time you see her you could say, "So, how are the soccer games going?"

We all appreciate it if someone expresses interest in us and remembers more than our name. Remembering someone's story makes that person both more tangible and more memorable to you.

Learning a person's story is far more complicated than the example I gave about the woman with the soccer-playing son. A person's life has layers like an onion that need to be peeled back.

To peel back layers of the onion, you have to negotiate your way through layers of etiquette and hesitancy on both of your parts. Think of the most minor response as an opportunity to find out more. When the woman in the previous example mentions that she has a 12-year-old son, you can try to peel back another layer, and more of her story will reveal itself to you. Ask something like, "So, how have the games been going? Does he enjoy playing?"

When she responds to your question about how her son is doing in his soccer games, she'll probably add something new, such as, "He's our first born," or "My husband usually goes to the weekend games." Whatever her response, you have an opportunity to venture farther into her story, thus making her a more memorable human being.

Fishing for the story that goes with a familiar face

Chances are, you've had the experience of seeing someone again whom you recognize and whose name you may even remember, but you forget the person's story — forget who they really are. As you stand there helplessly, you're at a loss for who they are behind the familiar face and name.

You may wonder why you may be able to remember a person's face or name and nothing else about them. Perhaps your memory of her face or name was coded into your memory without an association that cued you into anything about her story.

You don't want to be insulting and say, "I'm sorry, Sarah. I know we've met because I know your name, but I can't remember anything about you." You have to scramble to rediscover who this mystery Sarah is.

You need to develop a way to ensure that she'll tell you who she is without you letting on that you don't know. You'll need to somehow ask her questions that will lead her to believe that you're interested in what she has been up to. (The fact is, you *are* interested — but in a far more complicated way than she thinks.)

Ask open-ended and generic questions. Open-ended questions require elaboration, giving you an opportunity to find out more about the person. As she answers the questions, you'll have the opportunity to jog your memory, looking for cues and associations.

For example, you may ask, "So, how have you been doing lately?" But this question doesn't provide you with much information. It's a closed-ended question that may give you a simple answer, such as, "Oh fine." This answer gives you little to go on.

Closed-ended questions can be a conversation stopper. Avoid them if you really want to get a good conversation going. (Ironically, the question, "How are you doing?" could be an open-ended question. But few people expect an open-ended response. Most people expect a "Fine. And how are you?" In this case, it has become a closed-ended question that's appropriate for passing someone on the sidewalk but not for trying to start a meaningful conversation.)

You need a question that can produce more information for you. Open-ended questions, such as, "So, what have you been doing?" ask for more information than a simple answer. You need something to work with.

Stay with open-ended questions instead of closed-ended questions because they keep the conversation going. These types of questions provide you with a way to slowly unzip the story of the person you need to remember.

If you ask the person an open-ended question, chances are she'll inadvertently give you some clues to her identity by saying something about who she has seen or what specifically she has been doing that will serve as a link. If she says, "I had coffee with Jack," the name *Jack* may spring forth a whole association of memories.

If her answer still doesn't yield usable links, ask questions about her answers, such as, "Oh, that sounds like fun. How did you manage the time?"

Hopefully she won't say anything like, "What do you mean? I'm unemployed and alone. I have all the time in the world!" in which case she provides you with a slap-in-the-face cue.

You may luck out, and she may drop a clue about her job or family that can provide a memory link. Eventually, like peeling the layers of an onion, you'll soon get down to her identity. (Unlike an onion, you won't have to suffer the tears going through it.) She'll believe that you're truly interested in her answers, but she won't know that, all along, she has been having this warm conversation with someone who forgets who she is.

Being in the mental health business for more than 25 years has permitted me to meet literally thousands of people. Moreover, because my business is finding out about people's stories before I can help them, that's a lot of stories to remember. My confession is that, from time to time, I forget who I sit down with for the first few minutes of the session. But I ask a few questions and out pops the person. All I need is a few cues and a few comments about the person's mother or husband, and the whole story unfolds like a solved mystery.

My point is that this technique works even in a professional environment. You likely meet different people all the time and may have difficulties remembering details about the lives of various colleagues, clients, and acquaintances.

Even if you don't get the big picture immediately, don't give up. The key is to continue asking follow-up questions. Follow-up questions feed on the answers she gives. For example:

> "So, my husband and I spent a nice weekend at Tahoe."

> "That sounds nice. How did you find the time?"

> "Well, we managed to get Jim's parents to take care of the kids."

Aha! Two memory cues for you:

- ✔ She has a husband named Jim.
- ✔ She and Jim have children.

If those two clues still don't provide you with memory associations, you can use her answers as prompts for more open-ended questions.

> "So, what has Jim been up too?"

When she tells you about Jim's recent job stress or the kids' music recitals and ball games, you may have the necessary memory cues to develop a whole picture. You remember that Sarah and Jim recently moved from Lincoln, Nebraska, when Jim took a new job at the Microspot computer chip company and were riding high until the economic downturn.

Grasping the importance of the person

You remember information more easily when you find that it's relevant and meaningful. This fact applies to how well you remember people, too. If you find that a person has meaning and relevance to your life, you're more inclined to remember that person in contrast to someone who doesn't have meaning and relevance to your life.

Be careful about who you regard as relevant and meaningful when you meet someone new. You may think that you'll never see someone again, and, thus, not pay much attention to what you find out about that person. However, later, when you meet that person again and don't recognize him or her, it may cost you a potential business or job-related advance, not to mention provide you with a lot of embarrassment. In this case, the person was meaningful to you, and you didn't know it.

You may wonder how you're going to develop a sense of meaning and relevance in a person who seems totally nondescript. Find something, however remote and hidden, to relate to in the people you meet. Even if you have to fabricate a sense of meaning and relevance in them, you'll see your memory of people improve.

Sharing Memories: How People See Things Differently

The way that you remember a person may be quite different from the way I remember the same person. Because we're unique people with unique interests, sensitivities, and ways of expressing ourselves, that person may respond differently to you than he will to me. In other words, there's a tremendous amount of variation in what we remember about other people.

The differences in the ways we perceive people have a great deal of effect on the way we remember them. So when your spouse or friend tries to remind you of a person both of you met, he may attempt to jog your memory with cues that are relevant to him but not to you.

For example, he may say, "Remember that obnoxious guy who talked so much at the party?" You have no idea who he's talking about and look at him perplexed.

He looks frustrated and goes on, "The guy who was in your ear, talking about scuba diving. *That guy!*"

You remember him immediately. He was anything but obnoxious. In fact, he was quite charming. You laugh, realizing why you have such a difference of opinion. Then you say, "There's no reason to be jealous. He was telling me what a great time he and his wife had diving in Belize."

Sometimes, you may share the same memory cues as someone else. Usually, these cues are based on more obvious characteristics of the person. Both people easily remember that the person was tall and slim or short and plump. It's when two people try to remember someone's personality that things get distorted.

When you and another person attempt to remember someone you've both met, try to use the concrete characteristics, such as physical appearance. Unless the person you're both trying to remember possesses obvious personality characteristics, avoid using them as memory cues because everyone tends to perceive an individual differently.

Putting People in Pigeonholes

During the past 40 years, stereotyping people has become politically incorrect. With that disclaimer aside, let me acknowledge that you, I, and everyone else remember people by the categories we assign them to.

You may have organized your perceptions of other people around broad categories, such as whether the person is nice, mean, arrogant, shy, and so on. Remembering people in these overly basic ways helps you prepare yourself for the next encounter with them.

For example, if you have come to believe that Zachary is a mean person and he approaches you with a request to do him a favor, your defenses go up. You fear that he may retaliate if you don't accommodate his request.

Placing people into broad categories may help you make a memory association of them for future use. Try these broad categories:

- Occupations
- Hobbies
- Who they know
- Where they vacation
- Where they live

As you meet or come into contact with people, ask them their occupation. Try to imagine them at work to give yourself an idea of part of the person's life.

Most people spend much of their daily time adapting to their occupations. I know, for example, that I'm a very different person as a psychologist than I would have been had I gone ahead and become a lawyer as my family expected.

Lawyer jokes aside, I'm not making a qualitative statement about lawyers. You, too, have been shaped by the demands and culture that surround your job. Therefore, when you remember a person by his or her occupation, you remember more about that person than a cardboard stereotype.

This link allows you not only a way to remember a person but also a way to begin a conversation with that person at your next meeting.

If the person's a court reporter, for example, you can ask, "So, how's court been treating you?"

She may respond by saying, "Oh, we had a horrendous case last week."

Some people say that they live for their weekends and vacations. During these times off from work, your hobbies define your interests, and your interests define who you are.

Therefore, when you find out what a person's hobby is, you're finding out more than trivial information. You're finding out how they define themselves.

Suppose that you meet Jennifer at a social gathering. In the course of your very brief conversation, she mentions that she's a quilter. She belongs to quilting groups and has even participated in national quilting associations. You'll remember her as a crafts person. The next time you see her, you can ask her about quilting.

However you decide to remember who a person is, try to make sure that your method is foolproof. In other words, make sure that your method is durable and can work in many different conditions. The more variations and perspectives you use, the more flexible and versatile your memory of people can be.

Car Talk — Wheeling in the Person

We're an increasingly mobile society. Most families have more than one vehicle. You probably own a car, and most people you know own one. If you live in an area like Southern California, you're surrounded by freeways with six lanes and interchanges with banked multi-level bridges, all with cars too often containing just one person who thinks of his car as an extension of himself.

Though perhaps you and I don't live in an environment like that, you've probably noticed that people often drive vehicles that mirror their personalities in some way. A *true* environmentalist doesn't drive an SUV, a CEO of a major corporation doesn't drive a beat-up 1969 Volkswagen, and a carpenter usually doesn't drive a two-seater sports car (unless he's taking his wife's car out for a joyride).

When you associate a person to his or her vehicle, you may cue in the memory of that person just driving into the parking lot. As you see that person's car sitting in the parking lot, you allow yourself time to cue up other memories of the person in preparation for meeting him or her.

Associate something about the person you hope to remember with the vehicle he or she drives by doing the following:

- Rhyming the person's name with the vehicle's name
- Associating the style of the vehicle with the person's personality
- Connecting the color of the vehicle with the mood you find yourself in after talking to them

When you rhyme a person's name with their vehicle, try to put a whimsical spin to it. For example: Mary's Mustang or Gretta's Jetta.

If you meet someone named Michael and notice that he drives a sports car, look for some aspect of his personality that connects to the car. You may find that he seemed very animated as he talked about the upcoming Superbowl game. The connection becomes: Michael's **sports** car.

When you meet Don, you note that he drives a bright yellow coupe. He seems like a bright and sunny person, hardly capable of being in an overcast mood. In fact, when you talk to him you feel uplifted. So, Sunny Don drives a sunny-colored car.

Try to describe yourself based on the car you drive. You may be surprised by what you come up with. Somehow, I don't feel like a bland-colored Honda Accord! Perhaps I do to other people . . . .

Remembering the Pecking Order

Many organizations have so many people within them that keeping everyone straight is quite hard. Remembering those people whom you meet can help you move up in the organization, but forgetting people can stall you out.

In addition to using the various techniques described earlier in this chapter to remember names, faces, and stories, you may also need to remember the pecking order. Remembering the pecking order doesn't mean that you're placing value on the people you meet within your organization, but that you're remembering people by using a kind of organizational map.

Large corporations are composed of a cast of personalities. Your task is to place people you meet within the layers of the organization. Like a map or a flow chart, if you can remember both a person and her position together, you'll also learn the organization.

When you meet someone within the organization, find something about the way that person looks or his name and associate it to either the title of that person's position or the function of that position.

For example, when you met Edgar at the company Christmas party, you found out that he had recently been hired as a clerk in the accounting department. You know that he just graduated from college with an accounting degree and wants to move up to an accountant position. You can remember him as Eager Edgar, the aspiring accountant.

When you met Victor at the same party, you found out that he's one of the dozen vice presidents. On one level, you can try to remember him as Vic the vice president. On the other hand, you can watch him for personality characteristics. You notice that he chain smokes with one hand and clutches a tumbler of whiskey with the other. You may remember Vic for his vices.

Making Connections at Meetings

I don't know about you, but I attend a lot of meetings. I go to big ones, small ones, and medium-sized ones. I go to stimulating ones and boring ones. Someone else moderates many meetings, and I moderate some. It can be darn hard to keep everyone straight.

Periodically, I moderate a meeting of the Training Directors from 20 different medical centers in Northern California. My job is to oversee it all and, at the very least, make informed decisions about budgets and programs. But doing that job depends on my keeping everything straight.

Twenty people isn't a huge number to handle and remember, but, at times, people are out or on extended leave, some come with co-directors, other directorships rotate — meaning that, at times, people come and go. I've been fortunate that all of them are very likable and excited about what they're doing and about our joint mission, which makes these people more memorable. At times, a meeting can be like a game of musical chairs. I' have to remember all the players and the people in their programs. You may have experienced something similar to this predicament, or, perhaps, you're an attendee at regular meetings.

To remember people you see at meetings, try the following:

✔ Pay close attention to the introductions.

✔ Associate the person with some involvement outside the meeting.

✔ Have follow-up contact.

Many large meetings start with a round-robin introduction. Each participant is asked to introduce himself and his position or location. Often, this part of the meeting stirs up some anxiety because few people like to be onstage. Nevertheless, your task is to key in to those people you don't know, writing down their names and locations or repeating them to yourself (not out loud, of course!). Later, during the break or after the meeting, reintroduce yourself by saying something like this: "So Jim, you're from the manufacturing department in Tulsa."

This interaction brings you to another level of how to code this person into memory. You need to associate him with something else outside of the context of the meeting. With Jim from Tulsa, you may ask him about his hometown with a question like, "So, how do you like Tulsa?" He may respond by saying something like, "Well, we moved there from the Ozarks region and aren't used to living in a big city." You'll remember Jim not only because he's from Tulsa but also because he's not used to living in the city.

You may not see people you meet at the meeting until the next time you all meet. Consequently, rekindling your memories of them may take a little while. However, if you follow-up on your contact after the first meeting, your memory will be firm.

For example, if you know that a colleague of yours is moving to Tulsa, you may call Jim to establish a connection for her. When you see Jim months later at the next meeting, you can ask, "So, how is Kathy doing?"

The bottom line is that knowing something about a person outside of the context of the meeting allows you to form a solid memory of that person. So, the next time you dread going to yet another meeting, just remind yourself of all the interesting people you're going to see again and remember.

Remembering All Kinds of People

People come in all sizes, shapes, and colors and have different lifestyles. When you try to remember people, take into account this diversity.

For more than 20 years, I've taken part in committees that have addressed diversity. Taking advantage of the broad diversity of perspectives from people of different ethnic, racial, religious, and sexual orientations enriches the broad fabric of society. So, hungry for different perspectives, I've traveled to 40 countries, and I've been to half of those countries at least twice.

When I meet with people from diverse backgrounds, I try to zoom in on how their unique experience has shaped them. Of course, that's my job, and I can't help them without this understanding. But doing so also helps me remember them.

You, too, can remember more clearly the people you meet by factoring in details of their backgrounds. You may already try to do that in terms of broad categories of race and sexual orientation.

However, broad categories alone aren't enough. California, for example, is now more than 50 percent non-white. So, remembering people by their race alone is an overly crude way to remember them and, now, not even enough to pick up the most basic information. In fact, general references to heritage such as African, Latino, and Asian are so broad that they provide little variation for your memory.

When you meet people of African, Latino, Asian, or so-called White backgrounds, you need to be able to perceive the differences of the people within each of these broad groups. Not only do they become individuals, but they also become more memorable. Look for diversity within diversity.

Try to look for:

✔ What differentiates the people you meet from other people in their particular ethnic groups

✔ How they might be seen by people within their racial or ethnic groups

✔ How they might see themselves as members of those groups in contrast to the group that you belong to

When you meet a person from a particular racial or ethnic group, focus on what physical characteristic sets them apart from other people you've met from that group.

Suppose that you meet Yoshi, and you note that he's a lot taller than most Japanese men. You'll remember him because of his height.

When you meet Diane, a woman of African heritage woman, you note that she has particularly light skin. You begin to wonder how other people in her ethnic group view her.

You meet Carlos at the local coffee shop. He seems like a very kind and gentle person. You, however, are struck by his shyness. Halfway through your conversation, three Latino men walk into the coffee shop. Carlos greets them in a spunky and animated manner. He seems like a totally different person. You'll remember Carlos because of how differently he responded to you compared to how he responded to people of his own ethnic group.

You can remember people in an infinite number of ways if you concentrate on the diversity within diversity. Put your sensitivity to work, and your memory of people will be enhanced.

Chapter 15

Taking Stock of Important Dates and Strings of Numbers

· ·

In This Chapter

▶ Figuring out how to remember birthdays and anniversaries

▶ Knowing how to keep historical dates straight in your head

▶ Discovering how to make your appointments

▶ Uncovering ways to recall recurring events

▶ Diving into strings like telephone numbers and personal ID codes

· ·

One of the most frequently reported memory nuisances is forgetting dates: birthdays, anniversaries, an endless number of different types of appointments, and those pesky PINs (personal identification numbers).

Like many people, you may forget dates because they involve numbers. Don't worry! Remembering dates and strings, numbers or not, is easier than you think. Just like other bits of information, such as people's names or faces, you can use certain techniques to improve your memory of dates and long numbers. In this chapter, you discover tricks that put all your important dates and numbers at your fingertips.

Getting Briefed on the Technique

If you need help remembering long strings of numbers, such as phone numbers or your social security number, give that number some CPR:

✔ Chunk it

✔ Peg it

✔ Rhyme it

You can code important dates and times of appointments in a number of ways. For example, you can

- Associate the dates with something else important to you.
- Use rhymes.
- Match the date with seasons, holidays, or vacation.
- Associate the date with a reward.

You can also use established mnemonic techniques to help you recall information. Mnemonics are memory cues that have been used for a few thousand years. (See Chapter 8 for all the details on mnemonics.) You can use any one of the following mnemonic tricks to remember the appointment, birthday, or anniversary:

- **Peg:** This technique involves using a letter or number in association with the date or event.
- **Loci:** Here, you use the location as a cue for the appointment.
- **Story-link:** This technique involves telling yourself a story to remember the appointment.

Celebrating Those All-Important Days

You probably don't forget your own birthday, but you may forget those of others who expect you to remember. As for anniversaries, your spouse may consider this lapse in your memory as a sign that you don't love him or her.

Birthdays

Birthdays have different meanings to different people. Your birthday and those of your friends and relatives may represent multiple meanings for each person: For your 6-year-old daughter, her birthday may represent a time to have a birthday party and probably plenty of presents.

For your aging parents or grandparents (or, perhaps, even you!), birthdays can represent a time for a heightened focus on mortality. Your grandmother, who turns 93, may wonder how many more birthdays she has ahead of her. (See the related sidebar titled, "Birthdays make us refocus on *Life*," later in this chapter.

Remembering your own birthday isn't difficult, but remembering other people's birthdays is another matter. The difficulty is partly because you may have so many to remember. With close friends and family members, you probably have the month down but may slip on the day.

The costs of forgetting may be great, especially if that person is close to you. Perhaps by forgetting, you soon no longer will be close to her. At the very least, she'll wonder how important she is to you.

You can use a number of ways to remember birthdays:

- ✔ Connect the birthday date with a physical or personality trait of the person.
- ✔ Rhyme the date with a reference to the person.
- ✔ Associate the birthday with yearly, seasonal events.
- ✔ Use locations as cues.
- ✔ Tell a story about the event.

Plug a personality or make a rhyme

When you associate someone's birthday with a seasonal event, connect a characteristic of that person with the season. For example, let's say that your friend Carl's birthday is in midsummer. You reflect on Carl's personality and decide you want to connect Carl's sunny, optimistic, personality with summer. When the hot summer nights come to dominate the season, you are reminded of Carl's approaching birthday in late August.

When you rhyme a person's date of birth with her name, try to rhyme her name with the date as an event approaches. For example, if May 7 is Kay's birthday, you can say, Kay's birthday isn't until the 7th of May.

Tie into seasonal events

Sometimes, you have to think hard to build an association between an event and a person's birthday. Some events, like holidays, are good markers because they occur annually. Nevertheless, what do you do if the link between the person's birthday and the holiday seems nebulous? If it's too farfetched, you may not get the connection you need. If you provide a connection between the person and the holiday, however, you may find the process fun.

Birthdays make us refocus on *Life*

A good friend of mine, who just turned 60, told me he found himself reviewing his life, accomplishments, and regrets. Two other friends and I took him out for dinner after a rigorous 10-mile hike in the Point Reyes National Seashore in California. Remembering his birthday in this way inclined my friend to remind us of the other hikes he had taken with us, including the Escalante Canyon in Utah, the Lost Coast in Northern California, and the Grand Canyon. His mortality and reminiscing centered on friendship, hopes for future hikes, and his battle with cancer.

For example, say that Jim's birthday is October 31. You know that the 31st is also Halloween. When you think of your friend, Jim, however, you can't make any immediate associations between Jim and Halloween because he is one of the least dramatic people you know.

Now is the time to turn your image of Jim upside-down. Because Jim is so unassuming and typically wears the most non-descriptive clothes of any person you know, imagine him doing the opposite. The thought of Halloween then becomes a paradoxical cue for Jim's birthday. In your head, Jim is dressed in his birthday/Halloween costume of the most "normal" person that you've ever met.

Jim, of course, may surprise you someday and come to your Halloween party with the most outrageous and bizarre costume of the party. You won't recognize him. At that point (when you lament to another person at the party that it was meant as a surprise party for Jim and he didn't have the courage to show), make sure that he's not the one you're complaining to.

Use the Loci technique

Speakers or performers traditionally use the Loci technique (which involves associating locations with important information) to remember their lines. You can use locations as a way to remember an important date such as your spouse's birthday. (See Chapter 8 for details on the Loci technique.)

For example, on your drive to work for the month before the birthday, note landmarks along the way to remind you of the date:

1. **Your spouse's birthday is in November.** In most areas of the temperate regions of the northern hemisphere, deciduous trees lose their leaves by November. Your clue will be the bare trees on the way to work.

2. **You pass four barns along the highway.** You decide to cue into those barns every day after you notice the leafless trees. The four barns cue you to the fact that her birthday is on the 4th of November.

3. **You also want to remember to buy her a birthday present.** You notice almost as many billboards as trees along the journey. You set aside your general distaste of the crass materialism of American society and reflect for a moment on a purchase of some kind. In this case, you can use the presence of the signs as a paradoxical cue, meaning that you want to remember to buy her something that is more meaningful than some trendy purchase like a black leather jacket.

Of course, you may have to change your location cues over the years, because the four barns may be torn down to accommodate 600 tract homes. The billboards may someday feature political slogans or attack ads, in which case, you may find your anger sidetracking you into forgetting all about her birthday in order to campaign for the candidate with the fewer attack ads.

Create story links

Using a story link to remember a birthday may be a little more tricky, but still potentially useful. Your task is to construct a story that will remind you of the birthday.

Maybe you could combine the location cues that you used in your Loci mnemonic technique. As you drive past the trees going through their bright fall colors each day in late October, remember a story about the bright and colorful times you've had together over the years. Each day, add a new story.

As you pass the first three barns, note that the fourth barn (or November 4) is approaching. Then, as the leaves drop, tell yourself a story about how your relationship will fall if you forget your special person's birthday.

Anniversaries

Anniversaries mark all kinds of notable events: The day you were hired at work, the death of a beloved pet, or — for the example I use in this section — the day you got married. If you're married, every year you have the opportunity to acknowledge and celebrate your anniversary. First, you need to remember it. Forgetting your wedding anniversary can be a source of hurt and pain.

To make sure you remember your anniversary date, you need a way to structure the anniversary into your year. Like Christmas, Hanukkah, or Ramadan, it's a time of reverence. Although not related to religion, a wedding anniversary is a day that must symbolically resonate with a remembrance of your commitment to each other.

You probably have little trouble forgetting Christmas, Hanukkah, or Ramadan if you live in the West, because that society provides constant reminders of the approaching date. Especially for Christmas in the United States, advertisements on television and the news warn you that if you don't participate in the commercialism and buy your gifts soon, "you're going to be in deep trouble with those you love."

You get no such reminders for anniversary dates. The minimum reminder may be a quick note jotted down on the calendar — that is, if one of you remembered to do that. Even if the date is highlighted on the calendar, you may not be in the habit of checking it until the date itself. For example, if you look at the calendar only one day at a time — checking to see what appointment you may have for the day — you'll be ill-prepared to plan for a night out to celebrate.

Thinking of a seasonal day of reverence may not be enough to help you remember the anniversary. You need a mnemonic or a general memory cue to help you remember the month and the day.

You actually have two goals when it comes to remembering your wedding anniversary: (1) remembering the date, and (2) remembering that the date is coming up so that you can make plans to celebrate.

Map out a plan and peg it into your memory

Certainly, remembering the date on the day of the wedding anniversary is better than forgetting it entirely. At work, as you get ready for the day, you look on the calendar noting the date and remember, "Oh, today is our anniversary! I'd better get some flowers or a gift." Given the lack of time (you have two meetings, a working lunch, and a report to get through), a single rose wrapped in cellophane that you can pick up at the gas station seems the likely solution. (Uh-oh. Do you know how to spell t-r-o-u-b-l-e?)

However, if you remember ahead of time, you'll be able to plan for the event. You may say to your spouse, "You know our anniversary is coming up next week. Wanna go away for the weekend?"

Associate your anniversary with an opportunity to do something you don't normally do often. For example, associate it with

✔ A chance to go away for the weekend.

✔ A chance to go to that expensive restaurant reserved only for special occasions.

✔ Justification for the in-laws to come to baby-sit.

✔ A reason to buy both of you a present that would otherwise seem extravagant.

You can use the peg technique (see Chapter 8) to remind yourself of scheduling a night out for your anniversary. Use the first-letter peg to associate a word that you'll encounter on a regular basis.

Let's say you want to use the word *toast* as a way to remember the day. If your anniversary is on October 2, you can use the first letter of the following words:

Two

October

Anniversary

Schedule

Trip

The first letters of these words combined spells TOAST. Every morning in the fall, make sure your breakfast includes a slice of toast. Another way to think of this is that you're going to be toast if you don't remember.

Meet my associate . . .

For years, I had trouble remembering our wedding anniversary day. I knew it was March 29, 30, or 31. However, for some reason I couldn't pin down the exact day. Year after year, I would ask my wife "Now what day was it again?"

She'd say, "The 31st! Why can't you remember?"

The reason I couldn't remember the exact day was that I had yet to develop an association for the 31st with something relevant to the marriage. I decided that I'd take the **1st** part of 3**1st** as an anchor. This was and is my first and only marriage. Making an association for my anniversary finally gave me a way to remember that date every year.

I didn't have trouble remembering the month of March. If I did, perhaps I'd use the word March as a memory cue. In this case, I'd remember marching into marriage.

For our honeymoon, we went to the Great Barrier Reef off Australia to go diving. I could further associate the date with marching into a barrier, but instead of being obstructed, we dove down to find a magnificent kaleido-scope of coral and sea life.

Mnemonics to the rescue

My wife seemed to have no trouble with remembering the date of the 31st. She, in contrast, couldn't remember the year. She'd always ask, "Now how many years has it been?" She asked this not because she had trouble with math, but she'd always forget that it was in 1984. (See the related sidebar titled, "Anniversaries aren't for fools," later in this chapter.)

As I wrote this book, we approached our anniversary, and again she asked, "How many years now?" I suggested she use a mnemonic. She came up with "In 1984 we walked through the door."

Here you have two examples of people who remember part of the anniver-sary date but not the entire date. Chances are you remember a part of yours or that of close friends or family members. Your task is to complete the loop and remember the whole date. Take the piece that you do remember and expand on it.

Complete the picture by using the following:

1. **Pick one piece of what you do remember** and make an association to a part of it that you don't.

2. **Make an association** between the part that you can't remember and the marriage itself.

3. **Tie the two together** in a comical but enduring image.

Anniversaries aren't for fools

You may never know how another person remembers events no matter how close they are to you. I thought my wife remembered our anniversary date of March 31 more easily than I because she, as she often reminds me, is better at details. She also notes that I'm oriented toward the "big picture" at the expense of the small. So I thought she had the 31st nailed down because of her detail orientation, and I always remembered the year we got married, 1984, because of my so-called big picture orientation.

Nevertheless, I was missing something. I asked her how she remembered our anniversary was on the 31st. She said it was because we decided to make sure that it didn't take place on the following day — April 1.

I asked, "But there's more to it isn't there?"

My wife said, "Don't you remember that we said it would be foolish to marry on April Fool's day?"

How foolish of me to forget.

Creating Rhymes for Historical Dates

Many people have trouble remembering historical dates because they're just a string of numbers. Historical dates may not grab your attention or hold meaning for you. On the other hand, perhaps the historical events hold meaning, but the link to the year probably doesn't grab your attention.

Teach yourself rhymes for historical dates. The rhyme you choose is more useful if it

✔ Is easy to remember.

✔ Ties the historical events to the words in the rhyme.

✔ Is short and to the point.

Many people have trouble remembering a date if they are only in the year form. The historical dates such as 1066, 1492, 1865, 1915, and 1948 may sound meaningless as numbers by themselves, but each of these dates has historical significance, because the events that followed them shaped either a nation's history or that of world history.

You may know these dates as:

✔ **1066:** William the Conqueror's invasion of Britain

✔ **1492:** Columbus' arrival in the West Indies

✔ **1865:** The end of the Civil War and the assassination of Lincoln

✔ **1915:** The first genocide of the twentieth century

✔ **1948:** The establishment of the United Nations

Construct or remember a rhyme for the date and its historical events such as:

- **1066 — In ten sixty-six, William the Conqueror made the Saxons sick.** You are, of course, omitting the fact that there were Celts and Angles there, as well, but that would mess up your rhyme.

- **1492 — In fourteen hundred and ninety-two, Columbus sailed the ocean blue.** This one is an old one you probably remember from elementary school.

- **1865 — In eighteen sixty-five, one of our forefathers didn't survive.** The use of the word father is a tie to the fact that most Americans are taught that the two most important presidents include Washington and Lincoln. Both earned their own national holidays.

- **1915 — In nineteen fifteen, something terrible went unseen.** This refers to the fact that the Turks slaughtered 1.5 million Armenians. Hitler was to make note of this genocide when he was planning the genocide of the Jews and said, "Well, no one remembers what the Turks did to the Armenians."

- **1948 — In nineteen forty-eight, all people for everyone's sake.** This, of course, marks the all too maligned effort to promote international justice through the development of a world legislative body.

You can use the rhyming technique for historical duties such as those listed above or with dates personal to you, such as your anniversary or the birthdays of those you love.

Tying a String around Appointments

You may have had trouble remembering to show up for an appointment. Dentist offices expect you to forget appointments, which is why some dentist offices direct one of their staff to call you the day before as a reminder.

Of course, there are always reasons why you unconsciously may be motivated to forget an appointment. Psychologists refer to this as repression or *motivated forgetting*. When I work with someone who complains about a memory problem that's not general but focuses on one event or issue like going to the dentist, I help him or her resolve those reasons why they tend to forget. (See the related sidebar titled, "Freud on repression," later in this chapter.)

Let's say your memory for most appointments is generally okay. However, for some reason you can't remember to show up for your dentist appointment. Maybe you had root canal work done on two separate occasions? Both experiences, to say the least, were ones that you'd like not to repeat.

You may fear that at your next dentist appointment you'll find out that you're due for another root canal. The irony is that if you don't remember to take care of your teeth, you'll need that dentist to fit you for dentures.

Like many people, you may have decided that a daily planner or handheld organizer is the only thing you can use to help remind yourself to get to an appointment. These tools are certainly helpful, but you have to remember to use them.

Perhaps you did bother to code the appointment into the handheld and look at it in the morning. How do you make sure that you'll remember it later in the afternoon? Tie a string around your finger?

Consider following these guidelines to remembering an appointment:

- ✔ Plan to organize your day around the appointment.
- ✔ Visualize attending the appointment.
- ✔ Make associations to specific cues.
- ✔ Use the time of day and its date as a code.
- ✔ Use a rhyme or jingle.
- ✔ Bait yourself.

Make a new plan, Stan!

If you plan your day around the appointment, it's structured into the day. For instance, you have a dentist appointment at 2 p.m. on Tuesday. It's your vacation, and you don't want the dentist appointment to kill the whole day. You may even feel some resentment that you have to go to a dentist appointment on your vacation. What kind of vacation is this?

Freud on repression

More than 100 years ago, Sigmund Freud drew attention to the phenomenon of repression. He shocked Victorian society with the discovery that the sexual repression of the era contri-buted to unconscious forgetting or the pushing back of thoughts, feelings, and memories that are too uncomfortable to reside in conscious awareness.

This concept helped theorists who followed Freud to understand a whole range of psychodynamics, including conversion disorders, certain aspects of dreams, and slips of the tongue (now sometimes called Freudian slips).

The general concept of repression also helped people to understand why we forget things, events, or appointments, especially those that are distasteful, such as going to the dentist for root canal work. The task is to deal with those fears so you don't have to forget them.

You can structure your activities around the appointment: You decide to have lunch with your friend, Walt, at a restaurant in the same area of town as the dentist just before the appointment. You also decide that you'll go to a bookstore in the same area of town after the appointment. You estimate that the dentist appointment will take approximately an hour. That will leave you with enough time to get home for dinner. Whew! You've taken care of your health, spent time with a friend, and fed your brain with books. Not bad for a vacation day, right?

Picture this . . .

When you use the technique of visualizing an appointment, try to imagine something that draws your attention. Make it something that really captures your attention. The image has to be something that is pleasurable rather than something you want to avoid.

For example, imagining the dentist's drill grinding away at your teeth isn't something you'd look forward to, but something you'd rather forget. Instead, imagine driving up to the parking lot and inspecting the rose garden next to the dentist office. Perhaps you're a rose gardener, and you know these roses are cared for by a very astute landscaping service. You know this service is very talented at keeping roses healthy and beautiful.

The bottom line is that visualizing going to the appointment needs to grab your interest. If you have something to look forward to, such as a rose garden, then you'd be motivated to remember to attend an appointment. The image needs to pique your interest.

Connect the cues

Use the technique of making associations to specific cues to remind yourself of the appointment throughout the day.

Let's say you decide to search for the "D" representing dentist all day. As you drive down the highway, you notice the Ds on the litter of billboards that obscures your view of the countryside. You notice the **D**unlap exit, the turnoff for the town of **D**avenport, and the **D**unbartten Bridge. You take **D**orn **D**rive to get to your office and drive into the **d**riveway to park near your office.

As you begin work, you decide to stamp "**D**one" or "**D**o" on papers that pass your way. Your boss comes by to ask you why you're doing this.

You answer, "Oh Mr. **D**oolittle, I'm just **d**oing my **d**uty!"

He sends you to the Employee Assistant Counselor because he's worried about you.

You greet Ms. **D**avey and explain that you're trying to remember the **d**entist appointment. Both of you realize that if you leave right away you'll get there on time.

Use numeric coding

The date and time code technique reminds you of when the dentist appointment is scheduled. In this example, your appointment is scheduled for Tuesday at 2 p.m., but you need to put it in a number code to remember it more easily.

You can use a code whereby each day of the seven days a week earns a position, such as:

Monday: 1

Tuesday: 2

Wednesday: 3

Thursday: 4

Friday: 5

Saturday: 6

Sunday: 7

Your dentist appointment will earn a 2 for Tuesday. It so happens that it is at 2 p.m. Therefore, you can remember it by remembering 2-2 or 22.

Some number code systems try to account for all 24 hours a day by using so-called *military time*. Military time, of course, has no a.m or p.m. It goes for 24 hours. Therefore, 2 p.m. becomes 1400. (Because I'm assuming that you're not in the military and, like me, you prefer to use the simpler system, you'll probably want to go with the 2 for 2 p.m.)

Jingle your memory

Maybe you want to try to use a rhyme or a jingle to remind you of the dentist appointment. To do this, you need at least a handful of words that associate with the appointment. Try these:

Today's

Tooth

Two

You can string these three words together by saying, "Today's tooth at two. You can also think of these as the Three Ts.

Consider positive reinforcement

Okay, let's say you're having trouble encouraging yourself to use a memory technique to remind yourself to get to the dentist appointment. The bottom line is that if you're motivated to forget it, you won't remember it. The only reason you're motivated to get to the appointment is out of fear.

Maybe it's time for a little bribery, um, make that positive reinforcement. Make remembering the dentist appointment worthy of something more to you than quelling your fear of greater dental problems in the future. Reward yourself for going.

Say to yourself that if you attend, you'll buy that pair of binoculars (or shoes, or whatever) that you've been wanting. Let's hope that you don't pass up this opportunity and remain shortsighted.

Getting a Handle on Recurring Events

You have many things to remember to do on a periodic basis. You have to remember to change the oil in your car, change batteries, rotate tires, get your teeth cleaned, and so on.

This demand to re-remember recurring events presents a challenge to your already cluttered life. Remembering to do things that you have scheduled is hard enough, but to remember to schedule something, that's another thing entirely.

To remember, recurring events look for the possibility of reminding yourself by doing one of the following:

✔ Impose a pattern.

✔ Make a joke out of it.

✔ Anchor at least one date to something memorable, and then work backwards.

Schedules that always change sometimes have a pattern to them and sometimes they don't. Obviously, remembering the appointment is much easier if the pattern is set rather than fluctuates.

For example, when I served on the joint executive committees for the psychiatry departments at two medical centers, we had a set meeting schedule. Our meetings occurred on the first Tuesday of each month. The location alternated between two sites. This set-up, of course, demanded that we remember not only to go to monthly meetings but also where to go. There often would be at least one of the team who would forget to attend.

Some set-scheduled-cycled meetings, such as ours, include an added cycle. We had delegates from two different medical centers and needed a way to ensure that one group didn't always have to do the driving. Therefore, we devised a way to schedule one meeting at one medical center and alternate it with the other on a different month. Because we were already prone to forget, we needed to impose a pattern that we'd remember.

We decided that on the even months, we would meet in Vacaville and on the odd months, we'd meet in Vallejo. Because my home base was in Vallejo, I was in the odd group. We formed a private joke that our odd group was odd because we hated these meetings in contrast to the even group that seem to enjoy them.

Working with Rotating Schedules

When you have layers of cycles, it can be hard to remember them unless you impose some kind of a pattern. Cycled schedules become even more complicated when you have to remember rotating schedules with a specified time span but no monthly reference.

Rotating schedules can occur as part of your work schedule, school, even your dental hygienist appointment. Rotating work schedules may include working six days and being off three days, then being on again for six days, and so on. This schedule leaves you constantly changing plans with family and rescheduling events that conflict with your work schedule. On the other hand, if you pay meticulously close attention to the calendar, you may minimize your frustration.

A rotating schedule, such as getting an oil change every 3,000 miles, requires that you remember the mileage reading of the last oil change and then calculate forward 3,000 miles. Many car manufactures assume you need a way to remind yourself to change the oil, so they created a small, color-coded device that changes as your odometer changes. As you reach 3,000, the device turns yellow; as you pass 3,000, it turns red.

When you try to remember to get your teeth cleaned every six months, you need to anchor in the date and somehow remind yourself of it before it comes and goes. Many dentist offices have their patients fill out a postcard and then they send it to you just before your next appointment.

All these types of rotating schedules require organizational cues so that you'll remember. You can:

- ✔ Use external cues.
- ✔ Sequence the appointments.
- ✔ Use mnemonics.

Clue into external cues

The easiest and perhaps the most efficient way to remember dates and times in rotating schedules is to rely on external cues. Even if you do try to remember these appointments, with the fluctuating dates, I recommend that you back yourself up with an external cue.

External cues can include:

- ✔ Daily reminders
- ✔ Wall calendars
- ✔ Mailing yourself reminders just like the dentist office

Seek out a sequence

If you can get your rotating schedules to clump together into a sequence or pattern, you'll have an easier time remembering. For example, annual health exams could include a general physical with your primary care doctor, a prostate exam for men, and a Pap test and/or mammogram for women. Don't forget your biannual dental exams and biennial vision tests. Why not schedule all these appointments for the same month? You could say April is your personal health month. Then schedule three appointments on three consecutive Fridays.

You can do the same thing with all the mechanical devices you regularly service, such as your car, water treatment system for your house, well maintenance, sprinkler system, or whatever. Select a month, and space out the appointments. Call it your maintenance month.

Nail it with mnemonics

You can combine a peg mnemonic to this monthly system. For mechanical devices, pick a month that sounds like maintenance: May.

For your health-related cycle, you can't use a month that starts with an H because, um, there are none. Choose the month of your birthday, instead, because all these annual medical appointments relate to your birthday.

If the appointments are biannual, then stay with the month you chose for the annual and schedule the other exactly six months apart. The calendar has 12 months in a year; you'll have no trouble doing that.

Because you have the annual health appointments pegged by the first letter of the month of your birthday, you need to come up with a memory association for the maintenance month that is six months away. For the May appointment, for example, the six-month interval is November. Try to imagine servicing the mechanical devices before winter hibernation.

Getting to Your Appointment on Time

You may be like thousands of other people who manage to remember an appointment but forget how long it takes to get there. Because of this memory glitch, you may arrive at that appointment late anyway. So much for remembering the time of the appointment!

After you schedule the 2 p.m. dental appointment into your Tuesday and use all or some of the memory techniques described throughout this chapter, make sure you can get there on time by doing one or all of the following:

✔ Pad the appointment time.

✔ Think of the date and time as 21 and a half

For your Tuesday, 2 p.m. dental appointment, you know that it will take you half an hour to get to the dentist's office. When you make your plans, think of 21 as representing the appointment day and time and ½ as the travel time. Therefore, by saying to yourself 21½, you have the second day of the week (2, for Tuesday) and the time (1½).

Remembering Strings of Numbers

Dates, anniversaries, and appointments are sometimes easier to remember than strings of numbers by themselves, because anniversaries and appointments have built-in associations. These built-in associations are the names of the people who are being honored (or the person you're meeting), and the name of the month.

These advantages aren't available for a string of numbers such as a social security number or a phone number. Sure, the telephone number and social security number belong to people, but very few links are available to use as a memory link.

The same goes for a major nuisance that has blown in on the hurricane of high-tech devices: the personal identification number (PIN). This PIN is essentially a personalized password. The concept of the PIN is built around "security." However, the security is often so extensive that you can't break in when you've forgotten your own PIN. Don't worry too much, though. Many companies have a PIN reset number available to you, so that you can think of yet another PIN. (In Chapter 16, I talk about rotating passwords and PINs and how to deal with the nuisance of the numbing high-tech blizzard.)

Let me make a very basic, surprisingly overlooked suggestion: Remember, this secret number is *your* PIN. Don't make it more complicated and difficult to remember than it needs to be. Choose a personal code word embedded within your number or a number that has personal significance. But make sure that it doesn't have obvious personal significance that can be tracked by hackers who can easily access all sorts of personal information readily available on the Internet. Use something like your dog's birthday or your in-laws' anniversary.

License plate numbers are often quite difficult to remember for several reasons:

- You're rarely asked to recite them.
- They are often long.
- They are often a mix of letters and numbers.

Many states offer personalized license plates not only because people like to advertise their personality, but also so that they can choose numbers and letters that they can remember.

For remembering numbers in general, use the following techniques:

- Chunking
- Pegging
- Rhyming

Chunk it

Chunking is useful when the string of numbers is long. Chunking is a method of breaking up the chain of numbers into chunks that you can remember more easily.

Psychologists have determined that most people can hold seven digits, plus or minus two, in their short-term memory. It's partly for this reason that phone numbers in the United States are seven digits long (excluding area code).

Most people rely on chunking to break up the seven-digit number, which breaks up even further if you have to remember the area code. For example, if your phone number is 7923485, you'll remember it more easily by having one chunk that is three digits and one chunk that is four digits: 792 3485.

The same principle is at work when you remember your social security number. These numbers have nine digits and are difficult to remember without chunking. So, with a social security number such as 952475718, you'll find that if you chunk it like 952-47-5718, you'll remember it more easily.

Peg it

Pegging numbers initially may seem more complicated than it really is. A useful way to use this technique is to associate a number with a letter. Then, with the letters, construct a word.

Start with the following letter-number matches:

A - 1	N - 14
B - 2	O - 15
C - 3	P - 16
D - 4	Q - 17
E - 5	R - 18
F - 6	S - 19
G - 7	T - 20
H - 8	U - 21
I - 9	V - 22
J - 10	W - 23
K - 11	X - 24
L - 12	Y - 25
M - 13	Z - 0

Suppose that you want to remember Steve's telephone number. His number is 577-1695. These numbers correspond to the letters "egg pie." So, when you think of Steve, think egg pie.

This method requires some thought, because you won't always have enough letters or, on the other hand, you may actually have too many. You're in luck if there's a match.

Rhyme it

You may have to resort to a rhyme to remember a number. If you do, you'll want to rhyme to associate with what the number represents. For example, when trying to remember Tony's phone number, you could exaggerate the pronunciation of Tony's name with the word *phone* and come up with:

T (two) - 2

O (letter o) - 0

N - 9

Pho - 0

n - 9

oo - 00

Alternatively, if you want to remember it in chunked form, it's 209-0900.

With this technique, you may end up pushing the envelope a bit to get this number association. But who cares, it's your number to remember and your rhyme. Chances are you can construct a better rhyme to your own numbers that will have more significance to you.

Whatever memory technique you use to remember numbers, anniversaries, dates, appointments, or even phone numbers, try to personalize it as if it is your own PIN.

Numbers and dates don't have to be difficult to remember. The only thing really holding you back from remembering them is that, until now, you had not developed a strategy to code them into memory.

Chapter 16

Keeping Your Memory Intact in a High-Speed World

In This Chapter

▶ Being present for memories

▶ Avoiding multitasking

▶ Relying on aids

Modern society is saturated with cell phones, e-mails, faxes, pagers, teleconferencing, and instant messages via your computer or hand-held day organizer. We communicate with one another across great distances in an almost dreamlike web of these technological buffers.

What's more, we entertain ourselves by vicariously involving ourselves in the movies and television. We allow people onscreen to play out parts of ourselves in fantasies created by someone else.

If you find the modern social climate appealing — and who doesn't from time to time? — your memory skills can't help but be strained as you go about everyday business. How do you know what to pay attention to, what to remember, and, for that matter, what's real and what's just entertainment?

In this chapter, you discover ways to allow your memory skills to weather the media and tech blizzard.

Staying Organized at the Center of the Cyclone

Contemporary society is charged with a whirlwind of activities that people somehow feel compelled to participate in. If you feel such an obligation, you may sacrifice some of your memory skills along the way.

Want proof? Tag along with a Soccer Mom as she zooms from the playing field to the music lesson to the dentist appointment and somehow gets home in time for dinner and, hopefully, the homework. Unless she's Supermom, chances are, she forgot a few things along the way.

A harried existence makes you less capable of memory.

You need to take control of three major factors if you expect to remember anything at the center of the cyclone. They are:

✔ **Pace:** Think of pace this way: As you race from one event to another, the quality of your involvement in each event diminishes. You're like a rock skipping the water. To be able to retain a memory of what you did, slow down and see where you are before moving on.

✔ **Depth:** Depth means prioritizing your activities and eliminating the items that are low on the list, thus freeing more time and permitting more depth for the top priorities. The more time you spend with an activity, the more vivid and accurate your memory of that activity becomes.

✔ **Organization:** You know a lot about organization already. But I give the word a special twist: understanding how to make a clean break between one activity and the next, helping to keep your memories clear.

Doing all these things may sound like a very tall order. You may feel that you have no choice but to satisfy all those demands upon you. But you have to ask yourself how willing you are to damage your memory skills by engaging in a whirlwind of activities. The cost to your memory is as great as the speed in which you dash from one event to another. In this case, speed kills — memory, that is.

Setting priorities

Overextending yourself can have memory-costing consequences. You essentially dilute your memory of each of the projects or engagements that you're racing between.

By imposing a sense of organization and simultaneously slowing your pace, you allow yourself an opportunity to remember what you did. To accomplish this ability, remember to:

✔ Prioritize your activities.

✔ Eliminate those activities that are low on your priority list.

✔ Increase the time that you're involved in the activities that you chose to stay with.

✔ Cultivate greater depth in that activity.

✔ Impose a coherent sense of organization to your activities.

For example, suppose that you're the secretary of the PTA, a member of the Rotary Club, a full-time employee, a wife, and a mother of two children ages 7 and 10. Obviously, you're a busy person. But chances are, you're also a person who may be at risk of forgetting a lot as you dart from one activity to the next.

By prioritizing your involvements, you can give each of your commitments the attention they need. Here's how you rank your priorities:

✔ Family

✔ Job

✔ PTA

✔ Rotary Club

As you increase the time you spend with your priorities, you realize immediately that something has to give. You have to cut out something. You decide that, because the Rotary Club is the lowest priority, it has to go. You also realize that your tenure as the PTA Secretary may have to go at the end of your term. You can still stay with the PTA, but now you'll be an attendee rather than an officeholder. These cuts leave you with more time and energy to increase the time you devote to your family and your job. You maintain your family as your highest priority, followed by your job, so now you have the ability to devote much more quality time with each commitment.

Organizing your memory of priorities

Everything that you do has a *context* — a surrounding set of circumstances — that gives the activity meaning and relevance. For example, when you recall the assignment your boss gave you yesterday, the context includes the project you're already working on, the goals of the project, the people involved, the project's relationship to the rest of the company, and so on.

If you begin work on one project but then shift to another project, when you shift back to the first project, you must rekindle your memory of the appropriate context.

Applying your memory skills when you alternate between projects can work best if you:

✔ Fully disengage from one context before moving on to another

✔ *Think around* the new project by reflecting on all the issues that are related to it and the people involved

✔ Talk to someone involved

You need a boundary and transition between one project and another to be able to make full use of your context-specific memories. Your memories related to one project probably don't apply to the next project. This brief gap in time between projects allows you to regroup and focus on the new task. Go to the bathroom or get a drink of water to give your mind a break. Then, when you get back to your desk, you're ready to tackle the next project.

Talking to another person involved in the same project helps jog your memory and puts you back in the frame of mind appropriate to recall memories. This person is, in fact, part of the context of the memories for the project.

By keeping your life organized and setting your own pace, you increase the depth of your involvement in those activities you find to be of high priority. As the quality of your involvement increases, so does your memory regarding each activity.

Dodging the Hazards of Multitasking

You may be one of the millions of people juggling several tasks at once like:

✔ Talking on the phone while e-mailing

✔ Reading while watching television

✔ Writing a memo during a meeting about something completely different

✔ Making or taking a cell phone call while driving

This kind of complicated juggling has been referred to as *multitasking* because you're doing more than one thing at time. Multitasking has become a normal way of functioning in the world.

If you're proud of being able to multitask, you should be concerned about what it's doing to your memory. Recent research has made clear that divided attention dampens memory. Though you and I may be able to glide through the day, touching bases and dealing with busy work, the depth to which we remember any of it reduces as we engage in activities that require more concentration.

Imagine yourself sitting at a meeting at work and feeling pressed for time with too many people wanting your attention. Twice, you get up to answer your pager. After you sit back down in the meeting, you decide that you'd better get that memo to the staff written.

From one ear, you hear the director of the company talk about getting more out of the workers. From the other ear, you listen to two of your fellow supervisors gossiping about how the director was dating his assistant, Debbie.

You decide that you'd better get this memo written before the end of the meeting because you have a teleconferencing meeting and have to return some e-mails while you return some phone calls.

You write the memo on your laptop. After the meeting, you hand the floppy disk to your secretary and ask her to have it printed out and delivered to everyone's mailbox.

After you go to the two teleconferences, you get an urgent call from the director. He summons you to his office. You arrive to see him glaring at you. He hands you a copy of your memo. It reads, "Debbie and the Director want you."

Having that memo fly back in your face in this way would be enough to make you reconsider whether you'll continue multitasking. However, you shouldn't wait to change your ways until you experience such a dramatic humiliation. Most likely, the memory mistakes you make while multitasking are far more subtle. Perhaps, they're so subtle that you don't even notice because you're so busy multitasking.

Multitasking decreases your memory ability. Each task that you're engaged in drains part of your mental energy. This drainage is why multitasking breeds absentmindedness. Your complete mind isn't present when you shift from one task to another and back again. You could say that your mind is absent.

The plain truth is that you don't have unlimited ability to pay attention to several things at once. With each new task you toss in to the juggling act, you dilute your investment in each task. Consequently, even if you do complete one of the juggled tasks, you may not remember how you did it.

You may ask, "Is the solution to avoid multitasking?" The simple answer to this question is *yes*. But, at times, you may think that you don't have a choice. However, you may have a bigger choice than you think. True, certain times, you may have to do some juggling — but these times are probably fewer than you think. Your challenge is to know the difference between the times you absolutely *do* have to multitask and the times that you don't.

Even if you're compelled to multitask, you still may be able to retain some memory of what you did on one task before you shift to another. You can make this shift successfully if you shift your pace. Yet, just slowing down isn't enough because you still need to break the pace up with islands of sanity. You need to come up for air periodically.

Consider the break in pace to be an opportunity to remember what you just completed. It's a time for you to integrate that task with all the other tasks you completed in the same project. As you fit in the latest tasks with the other ones, you can see how they all relate to the bigger picture.

If you don't take breaks, you may be spinning your wheels by either repeating the same task because you forgot that you did it before, or by doing work you don't need to be doing anyway.

Use the *stop and focus* technique to break the pace and remember what you did. You can do this technique simply by:

- ✔ Walking outside for a break
- ✔ Going to get a refreshment from the cafeteria or kitchen
- ✔ Taking notes on what you just did
- ✔ Telling a peer, supervisor, or friend what you've just accomplished

By doing any or all of the above simple things, you're shifting your attention to the next task you need to focus on. You allow yourself a brief moment to remember what you just did.

You can even take mini breaks, just a few seconds long, while you're in the process of completing a few tasks. Try any one or all of the following to establish boundaries between tasks you're juggling:

- ✔ If you've been sitting, stand up and stretch.
- ✔ Take a few deep breaths to slow down your heart rate.
- ✔ Clear your mind for a few moments of all the tasks you've been working on as well as the one's you've yet to accomplish.

Breaking Away from a Media-Crazed World

The movies and television programs that you're exposed to are increasingly sensationalistic, because producers assume that you're too numb to pay attention. The average movie you see may be packed with numerous car crashes, exploding bombs, and people being murdered.

Amidst this fast-paced, media-blitzed world, you may have a hard time knowing what to pay attention to. Your attention toward information and events in your life may be numbed by the blitz of over-stimulation. The numbness then hinders your ability to remember, because you're not absorbing information — you're just being bombarded by it.

To shake off this numbness, you have to regard it as a consequence of being over-stimulated. You have to be more discriminating about what you pay attention to.

For example, don't get caught up in feeling the "need" to keep every tech device (cell phones, pagers, electronic organizers, and so on) on and in use throughout the day, especially not while you're supposedly trying to concentrate on something else. Be selective in terms of what you expose yourself to and how you participate in this media-crazed world.

I'm not saying that you need to isolate yourself. What I am saying is to use all the gadgets and conveniences of this new world to benefit yourself instead of wear yourself down. If you watch television, be selective. Don't watch it all the time. If you use a cell phone, pager, e-mail, or whatever other tech device, use those tools selectively.

I e-mail once a day, keep my cell phone on only during the drive home so my family can reach me, and don't carry a pager unless I'm on-call for the hospital. When I watch television, I pick programs that interest me and decide well ahead of time to watch them. Without taking these steps, I'd suffer from memory problems because my attention, otherwise, would be divided, compromised, and numbed.

Remembering yourself

Forgetting your goals, tastes, interests, and even a sense of self is often too easy in this blizzard of overblown commercialism in today's society.

You can't watch the Olympic games on television without being bombarded by more commercials than actual games. What's more, the programming itself is hard to separate from the commercials because it seems that the "up close and personal" spots on athletes "with gold in their eyes" are indistinguishable from the commercials. When the actual commercial airs, some of the same athletes are featured with their "favorite" products.

You're taught to like the products because you, too, "want to go for the gold" in life. As you're bombarded by all the slippery commercial hype, you run the risk of being worn down and forgetting memories of your own tastes and interests.

To regain a memory of who you are and what your true interests are, you have to create islands of individuality. These islands allow you an opportunity to reconnect with yourself. And creating these islands is actually quite simple.

To disconnect from all the media and even from other people, try the following:

- ✔ Take long walks in places where you won't meet anyone you know and, preferably, anyone in general.

- ✔ Go to a local park and just sit and feel the sun on your back.

- ✔ Go into your backyard and just sit without thinking of all the things you need to do and people you need to talk to.

- ✔ Get away from the rest of your family for a few hours to take a long bath and relax.

The point of taking these mini-vacations is to regroup and gather perspective. Focusing on goals is fine as long as they're long-range goals, such as what you're working toward — not the immediate short-term goals of endless busy work.

You need to take these breaks to provide yourself with an opportunity to reflect on what's really important in your life rather than what you've been persuaded to believe is important.

Essentially, you're going off automatic pilot. When you're on automatic pilot, who sets the control parameters? Society? You need to get back into the driver's seat to ensure that you don't forget who you are.

Focusing on the here and now

Throughout this book, I point out the important role that attention plays in your memory skills. Simply put, if you're not paying full attention to what you want to remember, you won't remember most of it.

In this ADD society where the MTV format dominates the media, people are assumed incapable of paying attention for longer than a few minutes at a time. Scripts for movies and television are developed with fewer and shorter lines because producers are worried that you'll lose interest and either get up and walk out of the movie theater or change the channel on your TV set.

You may be asking, "How on earth can you fight this sea of change and be able to pay attention?" Perhaps you're one of the few people who get angry when intense, meaningful dialogue in a movie is disrupted by flashes of sensationalism like a murder, car crash, or a violent chase.

You're going to have to disconnect from the feverish frenzy periodically, at the very least to consolidate the memories of the details of what and who you've been involved with during the day.

You also can benefit from a methodology that allows you to be completely present, so that your attention is heightened. This frame of mind is the opposite of multitasking. You could call it "mono-tasking" because it involves being completely focused on the process of performing the task that you're doing. At first, your mind may wander. But with practice, you can learn to focus more easily and not worry about other awaiting projects.

You may also want to try a practice called *mindfulness,* which can be useful to help your focus. Mindfulness is actually a meditative technique that we teach in our medical centers to people wanting to learn relaxation, to people suffering from chronic pain, or even to people wanting to increase the quality of their lives. This practice helps you increase your presence and attention.

A great "side-effect" of mindfulness is improved memory. Because you're more deeply involved in what you're doing — being mindful of the task — your memory of the details of the task greatly improves.

Mindfulness involves completely absorbing yourself in whatever you're doing. That total absorption that concentrates your attention makes the task become a rich and pleasurable experience. Because you're completely invested in your task, you can remember more about it.

Think of how your mind wanders as you engage in any task. Everyone's mind has the tendency to wander, some people's more than others. You can pull back your wandering mind by engaging in the mindfulness technique.

As we all age, we become creatures of routine. This routine isn't necessarily a bad thing as long as we all leave some room for novel experiences and remain mindful of each task we do.

Think of the life of a monk and how meditative the experience of each routine can be. His mind isn't distracted. He's mindful of each experience. As a result, his memories are vital. Each experience resonates in the now and is remembered later with clarity.

If you do practice this level of concentration (of mindfulness), besides the improved overall quality of your experience, you'll remember more about it.

Here's how you can practice doing it: Take a very simple example, such as washing your car.

As you rinse the car before scrubbing, notice the power of the hose shooting out the nozzle and hear the water pounding on the surface of the car. Notice what parts of the car the dirt clings to, despite the power of the spraying water. Now, as you scrub the car with a soapy sponge, notice the difference in texture on the various areas of the car. The areas that the dirt still clings to are not as smooth until you scrub off the dirt.

When you go back inside the house later and your spouse asks you, "Did you clean those two spots that never seem to get clean?" You can respond by saying, "Oh yes, I remember those two spots. Yes, I did get them clean."

Had you not engaged in the cleaning job mindfully, your mind probably would've been elsewhere. When asked if you cleaned those two spots, you probably wouldn't even have been aware of the spots or remembered whether you got them clean However, you remember because you were mindfully involved in a task that may have seemed laborious and boring, otherwise.

The point that I'm trying to make doesn't mean that letting your mind wander is "bad." A wandering mind is perfectly natural. You drive down the highway, and your mind wanders. Now, you may forget that you've driven a few miles because your mind was wandering. If you want to remember the journey, being mindful can help. But if you don't, that's fine, too.

Flowing with memory

The more you can *flow* with whatever you're doing at the moment, the better you can remember it later. "Okay," you say. "But exactly how do I flow?" The answer may sound ridiculously impossible, but here it is: Achieve a state of ecstasy.

Mihaly Csikszentmihalyi (what a name!) has described the experience of enjoyment and engagement as "flow." To explain, flow results from your ecstatic experience of being "at one" with your actions. In fact, the term *ecstatic* comes from the Greek *es,* meaning, "stepping inside." You step inside yourself, and you feel so much at one with what you're doing that all other distractions fade away. What's so hard about that?

You can think of the flow experience as a *highly motivated* mindfulness. You experience a charged-up mindfulness. (I say that mindfulness flows because the charged-up part of it isn't overwhelmed with anxiety.)

So, motivation is a key ingredient of flow. Think of it as the drive, the energy that helps you stay focused because you're interested and invested in what you're doing at the moment.

Optimism helps, too. Psychologist Dr. Daniel Goldman points out that several "emotional" factors make up what he calls *emotional intelligence,* and optimism is one of them.

Ambition is also good. Ambition and optimism complement each other and help your memory. (The way I'm using the word, ambition has nothing to do with getting ahead of anyone else. It has to do with maximizing your potential and striving for personal goals.)

Put 'em all together (motivation, optimism, and ambition), and you're in the flow — prepared to remember all the details of a significant experience, even in the middle of a frenetic world.

Aiding Your Memory with External Cues

Even though you're doing everything you can to improve your memory, using external cues to help you remember isn't the end of the world. It doesn't mean you have a defective memory. In fact, the world is so cluttered with trivial information that even someone with a super memory can make good use of memory clues.

Sometimes, you will find that you don't have time to use a mnemonic technique. You need to rely on an external cue. Consider the following as potentially useful external cues:

- ✔ To-do lists
- ✔ Notes to yourself
- ✔ Post-Its (If Tatam Cooley can do it, so can you.)
- ✔ An outline for a speech with bullets
- ✔ Note cards
- ✔ Date books and daily organizers
- ✔ Hand-held computer planners
- ✔ Good old-fashioned calendars

Many of these external cues, such as lists and cue cards for speeches and lectures and even shopping lists, have a time factor built into them. When you're at the store or a class, you know that it's time to pull out your list or cue cards.

The book-by-the-door memory aide

I don't know about you, but I've often had the experience of remembering something I need to do the next day just as I try to fall asleep. Usually, I get up and try to write it down so that I won't keep myself up worrying that I'll forget it.

However, sometimes I'm just too tired to get up and write it down, but not too tired to struggle out of bed and prop a book against the door. I know that I need some kind of external cue to remember it the next morning. In the morning, you'll leave the room and wonder, "Why is that book there?"

It will dawn on you that you left the book there to remind you about something. At that point, you may say, "Oh yeah! I've got to remember to talk to Jean about that flight to Vancouver."

One now famous incident occurred when former President Clinton was giving his State of the Union speech, and the teleprompter broke. As his aides scrambled to fix it, Clinton felt that he couldn't wait any longer. To almost everyone's amazement, he completed his speech without a glitch as if the teleprompter had been on. Moral of the story: Don't rely solely on externals.

Date books and calendars are excellent ways to offload memories of important dates. By consistent updates, you can be confident that you at least have the dates down. But you need to rely on them on a regular basis.

I always carry a to-do list with me. But I need to update it constantly and make sure that I use it wisely. I now use my electronic organizer to record dates and schedules.

If you use to-do lists, try not to keep multiple lists. But if you do have more than one list, always keep and constantly update one master list.

Part V
The Part of Tens

The 5th Wave — By Rich Tennant

"Of course you're angry at me for springing a surprise memory quiz on you, but you've got to learn to forgive and forget."

In this part . . .

A Dummies book isn't complete without The Part of Tens, where you can find lots of useful, practical quick references on the topic at hand. Part V contains three chapters, covering, for example, the ten best things you can do to improve your memory. You can also find a list of ten helpful Web sites — addresses to remember as you spend more time improving your memory.

Chapter 17

Ten Best Ways to Improve Your Memory

*Y*ou can do a wide variety of things to improve your memory. However, no one thing alone can give you the memory skills that you want and deserve of yourself; you have to be willing to make various lifestyle changes.

In this chapter, I give you ten actions to take to improve your memory. Practice all ten suggestions, and you're sure to remember more!

Consume a Balanced Diet

You've probably heard this old saying: *You are what you eat.* Your brain depends on fuel (food) to operate. Just as you wouldn't expect to run your car on an empty tank or to run on improper fuel, you shouldn't expect to run your brain without proper nutrition. You want your brain to run at its optimum, so you have to feed it well to make sure that it can.

By eating three balanced meals a day, you give your brain the fuel that it needs — the right building blocks to function at its potential. A good diet is the most basic foundation you can provide for yourself to allow your brain to remember.

A balanced meal includes a:

✔ Complex carbohydrate

✔ Fruit or vegetable

✔ Protein

When you eat the right foods, you bring in the balance of amino acids that your brain needs to manufacture a balanced spectrum of *neurotransmitters*. These neurotransmitters are the basis of your brain chemistry (see Chapter 3 for details on neurotransmitters).

Each neurotransmitter allows you to think and feel in ways that make you not only feel good about your life but also make you capable of memory. The neurotransmitter *acetylcholine,* for example, is critically important for your brain's ability to process memory.

But you don't need to know all the chemistry and biology behind your brain's functions to know what to do. Just follow this simple advice: Eat (and eat well) to remember.

Relax Your Brain

You need a calm and alert mind to be able to use your memory skills to their full potential. The basic ways to tune yourself up to be ready to remember are to get enough of the following:

✔ Sleep

✔ Relaxation

If you don't get enough sleep and/or relaxation, you won't be able to maintain enough attention to code information into memory (see Chapter 7 for details about sleep and relaxation). Attention is the gateway to memory. If your ability to pay attention is compromised, the gate can't fully open. So, keep the gate open — relax and get enough sleep.

Exercise Your Memory

You need regular exercise to keep your body running properly. Your distant ancestors didn't sit around all day in chairs being couch potatoes! Of course, with today's modern conveniences, being inactive is much easier than it used to be. But, unfortunately, that's no excuse. You simply have to incorporate exercise and activity into your daily routine.

By exercising, you allow your body and your brain to keep all of your organ systems operating at their optimum. You rev up your cardiovascular system and metabolism, and you improve the flow of nutrients to your brain.

Exercise also helps you to sleep at night and minimize the stress you build up during the day.

Therefore, basically, exercise keeps your body in working order and helps you maintain a clear head — both of which can help you have better memory skills.

Take Supplements

A variety of vitamins, minerals, and herbal supplements can help your brain achieve the right biochemistry that it needs to remember well.

However, don't consider supplements to be a replacement for a balanced diet. Make sure that you always eat three balanced meals a day. If you take supplements, consider them to be just that — supplements.

Also, keep in mind that we live in a pill-oriented society. Don't buy into the idea that you need to take *every* supplement that has been reported to help boost your memory. If you take too many supplements and combine them with medications you take to treat various illnesses, you may run the risk of creating more health problems. Ironically, these problems may include memory problems.

If you take supplements, operate with the maxim: *Less is more.* The fewer that you take, the less at risk you are to set up potential problems.

Stick with the basics (see Chapter 5 for details on supplements). Take only those supplements that have been widely researched, such as:

- ✔ Vitamin C
- ✔ Vitamin E
- ✔ Calcium/Magnesium
- ✔ Omega 3

Stimulate Your Mind

If you want to improve your memory, you have to exercise your mind. A lazy mind produces lazy memory skills.

Whatever your age, make sure that you're always challenging yourself. Your brain responds not only by stimulating more connections between your neurons (through dendritic branching), but also by keeping you more alert and engaged in the world around you (see Chapter 3 details on dendrites).

If you sit and watch TV excessively, your mind will turn off. Also, if you spend an inordinate amount of time mulling over the trivial mishaps that happen through the day, you'll not only make yourself and those around you miserable, but you'll also make your memory skills suffer because you're preoccupied with irrelevant sidetracks.

Think of intellectual exercise as a way to keep your memory skills sharp. Engage yourself in the following:

✔ Reading

✔ Taking classes

✔ Traveling

✔ Engaging in stimulating conversation and debate

Focus on Memory

Can I have your attention, please? Remember to pay attention because you have to pay attention to remember. Attention is the gateway to memory.

If you don't pay attention, you won't be able to move short-term memory into long-term memory. When I use psychological tests that measure short-term memory, I'm also measuring someone's ability to pay attention.

Attention is so critical to memory that whatever you can do to improve your attention, do it. Don't leave home without it, or you may not find your way home!

Stay Organized

By keeping yourself organized, you'll be better able to code into memory that which you hope to remember (see Chapter 11 for details on the importance of being organized). Staying organized doesn't mean being rigid. It means being able to differentiate your experiences and code those experiences into relevant associations.

If your life is disorganized, your memory will be, too. By being disorganized, you won't know how to retrieve your memories, and worse still, you won't have any memories to retrieve.

Get organized, so you can remember to remember!

Associate, Pair, and Connect

Your brain has multiple systems that provide multiple ways for you to code memories. If you use several of these systems to code information, the richer and more easily remembered every memory will be.

The more ways you can remember one thing, the better chance you'll have to remember it. If, for example, you're trying to remember a car, you'll be far more successful at recalling it later if you take down the name, its shape, its color, and also how it feels to drive it.

Use Memory Aids

Using memory aids, such as mnemonics, provides you with ways to trick yourself into remembering. Here are three useful and easy-to-learn mnemonics that I recommend:

- ✔ Pegging
- ✔ Loci
- ✔ Story-link

The *Peg system* involves associating a letter or number with a word that you want to remember. For example, by associating each letter of the alphabet with a number, you can remember a string of numbers by remembering letters arranged as a word or vice versa.

Say that your name is Deb and you want to select a PIN number by associating it with your name — the peg system. If you assign a number to each letter of the alphabet in order, the PIN number is 4 (D), 5 (E), 2 (B). From now on, Deb is 452, and vice versa.

When you use the *Loci system,* you abide by the real-estate rule of importance: location, location, location. By coding your memories with specific locations, you can remember the contents of a speech. Then later, when you're giving the talk, you can look at those locations and be reminded of what you want to say.

When you look at the podium, you can remember the first part of your talk. The windows can cue you to the second part of the talk. Finally, the door can cue you to the last part of your talk.

By inventing a little story, you can link up information that you hope to remember later. Then, when you recall the story, you'll be reminded of the information you want to remember.

Suppose that you want to remember to alert your co-workers of an upcoming project, so that they can respond in a timely way. To ensure that you remember, you tell yourself a story about a cowboy who slept too long. When he finally woke up, he discovered that the cattle had scattered, and he spent the next two days rounding them up. In the meantime, neighboring ranchers filled the orders for beef on the hoof. The cowboy had lost his opportunity for the year's big sale.

A vivid little story can be as memorable as a nightmare.

Keep the Right Attitude

Your attitude doesn't only affect how you feel about life, but it also affects your approach to it. And how you approach life has a lot to do with how you think and remember.

When other psychologists and I give intelligence tests (that include measures of memory), we're not only measuring a person's cognitive (thinking) skills, but also assessing their personality. These cognitive skills have a major bearing on how they approach the world and remember their experiences.

The following characteristics of attitude can play a major part in your memory ability:

✔ Ambition

✔ Optimism

✔ Curiosity

These characteristics of a good attitude can keep your memory skills sharp. If you abide by them, you'll be engaged in a strong effort to attain your goals, keep yourself from giving up, and be open to the world around you along the way.

Chapter 18

Ten Frequently Asked Questions About Memory

In This Chapter

▶ Uncovering common memory misconceptions

▶ Knowing which techniques really work to improve memory

We're all curious about our memory. Using your memory is a mysterious skill that, at times, works well and, at other times, not so well. That mystery may make you wonder why, how, and under what circumstances your memory is what it is.

In this chapter, you find out what some of the most frequently asked questions about memory are along with their answers.

As I Grow Old, Are My Memory Skills Going to Wither Away?

The short answer is, *not necessarily.*

The long answer is, *yes,* your brain does shrink with age. However, reduced brain size doesn't necessarily translate into reduced memory. If you take care of yourself, your memory can acquire some nice new character lines as you age. By taking care of yourself, I mean:

- Maintaining a balanced diet
- Avoiding alcohol
- Exercising
- Challenging yourself intellectually
- Supplementing with vitamins and minerals

If you do all these things, you just may rival the memory skills of someone much younger than you who doesn't do these things. So, take care of yourself. Your memory skills depend on it.

Can I Do One Thing to Improve My Memory?

No. You can do many things to improve your memory. However, no one thing can do the job all by itself. No magic pill, switch, or trick alone can create a super memory.

The reality is that you're a complex human being with many different facets to your memory. By doing many things all at once, you'll be far more capable of cultivating a wide range of memory skills.

Does My Brain Store Memories in Just One Place?

No. Your brain has multiple systems that all work together to code your memories. Certain parts of your brain specialize in different aspects of memory. For example, your *hippocampus* is involved in moving short-term memories into long-term storage.

Your *occipital lobes* specialize in processing visual information, your *temporal lobes* in auditory information, your *parietal lobes* in spatial information, and your *frontal lobes* in processing information connected to how you move (see Chapter 3 for details about your brain).

Your brain is the most complex organ on the planet; it is far too complicated to store all your memories in one place. Make sure you take care of your brain and take advantage of its many talents.

I Think I'm Losing My Memory. Can I Find It Again?

Your memory isn't something that can be lost and found, it's a spectrum of skills that you can figure out how to sharpen.

Your brain stores memories in various places, so it also gives you a variety of memory skills and ways of coding information into memory. The more ways you code a memory, the better able you'll be to remember it later.

For example, when you think about this book, you can remember its shape, its color, its title, the general category of information, the details of the information, and so on. (Most of all, I hope that you'll remember its contents. But you get my point.)

You can do a variety of things to improve your memory. In addition to improving your brain's potential to remember, you can try memory techniques like mnemonics, chunking, rhyming, and so on. Use all those techniques to make sure that you won't feel compelled to ask the question, "Where did my memory go?"

Can I Remember without Paying Attention?

No. Attention is the gateway to memory. If you're not paying attention, the information you hope to remember won't be remembered. You'll pick up fragments of information here and there, but as far as complete memories that will actually be useful, forget it!

Don't be lazy or try to rationalize. Pay attention and remember.

The proponents of sleep learning claim that you can learn while you're sleeping. They say that all you have to do is turn an audiotape on then go to sleep, and you'll be speaking Russian when you wake up. If you believe this claim, you'll speak as much Russian as I did on a recent trip. *Nyet!*

Do I Have Memories I Don't Know About?

Maybe. But this question is a complicated one with no single answer. If you're asking whether you have any deep, dark secrets that you don't know about, the answer is *probably not.*

The issue of *repressed memories* is riddled with a lot of hype and myth. It's not impossible (but highly improbable) that you have traumatic memories, long since repressed away in a hidden place in your mind. Most people who've been found to have so-called *repressed memories* have also been found to have been highly influenced by the person(s) helping them "recover" those memories.

Are My Memories Accurate Reflections of My Experiences?

Your memories aren't snapshots of objective information that are frozen in time. You're the one who looks back on those memories, and you've changed a lot since the experience you're remembering.

All the experiences that you've had since you laid down a particular memory shape your perception of yourself and your past experience. That perspective is always changing.

Looked at another way, if quantum physics has no complete objectivity, don't expect your memory to have it.

Should I Use Supplements?

Supplementing your diet with vitamins, minerals, and herbs may be helpful to your memory. But taking them is not an alternative to eating three balanced meals a day.

If you're considering taking supplements, take only the ones that have been thoroughly researched. When taking supplements, consider the following as good possibilities:

- ✔ Vitamin C
- ✔ A broad spectrum B complex vitamin
- ✔ Vitamin E
- ✔ Calcium and magnesium

Make sure that what you take doesn't create an adverse reaction to other supplements or medications you're taking. Use this simple guideline: Less is more.

Why Can't I Remember My Infancy?

The fact that you don't remember anything from your infancy is no cause for alarm. Few people have memories dating back to the time they were 2 years old. Most people can only remember back to the time when they were 3 or 4 years old. And these memories are still spotty and fragmented.

I've seen far too many people who think that something's wrong with them because their memories of childhood don't go back as far as they think they should. I tell them (in so many words), "Welcome to being a human."

The reason for this vagueness in memories from your early childhood is quite basic. You didn't have the equipment to remember any earlier. Your brain was just beginning to mature so that you could have memories.

The first parts of your brain to develop were the primary areas, which included those parts associated with your senses. Next to develop were those parts that established connections between the various senses. The tertiary areas that are involved in higher thinking aren't finished developing until late adolescence. So, not remembering those first two years makes perfect sense.

Should I Relax My Mind, So I Can Remember?

Yes and *no*. This question deserves a follow-up: Do you mean alternating periods of mental effort with relaxation such as meditation or taking a quiet walk? If so, the answer is *yes*. If, on the other hand, you mean "tuning out" by watching television, the answer is *no*. That's not the type of relaxation I'm talking about.

A relaxed mind is an uncluttered mind. Watching television or playing computer games hour after hour clutters your mind with often useless information.

Relaxation is best achieved by quieting your mind and focusing on one thing like the magnificence of a sunset, the tumbling of waves at the beach, or the gentle rhythm of your breathing.

Chapter 19

Ten Memory Web Sites

*T*he Internet is a rich and complex treasure. You can find a variety of Web sites that may be quite helpful in your effort to find out more about memory.

In this chapter, I present ten sites that give you another look at memory. Use these sites as a resource and click the links embedded within them for other helpful links.

exploratorium.edu/memory

This Web site is operated by one of the most creative museums in the country. The Exploratorium in San Francisco is a premier science museum that offers interactive and constantly changing exhibits. And most of these exhibits are interactive.

This site offers information on memory from a number of different angles and perspectives, including anatomy, psychology, interesting facts, history, and so much more.

www.demon.co.uk/mindtool/memory.html

The title of this site is "Memory Techniques and Mnemonics."

It's operated by Mind Tools out of the United Kingdom. It contains useful information on mnemonics. You find definitions of mnemonics and a wide variety of descriptions of mnemonic techniques.

The site also provides links to other Web sites, including Mind Tools itself, which is a resource for students, teachers, and parents.

www.cadre.sjsu.edu/switch/sound/ articles/wendt/folder6/ng621.htm

This site, entitled "The Art of Memory," highlights the history of memory techniques and offers references to the seminal works on the subject by Frances Yates.

Information is provided about major figures in the history of mnemonics, with links to pages for Giulio Camillo and Giordino Bruno. You can gain information about the long and fascinating history of memory techniques.

pseudonumerology.com

"Pseudonumerology" is operated by Dr. Allan Krill, a geologist and self-proclaimed pseudonumerologist, and professor of geology at Norwegian University of Science and Technology.

This page provides multiple tips and mnemonics for remembering numbers. You find tricks for remembering PINs, telephone numbers, historical dates, and more. He also offers word games and puzzles.

vcu.edu/psy/psy101/forsyth

This site is titled, "Memory and Cognition." It was developed by Dr. Donelson Forsyth, a professor of psychology at Virginia Commonwealth University.

The site provides multiple informational links to many subjects, such as repressed memories, physiology and memory, psychological testing, stress and memory, and many other topics.

www.apa.online.org

American Psychological Association Online — Public Affairs offers questions and answers on the controversial issue of repressed memories. It also offers information on how consumers can choose a qualified professional.

jimhopper.com/memory

This site is called "Recovered Memories of Sexual Abuse: Scientific Research and Scholarly Resources" and is a dense Web site operated by Dr. Jim Hopper, a psychologist and research associate at Boston University School of Medicine and Trauma Team.

It offers a large collection of papers and resources related to repressed memories and information on trauma. It also offers the other side of the debate surrounding repressed memories and memories of childhood sexual abuse. Here you can learn about people who have suffered from trauma and repressed those memories.

www.epub.org.br/cm/n01/ memo/memory.htm

The site is titled "Human Memory: What It Is and How to Improve It."

Dr. Silvia Helena Cardosa of the Center for Biomedical Informatics of the State University of Campinas, Brazil, offers pages on types of memory, the brain's growth, memory loss, and improving the memory. She also offers links to other sites on memory.

www.learnmem.org

This site, titled "Learning and Memory," is jointly operated by people from Coldspring Harbor Press and Stanford University. It contains several research papers on neurobiology, learning, and memory.

www.memory.rutgers.edu/memory/

"Memory Disorder Project" is operated through Rutgers University and contains information on memory disorders, frequently asked questions, and the way that memory works.

Index